DEFECTIVE PARADIGMS
Missing forms and what they tell us

PROCEEDINGS OF THE BRITISH ACADEMY · 163

DEFECTIVE PARADIGMS
Missing forms and what they tell us

Edited by
MATTHEW BAERMAN
GREVILLE G. CORBETT
DUNSTAN BROWN

Published for THE BRITISH ACADEMY
by OXFORD UNIVERSITY PRESS

Oxford University Press, Great Clarendon Street, Oxford OX2 6DP

Oxford New York

*Auckland Cape Town Dar es Salaam Hong Kong Karachi
Kuala Lumpur Madrid Melbourne Mexico City Nairobi
New Delhi Shanghai Taipei Toronto*

*With offices in
Argentina Austria Brazil Chile Czech Republic France Greece
Guatemala Hungary Italy Japan Poland Portugal Singapore
South Korea Switzerland Thailand Turkey Ukraine Vietnam*

*Published in the United States
by Oxford University Press Inc., New York*

*© The British Academy, 2010
Database right The British Academy (maker)*

First published 2010

*All rights reserved. No part of this publication may be reproduced,
stored in a retrieval system, or transmitted, in any form or by any means,
without the prior permission in writing of the British Academy,
or as expressly permitted by law, or under terms agreed with the appropriate
reprographics rights organization. Enquiries concerning reproduction
outside the scope of the above should be sent to the Publications Department,
The British Academy, 10 Carlton House Terrace, London SW1Y 5AH*

*You must not circulate this book in any other binding or cover
and you must impose this same condition on any acquirer*

*British Library Cataloguing in Publication Data
Data available*

*Library of Congress Cataloging in Publication Data
Data available*

*Typeset by
New Leaf Design, Scarborough, North Yorkshire
Printed in Great Britain
on acid-free paper by
Cromwell Press Group
Trowbridge, Wiltshire*

*ISBN 978–0–19–726460–7
ISSN 0068–1202*

Contents

Notes on Contributors		vii
Acknowledgements		xi
List of Abbreviations		xiii
1.	Introduction: Defectiveness: Typology and Diachrony MATTHEW BAERMAN AND GREVILLE G. CORBETT	1
2.	Failing One's Obligations: Defectiveness in Rumantsch Reflexes of DĒBĒRE STEPHEN R. ANDERSON	19
3.	Defectiveness as Stem Suppletion in French and Spanish Verbs GILLES BOYÉ AND PATRICIA CABREDO HOFHERR	35
4.	Defective Paradigms of Reflexive Nouns and Participles in Latvian ANDRA KALVAČA AND ILZE LOKMANE	53
5.	Relative Acceptability of Missing Adjective Forms in Swedish JOHN LÖWENADLER	69
6.	Defective Verbal Paradigms in Hungarian—Description and Experimental Study ÁGNES LUKÁCS, PÉTER REBRUS, AND MIKLÓS TÖRKENCZY	85
7.	On Morphomic Defectiveness: Evidence from the Romance Languages of the Iberian Peninsula MARTIN MAIDEN AND PAUL O'NEILL	103
8.	The Search for Regularity in Irregularity: Defectiveness and its Implications for our Knowledge of Words MARIANNE MITHUN	125
9.	Ineffability Through Modularity: Gaps in the French Clitic Cluster MILAN REZAC	151
10	Interactions between Defectiveness and Syncretism GREGORY STUMP	181

Index of Authors 211
Index of Languages 214
Subject Index 215

Notes on Contributors

Stephen R. Anderson is the Diebold Professor of Linguistics at Yale University where he has taught since 1994. He is the author of six books, the most recent of which is *Aspects of the theory of clitics* (OUP, 2005). He is a Fellow of several scientific societies and was President of the Linguistic Society of America in 2007.

Matthew Baerman is a Research Fellow in the Surrey Morphology Group, University of Surrey. His work focusses on the typology, diachrony, and modelling of inflectional morphology.

Gilles Boyé is *maître de conférences* at the University of Bordeaux. His work focuses on the description of regular and irregular behaviours in the inflectional morphology, principally in Romance languages.

Patricia Cabredo Hofherr is a Researcher at the *Centre National de la Recherche Scientifique* (CNRS), based at the UMR 7023 (*Structures formelles du langage* CNRS/Université Paris 8). Her research is on different aspects of the syntax-morphology interface (preposition-determiner portmanteaux in French and German, the analysis of noun-less DPs, antecedentless readings of third person plural pronouns) and on the verbal morphology of Spanish (in collaboration with Gilles Boyé). Currently, she is visiting researcher at the Surrey Morphology Group.

Greville Corbett works on morphology and typology, particularly on grammatical features. He is a past president of the LAGB and a Fellow of the British Academy; currently he holds a European Research Council advanced grant. He has published monographs on gender, number, and most recently on agreement, with Cambridge University Press.

Andra Kalnača is Associate Professor of Linguistics at the University of Latvia, Department of Latvian and General Linguistics. She teaches Latvian morphology and morphonology, and the historical grammar of Latvian. Her research focuses on grammatical categories, morphemics, and morphonology.

Ilze Lokmane is Assistant Professor of Linguistics at the University of Latvia, Department of Latvian and General Linguistics. She teaches Latvian syntax, semantics and general linguistics. Her research interests are the syntactic, semantic and pragmatic structure of the sentence.

John Löwenadler completed his PhD in 2007 at the University of Gothenburg, studying the cross-linguistic distribution of gaps in certain areas of syntax. He is currently doing research on similar topics at the University of Manchester. The present paper describes some initial observations related to a study of morphological gaps in Swedish which will be presented in detail in an upcoming issue of the journal *Morphology*.

Ágnes Lukács is a Senior Researcher at the Department of Cognitive Science of the Budapest University of Technology and Economics and at the Research Institute for Linguistics of the Hungarian Academy of Sciences. Publications include *Language abilities in Williams Syndrome* (Akadémai, Budapest, 2004) and 'Spatial language in Williams syndrome: evidence for a special interaction? *Journal of Child Language* 34/2, 311–43 with C. Pléh and M. Racsmány (2007).

Martin Maiden is Professor of the Romance languages at Oxford University and a Fellow of the British Academy. His research interests are historical Romance linguistics (particularly Italo-Romance and Romanian). His recent research has been on the historical morphology of the Romance verb and the role of 'morphomic' structure in its evolution. Some recent publications in this area are 'Morpological autonomy and diachrony', *Yearbook of Morphology* 2004, 137–75 (2005) and 'Where does heteroclisis come from? Evidence from Romanian dialects', *Morphology* 19 (2009).

Marianne Mithun is Professor of Linguistics at the University of California, Santa Barbara. Her primary research interests are morphology, syntax, discourse, pragmatics and their interactions; language change, particularly the development of grammatical systems; language contact; and language documentation and description.

Paul O'Neill is currently a University Teacher in Hispanic Linguistics at the University of Liverpool. He is also an associate of the Research Centre for Romance Linguistics at the University of Oxford where he is a DPhil Student attached to the major AHRC funded research project entitled 'Autonomous Morphology in Diachrony: comparative evidence from Romance languages'. He is currently completing his DPhil on the verbal morphology of Ibero-Romance. His research is primarily concerned with verbal stem allomorphy in the Romance languages of the Iberian Peninsula from both a synchronic and diachronic point of view.

Péter Rebrus is a senior researcher at the Research Institute for Linguistics of the Hungarian Academy of Sciences. He teaches linguistics and mathematics at the Theoretical Linguistics Department of Eötvös Loránd University in Budapest. His recent publications include: 'Uniformity and contrast in the Hungarian verbal paradigms (with Miklós Törkenczy) in *Paradigms in phonological theory*, edited by Laura J. Downing et al. (Oxford University Press, 2005) and (with Miklós Törkenczy) 'Covert and overt defectiveness in paradigms in *Modelling ungrammaticality in optimality theory*, edited by Curt Rice (Equinox Publishing, London, 2007).

Milan Rezac is a researcher with the CNRS, based at UMR 2073. His research is on phi-features, the syntax of A-movement, the syntax and morphology of agreement and clitic systems across various languages, and the modular architecture of language.

Gregory Stump is Professor of Linguistics at the University of Kentucky. He is author of *Inflectional morphology* (Cambridge, 2001) and of numerous articles on the theory and typology of inflection. He has argued for the conclusion that a theory of inflectional morphology should be inferential and realizational, and has specifically advocated one such theory, that of Paradigm Function Morphology.

Miklós Törkenczy is Associate Professor at the Department of English Linguistics and at the Theoretical Linguistics Department of the Eötvös Loránd University in Budapest. He also works as a Research Professor at the Research Institute for Linguistics of the Hungarian Academy of Sciences. He is the co-author (with Pétar Siptár) of *The phonology of Hungarian* (Oxford University Press, 2000).

Acknowledgements

This volume is a selection of papers from a conference held at the British Academy, London, April 10–11 2008, sponsored by the British Academy and the Arts and Humanities Research Council (grant number AH/D001579/1). Continuing support was provided by the European Research Council (grant number ERC-2008-AdG-230268 MORPHOLOGY). The support of all these bodies is gratefully acknowledged. We would like to thank Angela Pusey and Joanne Blore of the Academy, as well as all the participants, for making the conference a success. In the preparation of the manuscript, special thanks go to Penny Everson, Lisa Mack and Claire Turner, our project manager, Janet English and our copy-editor, Rosemary Morlin.

Glossing Abbreviations

ACC	accusative
ACT	active
ABL	ablative
COM	common
COND	conditional
CONTR	contrastive
DAT	dative
DEF	definite
DESID	desiderative
DP	duo-plural
DIM	diminutive
DU	dual
ERG	ergative
ETH	ethical
EXCL	exclusive
F	feminine
FI	feminine-indefinite gender
FZ	feminine-zoic gender
GEN	genitive
IMP	imperative
IMPRF	imperfect
INCL	inclusive
IND	indicative
INDEF	indefinite
INF	infinitive
INS	instrumental
INTR	intransitive
IPFV	imperfective
LOC	locative
M	masculine
MID	middle
N	neuter
NEG	negative
NMLZ	nominalizer
NOM	nominative
OPT	optative
PASS	passive
PL	plural
PLUPRF	pluperfect
POSS	possessor
POT	potential

PRS	present
PST	past
PTCP	participle
R	coreferential
REFL	reflexive
REL.PRON	relative pronoun
SBJV	subjunctive
SG	singular
TR	transitive
VOC	vocative

1

Introduction: Defectiveness: Typology and Diachrony

MATTHEW BAERMAN AND GREVILLE G. CORBETT

1. Introduction

A DEFECTIVE WORD IS, according to Matthews (1997: 89), one 'whose paradigm is incomplete in comparison with others of the major class that it belongs to.' For example, in standard Russian the word *mečta* 'dream' is defective according to normative dictionaries, lacking a genitive plural (1a). And corpus data do confirm that the genitive plural is indeed avoided (1b). In the Russian National Corpus (RNC), out of 8,722 tokens of this lexeme, only thirteen are of the genitive plural, and most of these are clearly jocular or ironic, playing on the incongruity of the form.

(1)   Russian 'dream'

	a. normative paradigm		b. tokens in the RNC (queried 10/2008)	
	singular	plural	singular	plural
NOM	mečta	mečty	2,771	1980
ACC	mečtu		929	
GEN	mečty	-----	996	13 (mečt)
DAT	mečte	mečtam	362	221
LOC		mečtax		459
INS	mečtoj	mečtami	643	348

There is nothing about the meaning of the word that would account for this gap, since the plural is otherwise well attested, while the genitive is required in plenty of contexts. Instead, it is the form itself which seems to be rejected. In its place, various alternative strategies are employed, such as using a different lexeme[1] or

---

[1] Such as *mečtanie* 'dreaming, dream', whose genitive plural is unusually frequent: 628 tokens in the RNC (queried 10/2008) out of a total 1,230 tokens for the lexeme as a whole. Presumably it is taking some of the load off *mečta*.

a non-canonical syntactic construction,[2] or framing the sentence such as to avoid any context which would call for the genitive plural.

On most views of how the components of language interact, this is getting things backwards. Morphology ought simply to be the handmaid of grammatical meaning, producing forms where other components require them. By the principles of Phonology-Free Syntax and Morphology-Free Syntax, syntax should operate independent of the properties of individual word forms. Defectiveness represents an unwanted intrusion of morphological idiosyncrasy into syntax. From a morphology-internal perspective it is also problematic, since any coherent model of inflectional morphology assumes that there will be productive, default mechanisms that permit the generation of a paradigm from any item whatsoever. Defectiveness is hardly a newly discovered phenomenon; e.g. Neue and Wagener (1897, 1902) devote thirty-seven pages to earlier grammarians' accounts of defective noun paradigms in Classical Latin.[3] But clearly, it has been ill incorporated into our theories of language. It is encouraging then to see an increase in interest in the topic in recent years (as the references in the subsequent chapters show). The present volume brings together scholars from different theoretical schools for an overdue typological overview of the issues involved.

Any definition of defectiveness is of necessity open ended. If we take Matthews' definition above, both the notions of 'completeness' and 'major class' want precise clarification. For example, English modals lack non-finite forms *(*to may, *to can; *maying, *canning)*; whether this makes them defective depends on whether we say they belong to the class 'verb' (in which case we expect to find these forms) or to a smaller class 'modal' (in which case we need not expect to find these forms). Obviously, the more idiosyncratic and lexically restricted the gap, the more canonically defective it is, and the more canonically defective the gap is, the greater the analytical challenge.

In the present volume we concentrate on clear instances of idiosyncratic gaps as the best representatives of what might well be a broader phenomenon. Though we need not belabour the definitional criteria, it would be well to review the various ways in which a paradigm might be incomplete—at least according to superficial expectations—without quite achieving what might usefully be labelled as defectiveness.

First, there may be transparent semantic constraints that make certain values incoherent in a given context, and so naturally yield a reduced

---

[2] For example, various quantifiers such as *mnogo* 'many' normally take the genitive plural of count nouns, but the RNC contains examples of these quantifiers used with the genitive SINGULAR of *mečta*.

[3] *Deficientia casibus*, that is; singularia and pluralia tantum take up another 145 pages.

paradigm. Thus we would be little surprised to find an impersonal verb restricted to third person subjects. In a similar vein, pragmatic constraints may make certain forms unacceptable in the social context within which the language is used (as with the Mohawk kinship terms described by Mithun, this volume §2.1).

Second, general syntactic rules may dictate that a morphosyntactic value is not relevant for some lexeme. For example, Tschenkeli gives the following paradigms for the three Georgian words for 'nobody', in which one of them, *nuravin*, lacks an ergative. (Warning: the variety Tschenkeli describes is different from the standard Georgian normally described in other sources. In the standard variety, the ergative of *aravin/veravin/nuravin* is identical to the nominative.)

(2) Georgian 'nobody'

	aravin	*veravin*	*nuravin*
NOM	aravin	veravin	nuravin
ERG	aravin-ma	veravin-ma	———
DAT/GEN	aravi-s	veravi-s	nuravi-s

₁ *aravin*: used with negator *ar* 'not' (general negator)
₁ *veravin*: used with negator *ver* 'not able'
₁ *nuravin*: used with negator *nu* 'not' (in prohibitions only)

Significantly, *ar* and *ver* can be used with any tense, while *nu* is restricted to present/future. But in Georgian, as will be familiar to many, case assignment is contingent on tense and verb class; subject case assignment is sketched in (3).

(3) Case, tense, and verb class in Georgian

	class I	class II	class III	class IV
PRS/FUT, IPFV/COND	nom	nom	nom	dat
AORIST	erg	nom	erg	dat
PRF, PLUPRF	dat	nom	dat	dat

Since *nuravin* is restricted to the present, and the ergative is used only in the aorist, there is no context that ever calls for an ergative of *nuravin*.

Third, there may be lexeme-internal syntactic constraints, i.e. where the lexeme is restricted to certain collocations or constructions. For example, words such as *midst* or *quoth* occur in constructions where one may otherwise find a noun or verb, respectively (*in the midst of* ≈ *in the middle of*, *quoth she* ≈ *said she*), but do not occur outside these constructions. One might choose to see these as nouns or verbs with restricted valence, or as members of some other, non-inflecting word class (bound preposition, quotative particle). In either case, though, the lack of a full paradigm is a direct consequence of the fact that such words have no need of one.

Finally, degrees of productivity may differ for different types of paradigm. One of the commonly understood distinctions between inflection and derivation is that inflection is fully productive across a word class, while derivation is applied in a piecemeal fashion. On that assumption we expect to find gaps in derivation. But of course in the real world things do not necessarily line up so neatly, and we may find both fully productive derivational processes and semi-productive inflectional ones (see in particular Löwenadler, this volume). For the present purposes we understand defectiveness as gaps which are decidedly exceptional, occurring in the context of productive morphosyntactic or morphosemantic oppositions.

In the sections below, we outline a typology of defective paradigms. First, we look at appropriate terms to describe defectiveness in synchronic terms. Second, we sketch the possible diachronic origins of defective paradigms, to the extent that they can be plausibly reconstructed. The intent is to offer a surface taxonomy, rather than a typology of explanations or analyses. For these we defer to the contributions in the subsequent chapters.

2. Synchronic Typology

Following Fraser and Corbett (1995: 125–32), Brown, Corbett, Fraser, Hippisley and Timberlake (1996), Stump (2002: 149–50) and Stump (this volume), we can see inflectional morphology as consisting of three components: (i) a set of forms (the form paradigm), (ii) a set of meanings or functions, be they syntactic or semantic (the content paradigm), and (iii) the mapping between the two.

(4)   Three components of an inflectional paradigm

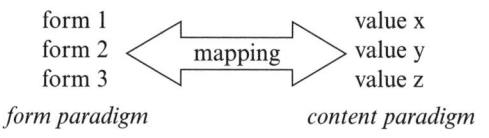

```
     form 1                        value x
     form 2  <  mapping  >  value y
     form 3                        value z
  form paradigm              content paradigm
```

Correspondingly, different patterns of defectiveness can be ascribed to these different components. Defectiveness of the form paradigm represents the most clearly identifiable type, and the one most readily subdivided into neat typological parcels. But the other two also represent logical possibilities, and may have a good deal to say about the way our morphological models should be working.

2.1. Form paradigm

The most obvious example of a defective paradigm is one in which *some form* is missing, i.e. where the gap can be described as the absence of some morphological entity, and we can base our morphological typology on the typology of components. Of course, what constitutes a morphological component is itself a slippery notion, dependent both on theoretical framework and individual analysis. Below, we make a rough division between stems, affixes and whole word forms, and then consider some further components (in effect, subdivisions) which might enter into a typology.

2.1.1. Stem

An example of stem-based defectiveness comes from Finnish. The paradigm of many verbs in Finnish is based on the opposition of what Karlsson (1999) refers to as the *infinitive stem* and the *inflectional stem*. For those verbs for which this distinction is relevant, four classes can be distinguished, based on the relationship between the two stems, outlined in (5). Taking the infinitive stem as the base, the inflectional stem may differ by (i) changes to the stem-final segment, (ii) an alternation of a consonant within the stem, known as 'consonant gradation' (note here that the alternant of *k* is Ø), or (iii) suffixation.

(5) Alternating stem classes in Finnish

		infinitive stem	inflectional stem	inflectional stem formed by:
a.	'hew'	hakat-	hakkaa-	stem-final -*t* → *V*
	'lie'	maat- (maØat-)	makaa-	consonant gradation + stem-final *V*
b.	'think'	ajatel-	ajattele-	consonant gradation
c.	'need'	tarvit-	tarvit-se-	suffixation
d.	'get warm'	lämme-	lämpe-ne-	consonant gradation
	'be quiet'	vaie- (vaiØe-)	vaike-ne-	suffixation

Some verbs of type 'd' are said to lack an infinitive stem, and consequently all the forms based on it; though the list of such verbs varies with the source, they all agree on *erkanee* 'spreads out' as an example (Hakulinen et al. 2004; Kiparsky 1974; SKP). What is particularly important in the present context is the fact that the two stems are distributed in the paradigm in a way which does not correspond to any semantic or syntactic natural class, as illustrated in (6), comparing forms of defective *erkanee* with those of non-defective *vaieta* 'be quiet', which belongs to the same stem type.

(6) Distribution of stems: *vaieta* 'be quiet' (inflectional stem *vaikene-*, infinitive stem *vaie-*) and *erkanee* 'spread out' (inflectional stem *erkane-*)

	finite			non-finite	
	active	passive			
IND PRS	vaikenee	vaietaan	PRS PTCP	vaikeneva	
	erkanee	———		erkaneva	
IND PST	vaikeni	vaietiin	PST PTCP	vaiennut	
	erkani	———			
COND PRS	vaikenisi	vaiettaisiin	1ST INF	vaieta	
	erkanisi	———			
POT PRS	vaienee	vaiettaneen	2ND INF	vaietessa	
	———				
2SG IMP	vaikene		3RD INF	vaikenemaan	
	erkane	vaiettakoon		erkanemaan	
3SG IMP (and PL)	vaietkoon	———			
	———				

N.B. active additionally inflected for person-number, given here as 3SG unless otherwise noted

In the case of *erkanee*, the 'expected' infinitive stem *era-* (i.e. *erØa-*) is rejected by many speakers, and is not part of the normative standard.[4] (A possible aggravating factor is the anomalous shape of the base: verbs of this class typically have an inflectional base ending in *-e*, e.g. *lämpenee* 'gets warm', *vaikenee* 'is quiet', but *erkanee* has a base in *-a*.) The Romance patterns described by Boyé and Cabredo Hoferr (this volume), Maiden and O'Neill (this volume) and Anderson (this volume) represent particularly clear examples of this type of defectiveness, as do the Hungarian verbal paradigms described by Lukács, Rebrus, and Törkenczy (this volume).

2.1.2. Affixes

Gaps may also correspond to the normal distribution of affixes, independent of any stem alternations. An interesting though somewhat involved example comes from Chickasaw. There are three sets of argument markers used with verbs (I, II, and III in Munro's terms). All three can be used to mark the subject of intransitive verbs. Munro and Gordon (1982) and Munro (2005) treat them as three inflection classes, though there is a rough semantic correlation with agency (I ≈ agentive, II ≈ patientive and III ≈ dative subjects).[5]

---

[4] Roughly synonymous verbs based on the same root but belonging to different verb classes, such as *erota* or *erkaantua*, are said to be used instead.
[5] Typically the choice of affix set is fixed for a given verbal root, and this choice is not always semantically transparent.

(7) Person-number markers in Chickasaw (Munro and Gordon 1982)

	set I	set II	set III[6]
1SG	hopoo-**li**	**sa**-chokma	**an**-takho'bi
	'I am jealous'	'I am good'	'I am lazy'
1PL	**(k)ii**-hopoo	**po**-chokma	**pon**-takho'bi
	'we are jealous'	'we are good'	'we are lazy'
2[7]	**ish**-hopoo	**chi**-chokma	**chin**-takho'bi
	'you are jealous'	'you are good'	'you are lazy'
3	hopoo	chokma	**in**-takho'bi
	'he is jealous'	'he is good'	'he is lazy'

Two argument verbs use set I markers for the subject, set II for direct object and set III for dative or indirect object. Only one object is ever marked on the verb, so there are two possible structures for two-argument verbs:

(8) *set I + set II:* chi-sso-li *set I + set III:* chim-ambi-li
 2.II-hit-1SG.I 2.III.-scare-1SG.I
 'I hit you' 'I beat you'
 (Munro and Gordon 1982: 83, 85)

Difficulties arise with a small set of transitive verbs that take set II markers for their subject. So long as the object is third person there is no problem, as third person direct objects are zero marked in any case, e.g. *sa-nokfónkha* 'I remember her' (Munro 2005: 125). But first or second person objects ought to be overtly marked, which would yield a word containing two set II markers. This is indeed how such verbs behave in closely-related Choctaw:

(9) *set II + set II:* An-at-o chi-sa-banna-h
 1SG-NOM-CONTR 2.II-1SG.II-want-PREDICATIVE
 'I want you.'
 (Davies 1986: 67; see also Broadwell 2006: 145)

But Chickasaw permits only the affix combinations 'set I + set II' and 'set I + set III'. Consequently, such verbs are defective, so meanings such as 'I remember you' or 'I want you' can only be expressed through some paraphrase (Munro 2005: 125). This pattern of defectiveness can thus be seen as a restriction on the licit combination of affixes.

---

[6] Depending on the following segment, the final nasal of the prefix is variously realized as *n*, *m* or as nasalization of the vowel.

[7] Second person plural is marked by *ha-* prefixed to 2nd person marker, so long as it is in word-initial position (in two-argument verbs, where the 2nd person marker is preceded by other person markers, singular and plural are not distinguished).

2.1.3. Whole word form

Some examples will necessarily require reference to whole word forms. For example, Inkelas and Orgun (1995), citing their own work as well as Itô and Hankamer (1989), report that some speakers of Turkish observe a disyllabic minimal size condition on affixed words. In practice, this means a ban on forms involving a monoconsonantal suffix on a monosyllabic vowel final stem. Although where this situation obtains for the native lexicon, alternative morphological strategies are employed, real problems do arise with the names of letters of the alphabet and musical notes with the shape CV when combined with the 1st person singular (-*Vm*) and 2nd person singular (-*Vn*) possessive suffixes, as the initial vowel of the suffix is regularly deleted when attached to a vowel-final base. Note that (i) disyllabic possessive suffixes are acceptable, and (ii) monosyllabic suffixes are acceptable so long as the stem is consonant-final, as the resulting form ends up disyllabic.

(10)

		fa (note F)		*sol (note G)*	
default form		fa	'F'	sol	'G'
1SG	-Vm	*fa-m	'my F'	sol-üm	'my G'
1PL	-VmVz	fa-mız	'our F'	sol-ümüz	'our G'

Crucially, this gap depends on properties of the (potential) word as a whole, not of the stem as such or of the affix as such.

2.2. Content paradigm

Some gaps have no obvious correspondence in a language's normal system of morphological forms, but do correspond to a coherent class of items in the system of functional oppositions, i.e. morphosyntactic/morphosemantic features. Here the analytic interpretation becomes tricky, since such gaps may be attributed to purely semantic or syntactic restrictions that are independent of morphology. Examples of words with obvious semantic restrictions would be weather verbs and impersonals, restricted to third person subjects, or non-count nouns that have no number opposition. Syntactic rules may also prevent the combination of certain morphosyntactic features. Where such rules are general, they may best be treated as a purely syntactic problem, though they may well reach a point of quirkiness and lexical restriction sufficient to see them as morphological defectiveness (see Rezac, this volume).

A fairly clear example of a gap which corresponds to a functional distinction without having an obvious functional motivation comes from Witsuwet'en (Athabaskan). The verbs *n-wət* 'walk fast' and *c'-ł-tsi* 'give birth' are used only in the third person, both singular and plural. The gaps may be filled by alternative expressions, e.g. *ʔay nə-s-ye* 'fast <1SG>walk' in place of **nə-s-wət*

'<1SG>walk.fast' (Hargus 2007: 569). Note that the missing parts of the paradigm do not correspond to any morphological component otherwise observable in the language: there is no potential stem alternation, and while the various person-number affixes belong to different position classes, it is not third person which is distinct, but rather 1PL/3PL which occupy a position class to the left of the other prefixes, as shown by 'breathe' (Hargus 2007: 777) in (11).

(11) normal verb 'breathe' *s#giz*[8]   defective 'walk fast' *n#wət*

	SINGULAR	DUAL	PLURAL	SINGULAR	DUAL	PLURAL
1	s-əs-giz	s-dət-giz	ts'ə-sgiz	——	——	——
2	s-en-giz	s-əxʷ-giz		——	——	
3	sgiz		hə-sgiz	nəwət		hə-nəwət

And while a restriction to third person would be unsurprising in the case of verbs with inanimate or impersonal subjects, the semantics of these verbs restricts them to animate subjects. As far as one can tell this restriction is simply a stipulated property of these lexemes.

2.3. Mapping between form and content

The prior two types involve gaps that can be characterized entirely within their own domains, i.e. there is some particular form that is missing, independent of the values it might realize, or there are some values missing, independent of the forms that might realize them. Now we turn to patterns which involve the relationship between the two domains.

In Tamashek, subject person is marked on verbs by a combination of prefixes and suffixes, with some allomorphy depending on whether the verb base begins in a vowel or consonant. One set of verbs is an exception to this, the adjectival verbs (in Heath's terminology; other sources refer to them as statives or verbs of quality). Though their imperfective stem forms take the same prefixes and suffixes as other verbs, their perfective stem forms have suffixes only. By the logic of this system, the forms of the third person singular and the first person plural, which are normally distinguished solely by prefixes, should fall together, realized by the bare stem. However, speakers reject the first plural interpretation of the bare stem: 'Instead, a circumlocution or a specialized construction was offered to express senses like "we became black"' (Heath 2005: 437f.).

---

[8] Hargus gives the underlying form as the abstract *D-yiz*, from which *s-giz* can be derived by regular morphophonological rules.

(12) Tamashek 'adjectival' verb 'be black' (Heath 2005: 388, 431f., 437)

	short imperfective (V-initial)	long imperfective (C-initial)	perfective
1SG	ikwal -æɣ	tikwal -æɣ	kæwal-æɣ
2SG	t- ikwal -æd	tikwal -æd	kæwal-æd
3SG.M	ikwal	i- tikwal	kæwal
3SG.F	t- ikwal	tikwal	
1PL	n- ikwal	nə-tikwal	———
2PL.M	t- ikwal -æm	tikwal -æm	kæwal-æm
2PL.F	t- ikwal -mæt	tikwal -mæt	kæwal-mæt
3PL.M	ikwal -æn	tikwal -æn	kæwal-æn
3PL.F	ikwal -ænt	tikwal -ænt	kæwal-ænt

If we interpret this as an instance of homophony avoidance, then it crucially involves the interaction of form and content. The form itself—the bare perfective stem—is clearly unexceptionable, nor is there anything obviously untoward about the meaning. It is only when the two are combined and assessed with respect to the rest of the paradigm that a problem arises.

2.4. Unclassifiable residue

The typology just outlined presupposes that the pattern of defectiveness conforms to some coherent class of items within a domain. Were this always the case, we could claim that defectiveness was always parasitic off another structure, i.e. the absence of some discrete unit defined elsewhere. If not, we would need to allow the possibility that gaps might be encoded independently of other structures, i.e. that a gap was a morphological object. Some examples suggest we consider this second possibility. A case in point is the present tense paradigm of the verb 'to be' in the variety of Itel′men recorded by Bogoras, which is missing the first person (both singular and plural), as well as third person singular and second person plural.

(13) Itel′men 'be' (Bogoras 1922: 766)

	present	past
1SG	———	t-łi-k
2SG	či-ž-č	łi-č
3SG	———	łi-č
1PL	———	n-łi-k
2PL	———	łi-šx
3PL	či-ž-ši?n	ł-či?n

Semantically this distribution makes little sense. Nor does it follow from the morphology. There is root suppletion (in this verb) between present and past, plus a present tense suffix -ž, but the endings of present and past ought to be the same,[9] and these do not fall into any pattern corresponding to the gap (indeed, the missing 3SG should be homophonous with the 2SG). Assuming the basic correctness of the description, in such cases we can entertain three possible interpretations: (i) the forms have been incompletely described, e.g. the existing forms participate in a suppletive relationship with some other root, (ii) the functions have been incompletely described, e.g. there are good syntactic reasons for the absence of some forms that have not been recognized, or (iii) the gaps in the paradigm are indeed lexically encoded. In the case of extinct languages (such as Latin or the dialect of Itel′men described above), the first two interpretations are distinct possibilities, but contemporary examples such as Latvian reflexive nouns and participles (Kalnača and Lokmane, this volume) show that wholly random gaps may indeed occur.

3. Diachronic Typology

A survey of defectiveness leads us to the impression that morphological systems, far from being streamlined media for implementing grammatical meaning, are ad hoc assemblages of imperfectly coordinated parts. At least in some cases. This implies that a diachronic perspective on defective paradigms has an especially important place in characterizing their nature. Naturally, defectiveness poses a particular challenge for diachronic reconstruction, as overt evidence of gaps is seldom forthcoming. Nevertheless it is possible to construct a logical typology of the ways in which defectiveness may arise, with plausible examples to illustrate them.

Defectiveness occurs when (according to one's analysis) the form paradigm of some lexeme is smaller than its content paradigm. Logically, this can be a result of arrested development, or of decay. That is, it could be that the lexeme has had gaps from the very outset and never resolved them, or that it once had a viable paradigm, but has since lost parts.

3.1. Arrested development

In an inflected language, novel lexemes presumably do not arise with all of their parts already in place; rather, the new lexeme arises as an isolated inflected form, and other cells are filled as need arises according to the rules at hand. If the expected expansion of forms to the whole paradigm stops short, we have a case of arrested development. We can distinguish various

---

[9] The š ~ č alternation in the 3PL is conditioned by the preceding segment.

types according to the way in which the novel lexeme comes about in the first place.

Borrowing

A word is borrowed from some other language into a paradigm that requires a morphological alternation not found in the source. For example, many of the defective Spanish and Portuguese verbs described by Maiden and O'Neill (this volume) were borrowed from Latin or French into a conjugation class which requires stem-vowel alternations. The Turkish examples discussed above (10) presumably also represent the same sort of development.

Derivation

This is similar to borrowing, with the source being another lexeme rather than another language. For example, in Russian, there is a class of denominal verbs formed through null derivation into an inflectional class that requires a stem-final consonant alternation in the 1st person singular. For some verbs, especially novel ones, there may be some reluctance to apply the alternation, balanced by an equal reluctance not to violate the requirements of the inflectional class. An often cited example is *pylesosit'* 'to vacuum', derived from the noun *pylesos* 'vacuum cleaner'. According to the established pattern of this inflectional class, the final consonant of the stem should alternate from *s* to *š* in the 1st person singular; many normative dictionaries suggest that the 1st person singular is instead defective.

(14) Russian *pylesosit'* 'to vacuum'

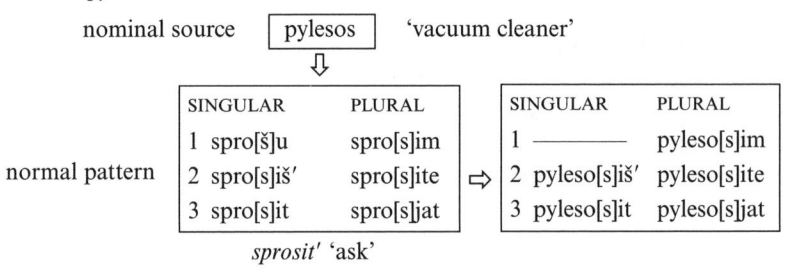

nominal source [pylesos] 'vacuum cleaner'
⇩

normal pattern

	SINGULAR	PLURAL
1	spro[š]u	spro[s]im
2	spro[s]iš'	spro[s]ite
3	spro[s]it	spro[s]jat

⇨

	SINGULAR	PLURAL
1	———	pyleso[s]im
2	pyleso[s]iš'	pyleso[s]ite
3	pyleso[s]it	pyleso[s]jat

sprosit' 'ask'

Baxturina (1966) discusses the varying range of judgements offered for such verbs, with some speakers. In practice, speakers (i) avoid the form, (ii) apply the expected consonant alternation (*pylosošu*), or (iii) anomalously forego the alternation (*pylesosju*).

Functional reanalysis

As discussed in §1 above, there may be good non-morphological reasons for the paradigm of a lexeme to restricted, e.g. semantic restrictions. Recategorization can remove semantic restrictions, as when mass nouns are recategorized as count nouns and appear in the plural (*two coffees*). In some instances though it may be argued that the non-morphological restriction has been removed but the morphology has not followed suit. One possible example is the German noun *Eltern* 'parents' which has only a plural form, and can only be used with referents that are both morphosyntactically and semantically plural.[10] The original justification was presumably because the term referred to the canonical pair of mother and father, i.e. to SOMEONE'S parents. As such the word was inherently plural, and any singular reference would have been to *mother* or *father*. In contemporary usage the word has as broad a remit as English *parents*; while the default interpretation may still be 'father and mother', it can also be used e.g. for a roomful of single parents, whose plurality results from sheer force of numbers, and not from inherent pairedness. As such, a corresponding gender-neutral singular is easily imaginable, as evidence by the (relatively) recent coinage *Elternteil* 'parental unit'. But this word has its own plural (*Elternteile*), and so cannot be seen as the singular of *Eltern* in any direct sense. On this interpretation, *Eltern* was formerly an inherently plural item which did not need a singular, and has since become an ordinary count noun whose lack of a singular has become lexicalized.

In some cases reanalysis may involve a shift in word class. One example involves the word *siromax/siromah/siromav* 'pauper, poor man', common to most of the South Slavonic languages. In most of the languages it is a masculine noun, but does show some syntactic overlap with adjectives in that it can be used as an attributive modifier (e.g. Bulgarian *siromax čovek* 'pauper person = poor person'), which is not a function freely available to most morphological nouns. In Macedonian, this has been taken one step further, and the word has been reanalyzed as a morphological adjective, as evidenced by the ending of the masculine definite singular form (adjectival *-iot* in place of nominal *-ot*). Nevertheless, its use has not been extended to feminine and neuter nouns.

	normal noun 'lion'		normal adjective 'beautiful'		defective adjective 'poor'	
	INDEF	DEF	INDEF	DEF	INDEF	DEF
M.SG	lav	lav-ot	ubav	ubav-iot	siromav	siromav-iot
F.SG			ubav-a	ubav-ata	—	—
N.SG			ubav-o	ubav-oto	—	—
PL	lav-i	lav-ite	ubav-i	ubav-ite	siromas-i	siromas-ite

---

[10] Again, as opposed to the typical plurale tantum count noun, whose reference is not semantically restricted; i.e. *scissors* may refer to a single item or multiple items, so long as it is used in a context where nothing needs to agree with it.

This could be seen as an arbitrary morphological restriction, or it could be seen as a semantically motivated restriction, with the adjective specified as [+MASCULINE]. Note though that no other adjectives are restricted by gender, so in either case it is an unusual restriction betraying the origins of the word.[11]

3.2. Decay

Conversely, a once healthy paradigm might decay over time.

'Spontaneous' loss
Forms of a paradigm may fall out of use over time, without anything else apparently having changed. This is at any rate how it seems on the surface, so we have termed this with a perhaps wilful ignorance 'spontaneous' loss. Nevertheless, it stands to reason that something must have happened, however covert, to the rules that govern the construction of the paradigm; e.g. reranking in OT terms. A more concrete example might be where a morphosyntactic value is itself in the process of being downgraded, so that latent problems in the paradigm of some lexemes may simply no longer be worth overcoming. This could account for the defective Greek genitive plural discussed by Sims (2006), since the genitive as a whole (on nouns) has largely yielded to periphrastic constructions with the accusative in the spoken language (Mackridge 1987: 60ff.).

Splitting
Where a paradigm involves some aberrant alternation, speakers may lose the sense of connection between different parts of the paradigm, leaving them stranded. A relatively clear example comes from Polish. The word *deszcz* 'rain' originally had a fairly extreme stem alternation, bordering on the suppletive, between nominative/accusative *deszcz* /deʃtʃ/ and *dżdż-* /dʒdʒ/ in the other cases (this was a direct result of regular sound change). This alternation was levelled out through the extension of the nominative/accusative stem to all forms. The old forms have persisted, but exclusively as a defective noun with the meaning 'drizzle'. For many speakers, there is no sense of the etymological relationship of the two stems.

---

[11] Morphologically, it is also distinguished from other adjectives by retaining a singular~plural stem alternation. Such stem alternations are found with a minority of nouns, but are otherwise not found with adjectives at all.

(15) Polish *deszcz* 'rain'

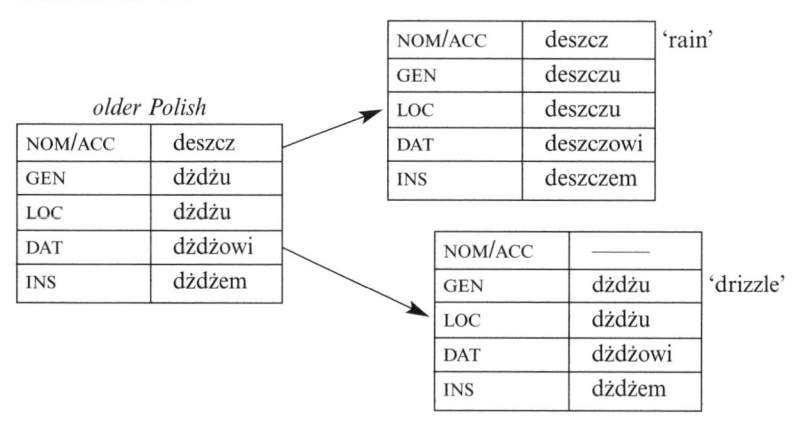

older Polish	
NOM/ACC	deszcz
GEN	dżdżu
LOC	dżdżu
DAT	dżdżowi
INS	dżdżem

		'rain'
NOM/ACC	deszcz	
GEN	deszczu	
LOC	deszczu	
DAT	deszczowi	
INS	deszczem	

		'drizzle'
NOM/ACC	——	
GEN	dżdżu	
LOC	dżdżu	
DAT	dżdżowi	
INS	dżdżem	

Gilliéron (1919) posits a similar development for the defective French verb *frire* 'fry', which originally had the stems *fri-* and *fris-*. On his interpretation, *fris-* was fleshed out into the non-defective verb *friser* 'curl (hair)'—i.e. fry with a curling iron—leaving only remnants of the paradigm with the meaning 'fry'.

Functional restriction
Inflected words may become functionally restricted over time. For example, they may end up used only in certain collocations, or they may drift to the point where we should rather consider them members of a different (uninflected or minimally inflected) word class (as with *midst* or *quoth*, described in §1 above). Here we need not speak of MORPHOLOGICAL defectiveness: the lexemes have as many forms as they need, which just happens to be not that many. But if such functional restrictions were not absolute, we might well get a situation where occasional forays were made into other functional (and hence morphological) territory. For example, the third person forms of the Latin verbs of saying *inquam* had, by Classical times, developed into a quotative particle (*inquit* 3SG, *inquiunt* 3PL), while the first person present (*inquam*) had become a discourse particle meaning 'of course'. Nevertheless, other inflected portions of the paradigm were attested, however rarely (Kühner 1955: 823), suggesting that, for at least some authors, there remained a feeling that this was still an inflectable verb.

3.3. Relativity of the direction of change

If we view defectiveness diachronically it is unavoidable that we see it in terms of arrested development or decay. But we should also bear in mind that the direction of change is relative to the object under observation. In particular, this involves the interaction of related idioms, affecting the interpretation of 'borrowing' and 'spontaneous loss'. Consider, in the abstract, that we have a language *X* with subvarieties *a* and *b*. Lexeme *foo* is borrowed from *a* to *b*, but never develops the full range of forms. From the perspective of the language as a whole this represents decay, as *foo* is a lexeme in *X* and has lost forms in one variety. But from the perspective of *b* it represents arrested development, as *foo* is a novel item. The more one's analysis keeps related idioms separate, the more arrested development one identifies; the more one's analysis merges them, the more decay one identifies.

One parameter is historical period. For example, the French verb *clore* used to be the default verb meaning 'close', with a full paradigm, but is now defective, having been supplanted by *fermer* (for a description of its paradigm, see Boyé and Hofherr, this volume). From this perspective it looks like decay. But according to Gilliéron's (1919) account, the word was completely obsolete by the seventeenth century and was later artificially resuscitated by the French Academy—and apparently, none too successfully. If one recognizes this break in historical continuity, then *clore* was a borrowed word, and its failure to fully adapt an instance of arrested development.

Another parameter is register. The early history of the Russian literary language is characterized by the interplay of two strains, vernacular ('Russian' in the strict sense) and ecclesiastical (Church Slavonic). Church Slavonic had in fact a distinct historical source, based originally on a South Slavonic variety (essentially Old Bulgarian), while Russian is East Slavonic. As such there were substantial morphological and lexical differences between the two, but enough mutual influence that it would be misleading to speak of two distinct languages. The codification of the modern Russian literary language in the eighteenth century saw the incorporation of a great many Church Slavonic elements, though not all of these withstood the test of time. One casualty appears to have been the bound verb stem *-bedit'* found in the verbs *ubedit'* 'convince' and *pobedit'* 'overcome' (for details, see Baerman 2008). These verbs belonged to the same inflection class described above (14), with a stem-final consonant alternation in the 1SG. But crucially, the two systems have different alternations here: Church Slavonic has *d ~ žd* and Russian has *d ~ ž*. The normative standard initially dictated the maintenance of the otherwise anomalous Church Slavonic alternation. This never found full acceptance, but neither has the Russian-style alternation, and these verbs have ended up as defective for many speakers (as indeed they are normatively). Again, whether this is to be construed as decay or arrested development depends on the perspective. If the object of study is literary 'Russian' in the larger sense, subsuming both vernacular and ecclesiastical varieties, then it represents decay, spurred by the imposition of new constraints (in particular, the obligation to adhere to vernacular norms). If the object of study is Russian in the narrow sense, then these verbs represent borrowings from Church Slavonic, and this is a case of arrested development.

4. Conclusion

The foregoing is an attempt to provide a descriptive framework for defectiveness, both as a way of establishing a context for the chapters that follow, and as a contribution to further research on the topic. Although based on the surface characteristics of the paradigms affected, there are obvious implications for the types of analyses which may be appropriate. Thus a gap which corresponds to a morphological stem that embraces an incoherent set of morphosyntactic values will require an analysis that focuses on properties of the form or phonology, while a pattern describable purely in morphosemantic terms will best be analysed as a restriction principally on feature values. We have foregone (we *forwent*?) a typology of possible ANALYSES, as this would seem to be begging the question; any given instance of defectiveness likely involves multiple factors, whose individual contribution we are seldom in a position to sort out. The elusiveness of a comprehensive explanation for paradigm gaps poses a special challenge, which the following chapters boldly take up.

References

Baerman, Matthew. 2008. Historical observations on defectiveness: the first singular non-past. *Russian Linguistics* 37/1. 81–97.

Baxturina, R. V. 1966. Morfonologičeskie uslovija obrazovanija otymennyx glagolov s suffiksom -/0–//-i-(t'). *Razvitie slovoobrazovanija sovremennogo russkogo jazyka*, ed. by E. A. Zemskaja and D. N. Šmelev, 113–26. Moscow: Nauka.

Bogoras, W. 1922. Chukchee. *Handbook of American Indian languages* (part 2), ed. by F. Boas. Washington: Government Printing Office.

Broadwell, George Aaron. 2006. *A Choctaw reference grammar*. Lincoln, Nebraska: University of Nebraska Press.

Brown, Dunstan, Greville G. Corbett, Norman Fraser, Andrew Hippisley and Alan Timberlake. 1996. Russian noun stress and Network Morphology. *Linguistics* 34. 53–107.

Davies, William D. 1986. *Choctaw verb agreement and universal grammar*. Dordrecht: Reidel.

Fraser, Norman M. and Greville G. Corbett. 1995. Gender, animacy and declensional class assignment: a unified account for Russian. *Yearbook of Morphology 1994*, ed. by Geert Booij and Jaap van Marle, 123–50. Dordrecht: Kluwer.

Gilliéron, Jules. 1919. *La faillite de l'étymologie phonétique: Étude sur la défectivité des verbes*. Neuveville: Beerstecher.

Hakulinen, Auli, Maria Vilkuna, Riitta Korhonen, Vesa Koivisto, Tarja Riitta Heinonen and Irja Alho. 2004. *Iso suomen kielioppi.* Helsinki: Suomalaisen Kirjallisuuden Seura.

Hargus, Sharon. 2007. *Witsuwet'en grammar.* Vancouver: University of British Columbia Press.

Heath, Jeffrey. 2005. *A grammar of Tamashek (Tuareg of Mali).* Berlin: Mouton de Gruyter.

Inkelas, Sharon and Cemil Orhan Orgun. 1995. Level ordering and economy in the lexical phonology of Turkish. *Language* 71/4. 763–93.

Itô, Junko and Jorge Hankamer. 1989. Notes on monosyllabism in Turkish. *Phonology at Santa Cruz* 1. Santa Cruz: University of California, Santa Cruz, Syntax Research Center.

Karlsson, Fred. 1999. *Finnish: an essential grammar.* London: Routledge.

Kiparsky, Paul. 1974. Remarks on analogical change. *Historical linguistics: Proceedings of the First International Congress of Historical Linguistics,* ed. by C. Jones and J. Anderson, 257–76. Amsterdam: North-Holland.

Kühner, Raphael. 1955. *Ausführliche Grammatik der lateinischen Sprache.* Hamburg: Hahn.

Mackridge, Peter. 1987. *The Modern Greek language.* Oxford: Oxford University Press.

Matthews, P. H. 1997. *The concise Oxford dictionary of linguistics.* Oxford: Oxford University Press.

Munro, Pamela 2005. Chickasaw. *Native languages of the Southeastern United States,* ed. by H. K. Hardy and J. Scancarelli. Lincoln, Nebraska: University of Nebraska Press.

Munro, Pamela and Lynn Gordon. 1982. Syntactic relations in Western Muskogean: A typological perspective. *Language* 58/1. 81–115.

Neue, Friedrich, and Carl Wagener. 1897, 1902. *Formenlehre der lateinischen Sprache.* vol. 1: *Das Substantivum,* vol. 3: *Das Verbum.* Leipzig: O. R. Reisland and Berlin: Calvary.

Sims, Andrea. 2006. *Minding the gaps: inflectional defectiveness in a paradigmatic theory.* PhD thesis, The Ohio State University.

SKP = Haarala, Risto (ed.). 1996. *Suomen kielen perussanakirja.* Helsinki: Valtion painatuskeskus.

Stump, Gregory. 2002. Morphological and syntactic paradigms: Arguments for a theory of paradigm linkage. *Yearbook of Morphology 2001,* ed. by Geert Booij and Jaap van Marle, 147–80. Dordrecht: Kluwer.

Tschenkéli, Kita. 1958. *Einführung in die georgische Sprache.* Zurich: Amirani.

2

Failing One's Obligations: Defectiveness in Rumantsch Reflexes* of DĒBĒRE

STEPHEN R. ANDERSON

COMPARED WITH SOME OTHER AUTHORS IN THE PRESENT VOLUME, I do not have an overall theory of defectiveness and the status of paradigmatic gaps to offer in this paper. As opposed to the rich and varied array of defectiveness documented by Boyé and Hofherr (this volume) and Maiden and O'Neill (this volume), for other Romance languages, I have only one poor little crippled verb to offer up on parade: a single verb in a relatively obscure language which lacks many of the forms other verbs have, forcing speakers to use a distinct, nearly (but not quite) synonymous verb in its stead. The broader context in which this situation arises is, however, of some interest, I think, and it provides an opportunity to raise (if not to resolve) the question of how gaps should be treated in the context of Optimality Theory.

The language in question is Surmiran, a form of Swiss Rumantsch, although as I will note, somewhat similar phenomena are attested in other related languages. Surmiran is of course a Romance language, and one of a range of farily closely related languages spoken primarily in the canton of Graubünden[1] in Switzerland. Beyond that, however, its affiliations within Romance are somewhat controversial. Traditionally, Swiss Rumantsch is grouped together with Friulian and the Ladin languages of the Dolomites as a 'Rhaeto-Romance' sub-group of Gallo-Romance. The languages in

---

* This work was supported in part by NSF awards #BCS–0418410 and #BCS 98–76456 to Yale University, and by awards from Social Sciences Research Fund at Yale. The Surmiran data here are drawn from dictionaries (Sonder & Grisch 1970, Signorell 1999, including the electronic edition of this work, version 2.0 [01.03.2004]), from the grammar of Signorell, Wuethrich-Grisch & Simeon 1987, and in part from my own field work in Salouf and Savognin during the summers of 2002–2008. Comments from the audience at the London Defectiveness Conference, and also from Martin Maiden and Andrew Carstairs-McCarthy have been useful in preparing this paper.
[1] 'Grisons' in French, 'Grigioni' in Italian, or 'Grischun' in Rumantsch.

Table 1. 'Rhaeto-Rumantsch'

	Swiss Rumantsch		Dolomitic Ladin	Friulian
Engadine	Central	Western		
Puter	**Surmiran**	Sursilvan	Gardena	Friulian
Vallader	(Bergün)		Gadera	
(Val Müstair)	(Obervaz)		Fassa	
	Sutsilvan		Livinallongo	
			Ampezzo	

question are shown in Table 1; among the Swiss Rumantsch languages, those with distinct literary and orthographic standards are unparenthesized, while several other quite distinct forms of Rumantsch (not at all an exhaustive list) are given in parentheses.

Haiman and Benincà 1992 argue that the evidence that the languages in Table 1 form a distinct genetic group within Gallo-Romance, as opposed to being simply a set of Gallo-Romance languages spoken within a comparatively well-defined area, is weak or non-existent. Since our concern will be primarily with Surmiran, these comparative considerations are not of great importance, however.

The verbal system of Surmiran falls well within the 'normal' range for a Romance language. The present indicative paradigm of a regular verb such as *cantar* 'to sing' as shown in (1) includes distinct forms for singular and plural in three persons, with a typical difference in the location of main stress in the first and second person plural as opposed to the rest of the paradigm which will be important in what follows below.

(1) *cantar* 'sing' (PRS IND): 1SG (ia) cant [kant]
2SG (te) cantas ['kantəs]
3SG (el) canta ['kantə]
1PL (nous) cantagn [kənˈtaɲ]
2PL (vous) cantez [kənˈtɛts]
3PL (els) cantan ['kantən]

In addition to the present indicative, Surmiran verbs show a number of other forms. These include the present subjunctive, illustrated in (2), in which the main stress is consistently on the stem.

(2) *cantar* 'sing' (PRS SBJV): 1SG (ia) canta ['kantə]
2SG (te) cantas ['kantəs]
3SG (el) canta ['kantə]
1PL (nous) cantan ['kantən]
2PL (vous) cantas ['kantəs]
3PL (els) cantan ['kantən]

There are also several other tenses, for which 1SG forms are given in (3); like the present subjunctive, these forms show a consistent location of main stress.

(3) **Imperfect** (ia) cantava [kənˈtavə];
   Future (ia) cantaro [kanˈtəro];
   Imperfect subjunctive/Conditional (ia) cantess [kənˈtɛs]

Non-finite forms include the gerund (*cantond* [kənˈtond]); a (potentially agreeing) Past participle (masculine *canto* [ˈkantə], feminine *cantada* [kənˈtadə]) and the imperative (singular *canta!* [kˈantə], plural *cante!* [kənˈte]). A number of other tenses are built periphrastically from forms of the auxilliary verbs *esser* 'be' and *aveir* 'have' together with non-finite forms of a lexical verb.

In this context, we can now examine our defective verb, as illustrated in (4).

(4) *dueir* 'should':
   a. Present indicative: 1PL. *duagn* [dʊˈaɲ], 2PL. *duez* (dʊˈɛts]; all singular forms and 3PL missing)
   b. Present subjunctive: missing
   c. Imperfect (*ia*) *dueva* [dʊˈevə]; future *duaro* [dʊəˈro]; imperfect subjunctive/conditional *duess* [dʊˈɛs]
   d. Gerund *duond* [dʊˈond]; past participle *duia, dueida* [dʊˈiə, dʊˈejdə]
   e. Imperative: missing

The absence of an imperative form of *dueir* 'should' (4e) is clearly a semantic fact and not in need of further explanation. The same is not true for the absence of a present subjunctive, however: this is the form that expresses reported speech, among other uses, and there is nothing about it that is either marginal or semantically inconsistent with a modal of obligation. Similarly, there is no obvious basis for the lack of singular or 3PL present indicative forms. What seems to be the case is simply that *dueir* lacks certain forms, as shown in (4), and that this idiosyncrasy is to be accounted for in some way on the basis of the verb's specific lexical representation. Before we can make a specific proposal along those lines, however, we must lay out the broader picture within which it is to be understood.

Some general considerations related to the analysis of the Surmiran verb are presented in Anderson 2008a. The 'regular' verbs of the language are not all like *cantar*, but belong to one or another of six classes (descended in obvious ways from the conjugation classes of Latin) as listed in (5).

(5)

INF	EXAMPLE	1PL PRS	IMPRF	FUT	COND	PST PTCP
-ar [-ar]	cantar 'sing'	-agn	-ava	-aro	-ess	-o/ada
-er [-er]	lascher 'leave'	-agn	-eva	-aro	-ess	-ea/eda

22   *Stephen R. Anderson*

-ier [-iər]	spitgier 'expect'	-agn	-iva	-aro	-ess	-ia/eida
-eir [-ɛjr]	tameir 'fear'	-agn	-eva	-aro	-ess	-ia/eida
-er [-ər]	tanscher 'reach'	-agn	-eva	-aro	-ess	-ia/eida
-eir [-ejr]	parteir 'depart'	-ign	-iva	-iro	-iss	-ia/eida

A large number of verbs show substantial conjugational irregularity; in some cases this falls into patterns of limited sub-regularities, but in any event must be indicated for the individual verbs in question. Some of the irregular verbs are illustrated in (6).

(6) eir 'go' neir 'come' (vu)leir 'want' deir 'say' star 'stay, live' saveir 'know'

	eir	neir	(vu)leir	deir	star	saveir
1SG	vign	vign	vi	dei	stung	sa
2SG	vast	vignst	vot	deist	stast	sast
3SG	vo	vign	vot	dei	stat	so
1PL	giagn	nign	lagn	schagn	stagn	savagn
2PL	gez	niz	lez	schez	stez	savez
3PL	von	vignan	vottan	deian	stattan	son

Members of a much larger class of 'alternating' verbs, however show a single basic deviation from the simple conjugation pattern in (2). In the present indicative these verbs, as illustrated in (7), have one stem in the first and second person plural and another with a distinct vowel in the remaining forms.

(7)

	ludar 'praise'	durmeir 'sleep'	lavar 'get up'	fittar 'finish'
1SG	lod	dorm	lev	fet
2SG	lodas	dormas	levas	fettas
3SG	loda	dorma	leva	fetta
1PL	ludagn	durmign	lavagn	fittagn
2PL	ludez	durmiz	lavez	fittez
3PL	lodan	dorman	levan	fettan

Apart from the present indicative, these alternating verbs show the same stem as that of the singular and third person plural in their present subjunctive paradigm and also in the singular imperative, as illustrated in (8).

(8)

	ludar	durmeir	lavar	fittar
1SG	'loda	'dorma	'leva	'fetta
2SG	'lodas	'dormas	'levas	'fettas
3SG	'loda	'dorma	'leva	'fetta
1PL	'lodan	'dorman	'levan	'fettan
2PL	'lodas	'dormas	'levas	'fettas
3PL	'lodan	'dorman	'levan	'fettan
2SG IMP	'loda!	'dorma!	'leva!	'fetta!

The remaining forms of these verbs, however, as illustrated in (9), are built from the same stem as the first and second plural of the present indicative.

(9) infinitive: ludar   durmeir   lavar   fittar
     1PL PRS ([-'aɲ]/[-'iɲ])   ludagn   durmign   lavagn   fittagn
     1SG IMPRF ([-'evə]/[-'ivə])   ludeva   durmiva   laveva   fitteva
     1SG FUT ([-ə'ro]/[-ɪ'ro])   ludaro   durmiro   lavaro   fittaro
     1SG COND ([-'ɛs]/[-'ɪs])   ludess   durmiss   lavess   fittess
     2PL IMP ([-'e]/[-'i])   lude!   durmi!   lave!   fitte!
     PRS. PTCP ([-'ɔnd])   ludond   durmond   lavond   fittond

A final form of the verb which has not been accommodated above is the infinitive. In general, the infinitive in Surmiran is built on the same stem as the first and second person plural present indicative, as can be seen in the verbs in (7). Exceptionally in this regard, 'Fifth conjugation' verbs, whose infinitive ends in [-ər], have infinitives built on the stem of the singular and third plural of the present indicative: e.g. *discorrer* [dɪʃ'korər] 'speak'; 1SG present *discor* [dɪʃ'kor]; 1PL present *discurrign* [dɪʃku'riɲ].

Lexically idiosyncratic forms of genuinely suppletive irregular verbs, like those in (6), are of course associated with specific bundles of morphosyntactic features. No coherent morphosyntactic characterization of the categories calling for one or the other of the stems of alternating verbs is available, though. This observation is reinforced by the fact that infinitives, as just noted, can call for one stem or the other depending on their ending.

On the other hand, a clear basis for the choice of stem does exist across all categories: one stem is used when main stress falls on the desinence (as in 1PL, 2PL present indicative and the other forms in (9)) while the other is used when main stress falls on the stem itself (as in (8)). The difference between infinitives like *discorrer* [dɪʃ'korər] 'speak' and others is that only in the 'Fifth conjugation' does stress fall on the stem.

Disregarding obvious loan words, stress in Surmiran is largely predictable from the phonological form of a word: main stress falls on the penultimate if the rhyme of the final syllable consists of [ə], possibly followed by [r], [l], [n], or [s]. If the final syllable contains a full (non-ə) vowel, or ə followed by some other consonant, it bears the main stress. Secondary stress falls on initial syllables separated by at least one syllable from the main stress; parts of compounds are stressed separately with main stress on the stress centre of the final element. Other secondary stresses appear to result from cyclic word formation, although the principles at work have not been fully worked out.

Vowel quality and stress are inter-related. Stressed syllables can contain a variety of vowels (long and short) and diphthongs. Unstressed syllables typically contain only short [ə] (written *a* or *e*), [ɪ] (*i*) or [ʊ] (*u*), though unstressed [ɛ, ɔ] are not rare. Looking at the relation between stressed and unstressed stems in alternating verbs like (7), then, it is reasonable to ask whether the stem alternation might not simply reflect the effects of a phonological rule of vowel reduction.

Reasons to reject this analysis are presented in Anderson 2008a, 2008b, and will not be rehearsed here in detail. Even confining our attention to simple alternation patterns like those illustrated in (7), the correspondence between the vowels in the two stems of verbs is many-to-many, and not unique in either direction. Each of unstressed [ə, ɪ, ʊ] in a stem can alternate with any of several vowels, and the correspondence between particular stressed vowels and their unstressed counterparts is equally non-unique. The same stressed vowel can correspond to more than one unstressed vowel (for [a] and [o], to all three). There is no stressed vowel whose unstressed correspondent is unique.

Furthermore, stem alternation can also involve consonants, with or without accompanying vowel changes; apparent metathesis (really V/Ø with subsequent epenthesis); and more complex, multi-vowel alternations such as those in (10).

(10)
Alternation	Infinitive	3SG PRS IND	gloss
a–ə ~ o–e	flammager	flommegia	'blaze'
e–ə ~ ə–e	declarar	daclera	'declare'
i–i ~ ə–e	angivinar	angiavegna	'solve'
i–i ~ ə–ei̯	misirar	maseira	'measure'
i–i ~ ə–i	ghisignier	gasigna	'taunt'
u–ə ~ ə–o	murmagner	marmogna	'murmur'
u–ə ~ ə–oi̯	suarar	savoira	'smell'
u–ə ~ ə–u	ruschanar	raschunga	'speak'
u–Ø ~ ə–ou̯	luvrar	lavoura	'work'

The simple vowel alternations in (7) are just part of a more comprehensive system of stem alternations which are idiosyncratically associated with particular lexical items. Each alternating word has two listed stems, one used when stress falls on it, and the other when stresss falls on an ending. The origins of these various patterns of alternation are in the historical phonology of the language, and especially in a simple rule of vowel reduction that once characterized the relation between the vocalism of stressed and unstressed syllables. However, complex phonological developments over time (cf. Lutta 1923, pp. 120–36, Grisch 1939, pp. 76–94, Haiman and Benincà 1992, pp. 56–63), plus the influx of German words with vowels other than [ə, ɪ, ʊ] in unstressed syllables have made the original vowel reduction regularity opaque. Stem alternation is the morphologized remnant of that process, and can no longer be reduced to the effects of a phonological rule of vowel reduction.

A tempting possibility is to suggest that the alternations are an instance of the morphomic 'N-pattern' of Maiden (1992, 2004, 2005, Maiden and O'Neill, this volume), instantiated (as Maiden shows) in numerous Romance languages. On that analysis the difference between the categories calling for one stem or the other corresponds not to a coherent set of morphosyntactic categories, but rather to a language particular set, a *morphome* in the sense of Aronoff 1994.

While that analysis is appealing for many other Romance languages, it is much less so for Surmiran. First of all, the distribution is clearly correlated with an obvious phonological factor, stress: one stem is used when main stress falls on the stem itself as in (8), 'Fifth conjugation' infinitives, and the singular and 3PL present indicative. The other is used when main stress falls outside the stem, as in 1PL, 2PL present indicative and the other forms in (9), and other infinitives. Not only is the phonological conditioning compelling and clear, it also contradicts any morphologically based categorization, in the case of the infinitive.

Furthermore, we find the same patterns of alternation, again correlated with the location of stress, in derivationally related non-verbs, to which the 'N-Pattern' morphome would not apply. Where the forms involved are related to a verb, the stems that appear are generally the same as those that are found in the verb's paradigm, as in the lexical sets in (11).

(11) a. burschanar 'brush' 3SG PRS barschunga
     barschung 'brush (N)'; (la) burschaneda '(process of) brushing'
   b. cuglianar 'swindle' 3SG PRS cugliunga
     cugliung 'swindler'; (la) cuglianada '(act of) swindling'
   c. guttar 'to drip' 3SG PRS gotta
     got 'drop (N)'; gutella 'drip (N), (eye)drop', guttarada 'sudden snow-melt'
   d. néiver 'to snow' 3SG PRS neiva, PP. navia
     neiv 'snow'; navaglia 'big snowfall'; navada '(lots of) snow'
   e. véiver 'to live' 3SG PRS veiva, 2PL PRS vivagn
     veiv 'alive'; vivent 'one who lives'

At least one alternating verb has related non-verbal forms with a different alternation, illustrated in (12).

(12) suarar 'to smell' 3SG PRS savoira
     savour 'smell (N)'; savurous 'fragrant'

In a significant number of forms, however, the 'stressed' stem appears in a form where it does not take the stress, as shown in (13).

(13) a. ˈsfend[ər] '(to) split' 1PL PRS sfandagn
     sfandia 'cracked (adj)'; sfendibel 'splittable'
   b. durmeir '(to) sleep' 3SG PRS dorma
     durmigliun 'late riser' dormulent 'sleepy'
   c. satger '(to) dry [intransitive]' 3SG PRS setga
     setg(a) 'dry (adj.)'; setgantar '(to) dry [transitive]'
   d. anganar 'defraud' 3SG PRS angiona
     anganous 'fraudulent'; angion 'fraud (N)'; angionareia 'deceit (coll.)'

e. preschentar '(to) present' 3SG PRS preschainta
preschentaziun 'presentation; preschaint 'present (adj)'; preschaintamaintg 'presently'

Some of these are clearly derived from other words in which the stressed base is motivated: *setgantar* 'to make dry' is de-adjectival, from *setg(a)*; *preschaintamaintg* is an adverb derived (as in other Romance languages) from the feminine form of the adjective *preschainta*, etc. Others represent more compositional, word-level derivation, as opposed to (sometimes semantically idiosyncratic) stem-level derivation, comparable to the situation in English.

I assume here that morphology and phonology interact cyclically, on roughly the model of 'Stratal OT' (Kiparsky 2000; Bermudez-Otero Forthcoming). Each cycle of morphological formation provides the input to an appropriate constraint system which determines the corresponding phonological form—which may in turn serve as the basis for further cycles of morphological formation. Stem choice takes place on the first cycle to which a stem is subject, and once the stem is determined, that decision is not revisited on subsequent cycles. As a result, if the 'stressed' base is chosen on the first stem cycle, and this form is subsequently extended by further endings so that the vowel stressed on the first cycle no longer bears stress, the original stem will appear inappropriate. (cf. Kamprath 1987 for discussion of motivations for cyclic interaction in a closely related form of Rumantsch).

Word-level morphology is based on an input from the stem level, where the stem choice (in the absence of stress-attracting stem extensions) will favour the 'stressed' stem. Subsequent layers of word-level morphology will render this choice opaque. Consistent with this picture, note that such opaque or 'incorrect' stem choice never involves the appearance of the 'unstressed' stem in a word where it would bear stress.

In addition to the stem alternations we have seen above, a great many verbs in the 'productive' [-ar] and [-ejr] conjugations form their 'stressed' stem with the extension *-esch*, as illustrated in (14).

(14) *luschardar* ([lužər'dar]) 'strut':

1SG	luschardesch
2SG	luschardeschas
3SG	luschardescha
1PL	luschardagn
2PL	luschardez
3PL	luschardeschan
PRS SBJV	luschardescha, etc.
IMP SG	luschardescha!
IMP PL	luscharde!
IMPRF	luschardeva, etc.

For such verbs, the 'stressed' stem is always formed by extending the 'unstressed' stem with *-esch*, and the stress itself falls on this extension. As a result, of course, no other stem alternation occurs in these verbs. The distribution of *-esch* obviously follows the same pattern as that of the 'stressed' stem in alternating verbs, but this does not in any way compromise the observation that it is the location of main stress that conditions the appearance of one stem as opposed to the other.

The 'stressed' stem in *-esch* is clearly a matter of *verbal* morphology: it never shows up except in verbal inflection. Verbs that take *-esch* in their stem-stressed forms always use the 'unstressed' stem as the base for derivation (e.g. *fixar/fixescha* 'fix, harden'; *fix* 'fast, unmoveable', *fixaziun* 'fixation').

Verbs in *-esch* include many recent borrowings. Some verbs listed as alternating in Sonder and Grisch 1970 appear in Signorell 1999 with *-esch* (and current speakers extend this trend to additional verbs). Sometimes when speakers do not know or cannot recall the correct alternation pattern for a given verb, they produce *-esch* forms instead. It seems plausible that the absence of (internal) stem alternation in verbs with *-esch* is related to their use in these 'default' conditions. Of course this observation does not in itself constitute an analysis, though one will be proposed below.

I conclude that, although the stem alternations in Surmiran (and their parallels in the other Swiss Rumantsch languages) have their origin in strictly phonological processes, those have become opaque, and are now lost as phonological rules. The residual allomorphy, however, is governed by a strictly phonological condition: one stem or the other is chosen depending on the location of main stress in the output form. Unlike many other instances of phonologically conditioned allomorphy (Carstairs 1986, 1988), this pattern affects most content words in the language, not just a small set such as a few affixes, or the 'mobile diphthongs' of Italian (van der Veer and Booij 2009). Since it is stems, and not affixes that alternate, a sub-categorization solution (Paster 2009; Bye 2007) does not seem appropriate. Instead, I adopt an approach that treats stem choice as a matter of optimization based on phonological conditions (as in Kager 2008; Rubach and Booij 2001).

The analysis I proposed for these facts in Anderson 2008a is as follows. First, let us assume the distinctions [a] *vs.* [ə], [i] *vs.* [ɪ], [u] *vs.*[ʊ]. The first member of each pair should only appear in stressed position, the second only in unstressed position. The phonology of Surmiran includes a set of (Optimality Theoretic) constraints that express these preferred associations between stress (or its absence) and vowel quality, as well as others that describe the location of stress itself.

Stems have two (listed) alternants in the lexicon. In one of these the last vowel is generally from the set [ə, ɪ, ʊ], and in the other the last vowel is a full vowel or diphthong. In the derivation of a given verbal (or other) form, the input consists not just of a single stem, but rather of both listed stem possibilities, together with the remaining affixal material associated with the form in question. This provides two sets of candidate forms, one set based on each of the possible stems for the word in question. The constraints that associate full vowels with stressed syllables and reduced vowels with unstressed ones then function to choose the optimal form from the union of these two sets on the basis of the location of main stress.

This approach allows us to reduce the amount of arbitrary specification even in the case of verbs showing idiosyncratic patterns of suppletion, for most of which the actual idiosyncrasy is quite circumscribed. The verb *pudeir* 'can, be able to' for instance, as illustrated in (15), can be treated as having two stems like any other verb, but with three additional forms listed for specific morphosyntactic circumstances.

(15) 1SG   ia poss
     2SG   te post
     3SG   el pò
     1PL   nous pudagn
     2PL   vous pudez
     3PL   els pon
     Stems   {/pɔs/, /pud/}
     Listed: 2∅SG, 3SG and 3PL present indicative (/pɔst/, /pɔ/, /pɔn/)

Verbs in *-esch* can now be described as having only an 'unstressed' stem. The morphology includes a rule introducing *-esch* in verbs, formulated roughly as in (16).

(16)   /X/ → /Xɛʃ/ $\left[+\overline{\text{VERB}}\right]$

According to normative descriptions such as that of Signorell et al. 1987, this rule is limited in its application to [-ar] and [-ejr] verbs. That is generally true, although I have recorded instances of *-esch* forms for a few other verbs.

Rule (16) would appear to be much too general, but in the context of an Optimality Theoretic description its actual application is quite limited. Notice that it mandates the introduction of phonological material into a verbal form, material that corresponds to no aspect of the form's morphosyntactic or semantic content. As a result, higher ranking **Dep** constraints (requiring that material in the output correspond to material in the input) would always disprefer the application of this stem addition, unless some other constraint were satisfied exactly by the presence of the otherwise gratuitous suffix material. Of course, that will be the case exactly when the presence of *-esch* results in a prosodically preferred form, by avoiding stress on the unstressable vowel in the last syllable of such a verb's only lexical stem. Ranking the constraints relating stress and vowel quality above the relevant **Dep** constraint (itself ranked above (16) construed as a constraint) will thus have the effect of introducing *-esch* in exactly those verbal forms where it would bear the main stress.

With this overall framework in place, we can return to the specific problem of *dueir* [dʊɛjr] 'should' (cf. (4) above). The descriptive generalization regarding this verb is as follows: all and only the forms built on the 'unstressed' stem /du/ exist, and these are constructed in completely regular fashion.

We might ask what we would expect the 'stressed stem' forms of *dueir* to look like. The only other verbs of the shape [C₀uɛjr] are suppletive in their 'stressed stem' forms, as illustrated in (17) for *stueir* 'must, should'.

(17) 1SG   stò
      2SG   stost
      3SG   stò
      1PL   stuagn
      2PL   stuez
      3PL   ston

Superficially similar verbs that use the stem extension *-esch* in the stem-stressed forms (e.g. *cueir* 'allow'; *flueir* 'flow'; *prueir* 'sprout', etc.) differ from *dueir*, *stueir* in that they end in [-ejr], and thus (unlike *du*[ɛ]*ir*, *stu*[ɛ]*ir*) fall within the conjugation class for which this stem extension is possible (as opposed to [-ɛjr] verbs like *dueir*, to which rule (14) is generally inapplicable).

In terms of the classification of defectiveness given by Baerman and Corbett (this volume), the aetiology of the gaps in the paradigm of this verb is morphological, consisting in the lack of a stem present for other comparable lexical items. It is thus similar to Baerman and Corbett's example of the absence of the infinitive stem of *erkanee* 'spread out' in Finnish. *Dueir* is defective in having no 'stressed' stem, and no valid model on which one can be constructed. That is, *dueir* only has a single stem (/du/). Where stress would fall on this stem, the form is missing.

The gaps in the paradigm of *dueir* do not leave a speaker of Surmiran silent: where one of the missing forms would be required, a corresponding form of the nearly synonymous verb *stueir* 'must' is substituted. This verb is itself suppletive, as shown in (17). It is tempting simply to see the forms of *dueir* and *stueir* as constituting a single paradigm displaying internal suppletion, but this is probably not correct. For one thing, *stueir* itself has a full paradigm independent of that of *dueir*, and where both forms exist (e.g. *nous duagn/stuagn*) there is a subtle semantic difference between them linked to the degree of obligation implied. It seems most reasonable to say simply that *dueir* lacks certain forms, as shown in (4), and that where one of the missing forms would be required, the meaning is expressed by a form of the semantically very similar verb *stueir* instead.

This conclusion is somewhat problematic within an Optimality Theoretic account. The essence of that theory is that the constraints constituting a grammar are ranked, and violable; and that the observed form corresponding to a given input will be the one that represents the best possible compromise with the requirements of the constraint system. That implies that for any given input, there ought to be *some* possible output, even if this is phonologically and/or morphologically ill-formed to some degree. Such a theory is incompatible in its essence with absolute ungrammaticality of the type represented by defective paradigms, including that of Surmiran *dueir*. A substantial literature within the OT tradition has arisen attempting to provide compatible mechanisms for describing the absolute impossibility of certain forms; I will not review the various devices that have been proposed for this purpose in detail here, but simply note that no consensus has been reached that any particular proposal is satisfactory.

In a case such as this one, where the missing forms are substituted by ones from the paradigm of a semantically similar verb, we might at least describe the situation as follows. Perhaps the constraints associating vowel quality with stress (or its absence) outrank other constraints that require a given meaning to be lexicalized by a (form of) a specific verb. Let us call this '**Faith (Lexicalization)**', and assume that a minimal violation of it consists in employing a distinct lexical item whose meaning is as close as possible semantically to that of the intended word. Assuming that such a requirement could be outweighed by phonological considerations such as those relating vowel quality and stress, an input that included a verb whose only stem is /dʊ/ together with associated morphology that would cause the main stress to fall on the (reduced) vowel [ʊ] might be realized by a form of the distinct verb *stueir*, for which phonologically well-formed forms with stem stress are available. I do not pretend, however, that this constitutes a deeply principled solution to a problem which must remain for the overall approach represented by Optimality Theory.

The situation surrounding Surmiran *dueir* must be of relatively recent origin, and it may be useful to establish some of the historical and comparative context in which it has arisen. According to Decurtins 1958, earlier Surmiran had a fuller paradigm for *daveir*. F. DaSale (*Fundamenti della lingua Retica*, 1729, *apud* Decurtins 1958) had *dé, dest, de, dejen, deies, deien* for the present indicative; for the corresponding present subjunctive [1SG not attested], *deiest, deia, deiegns, deies, deien*; and Imperfect *daveva*. These show no stress alternations within a tense, but the verb seems to have stems [dəv] and [de] within a system in which stress may have been less predictable phonologically than in modern Surmiran. A 1768 *Catechism* has 1PL present indicative *deiagns*, surely with desinential stress. Subsequently, the forms with stem stress were lost (and replaced in usage by forms of *stueir*). Present indicative *duagn, duez* (with stem /dʊ/ < /dəv/) were presumably preserved because they had been rebuilt with stress on the endings.

It is interesting to compare these facts with those of the Rumantsch languages of the Engadine, where we find essentially the mirror image of the Surmiran situation. Consider the paradigm of Vallader *dovair* 'should' (cf. Tscharner 2000) given in (18).

(18) **Present Indicative:** 1SG   dess [dɛs]
     2SG   dessast [ˈdɛsəst]
     3SG   dess [dɛs]
     1PL   dessan [ˈdɛsən]
     2PL   dessat [ˈdɛsət]
     3PL   dessan [ˈdɛsən]

Present Subjunctive: 1SG   dessa [ˈdɛsə]
     2SG   dessast [ˈdɛsəst]
     3SG   dessa [ˈdɛsə]
     1PL   dessan [ˈdɛsən]
     2PL   dessat [ˈdɛsət]
     3PL   dessan [ˈdɛsən]

All other forms of this verb (that is, all those with desinential stress) are lacking. Although dictionaries cite it as a verb with a lexical entry indentified as *dovair* [doˈvajr], in fact this form is not a verbal infinitive and is only used as a noun meaning 'duty, obligation'. The **verb** identified as *'dovair'* lacks any forms with a stem like [dŏv-] where main stress does not fall on the stem. The missing forms include an infinitive **doˈvair*, and imperfect **doˈvaiva*, past definite **doˈvet*, future **dovaˈra*, etc. Puter *'dovair'* is the same, except that the 1PL forms (indicative and subjunctive) are both *dessans* [ˈdɛsəns].

In Vallader and Puter, this verb only has a single stem /dɛs/ (historically an intrusion from the conditional paradigm, but now used for the present), which is necessarily stressed. The pattern of defectiveness is thus exactly the opposite of that in Surmiran, but the analysis is entirely parallel: as opposed to other verbs in the language, this one has only one stem, a stem which is only phonologically appropriate for a restricted set of inflected forms. Where stress would not fall on the stem, this verb cannot be used.

The lack of a second, unstressed, stem is particularly remarkable in Vallader and Puter, because of the presence in the lexicon of a related noun which could provide /dɔv/ as an unstressed stem. Although surprising, this situation is not at all unprecedented in the language. Essentially, the stem alternation characteristic of a given verb is independent in principle of the alternations shown in derivationally related words. In (12) above, we already saw one word family in which the verbal alternation was distinct from that in non-verbal forms. Similarly, there are a number of verbs whose conjugation involves the stem extension *-esch*, and which on the present analysis therefore have only one lexical stem, but for which related non-verbal forms exist that would supply a model for a 'stressed' stem, as illustrated in (19).

(19) a. favoréir 'to favour' 3SG pres. favorescha
favour 'favòur'; favorevel 'favourable'

b. fludrar 'line (clothing)' 3SG pres. fludrescha
flodra 'lining (of an article of clothing)'; fludrader 'one who lines (clothes)'

c. sblitgier 'to bleach' 3SG pres. sblitgescha
sblatg 'bleach(ed) (N,A)'; sblitgider 'one who bleaches'

The fact that the stem of Vallader/Puter *dovair* 'duty, obligation' does not automatically become available to serve as the unstressed base of forms of the related verb in (18), then, is not isolated.

Other Swiss Rumantsch languages do not provide additional data points. Sutsilvan has a full paradigm for the verb *duer*: Present indicative *de, des, de; duagn, duez, den*; present subjunctive *degi, degias, degi; dueian, dueias, degian*, etc. with abundant alternations based on multiple lexical stems. Sursilvan (Western Rumantsch) also has a full paradigm. Defectiveness is thus limited to Surmiran and the Engadine languages. The artificially constructed language known as 'Rumantsch Grischun' has eliminated the stress alternations in most verbs, generalizing desinential stress throughout the paradigm. There are thus no stem alternations in verbs apart from a very small set. Not surprisingly, Rumantsch Grischun *duair* has a fully regular paradigm.

Surmiran *dueir*, like Vallader/Puter *dovair*, is a reflex of Latin DĒBĒRE, itself from DE+HABĒRE. In other 'Rhaeto-Romance' languages, this verb has competed unsuccessfully in many instances with semantically similar modals, in ways that are not always based on phonology. In the Dolomitic Ladin of the Val Gadera, for example (cf. Kramer 1990), it survives only in the present (formally a conditional as in the Engadine languages: *dess, desses, dess, dessun, desses, dess*), and the imperfect indicative (*dô, dôs, dô, dôn, dôs, dô*), with stem alternation. Elsewhere it is replaced by forms of *messëi* (from German *müssen*) or Northern Italian *cognèr*.

I suggest that the primary factor in the emergence of defectiveness in Surmiran *dueir*, as well as the complementary pattern in the Engadine languages, was the morphologization of the vowel alternations in Swiss Rumantsch. If we hypothesize that this was combined with reduced use of the verb due to competition with others such as *stueir*, it could well have led to the present situation with only one stem conserved. An understanding of that situation, however, is only possible on the basis of a comprehensive picture of the pattern of stem alternations in these languages, a particularly dramatic example of the replacement of productive phonology by a system of phonologically conditioned allomorphy.

References

Anderson, Stephen R. 2008a. Phonologically conditioned allomorphy in Surmiran (Rumantsch). *Word Structure* 1. 109–34.
Anderson, Stephen R. 2008b. Stress-conditioned allomorphy in Surmiran (Rumantsch). Paper given at OxMorph 1 Workshop, Oxford University, 27 August.
Aronoff, Mark. 1994. *Morphology by itself*. Cambridge, MA: MIT Press.
Baerman, Matthew and Greville G. Corbett. This volume. Defectiveness: typology and diachrony, 18.
Bermudez-Otero, Ricardo. Forthcoming. *Stratal optimality theory*. Oxford: Oxford University Press.
Boyé, Gilles and Patricia Cabredo Hofherr. This volume. Defectiveness as stem suppletion in French and Spanish verbs, 35–62.
Bye, Patrick. 2007. Allomorphy—selection, not optimization. *Freedom of analysis?*, ed. by M. Krämer, S. Blaho, and P. Bye. Berlin: Mouton de Gruyter.
Carstairs, Andrew. 1986. *Allomorphy in inflexion*. London: Croom Helm.
Carstairs, Andrew. 1988. Some implications of phonologically conditioned suppletion. *Yearbook of Morphology* 1. 67–94.
Decurtins, Alexi. 1958. *Zur Morphologie der unregelmäßigen Verben im Bündnerromanischen*. Vol. 62: Romanica Helvetica. Bern: A. Francke Verlag.
Decurtins, Caspar. 1982. *Rätoromanische chrestomathie*. Vol. X.1: Sursettisch, Sutsettisch. Chur: Octopus Verlag. Reprint of 1914 edition.
Grisch, Mena. 1939. *Die Mundart von Surmeir*. Vol. 12 of Romanica Helvetica. Paris: E. Droz.
Haiman, John and Paola Benincà. 1992. *The Rhaeto-Romance languages*. London: Routledge.
Kager, René. 2008. Lexical irregularity and the typology of contrast. *The nature of the word: Essays in honor of Paul Kiparsky*, ed. by K. Hanson and S. Inkelas. pp. 397–432. Cambridge MA: MIT Press.
Kamprath, Christine. 1987. *Suprasegmental structures in a Raeto-Romansh dialect: A case study in metrical and lexical phonology*. PhD thesis. University of Texas at Austin.
Kiparsky, Paul. 2000. Opacity and cyclicity. *The Linguistic Review* 17. 351–67.
Kramer, Johannes. 1990. *Etymologisches Wörterbuch des Dolomitenladinischen (EWD)*. Hamburg: Helmut Buske Verlag.
Lutta, C. Martin. 1923. *Der Dialekt von Bergün*. Vol. 71. Beihefte Zur Zeitschrift für romanische Philologie, Halle (Saale): Max Niemeyer.
Maiden, Martin. 1992. Irregularity as a determinant of morpholigcal change. *Journal of Linguistics* 28. 285–312.
Maiden, Martin. 2004. When lexemes become allomorphs—on the genesis of suppletion. *Folia Linguistica* 38. 227–56.
Maiden, Martin. 2005. Morphological autonomy and diachrony. *Yearbook of Morphology 2004*. 137–75.
Maiden, Martin and Paul O'Neill. This volume. On morphemic defectiveness: evidence from the Romance Languages of the Iberian peninsular, 103–24.

Paster, Mary. 2009. Phonologically conditioned suppletive allomorphy: Cross-linguistic results and theoretical consequences. *Tranel* (2009).
Rubach, Jerzy and Geert Booij. 2001. Allomorphy in optimality theory: Polish iotation. *Language* 77. 26–60.
Signorell, Faust, ed. 1999. *Vocabulari surmiran-tudestg/Wörterbuch Deutsch-Surmiran*. Coira: Departamaint d'educaziun digl Grischun.
Signorell, Faust, Mena Wuethrich-Grisch and Gion Pol Simeon. 1987. *Normas surmiranas*. Coira: Tgesa editoura cantunala per stampats e meds d'instrucziun.
Sonder, Ambros and Mena Grisch. 1970. *Vocabulari da Surmeir*. Coira: Leia Rumantscha.
Tsharner, Gion. 2000. *Verbs Valladers*. Cuoira: Chasa editura per mezs d'instrucziun dal chantun Grischun.
Tranel, Bernard, ed. 2009. Understanding allomorphy: *Perspectives from optimality theory*. London: Equinox Press.
van der Veer, Bart and Geert Booij. 2009. Allomorphy in OT: The Italian mobile diphthongs. *Tranel* (2009).

3

Defectiveness as Stem Suppletion in French and Spanish Verbs[1]

GILLES BOYÉ AND PATRICIA CABREDO HOFHERR

1. Introduction

WE EXAMINE A PARTICULAR TYPE OF DEFECTIVENESS in French and Spanish verbs. In the cases considered, the gaps in the paradigm cover the same zones as the stem suppletion patterns observed in irregular verbs: in these examples defectiveness runs along the same lines as the systematic stem syncretisms of the verbal system (see Stump, this volume). For verbs that are defective for all the forms in a zone of systematic stem syncretism we propose that defectiveness is associated to the level of the stem. Following Aronoff (1994 ch2., pp 54–5), we propose to analyse this phenomenon on a par with stem suppletion. More specifically, we propose that some of these cases should be analysed as the lexicalization of a gap in the stem space.

The paper is structured as follows. In section 2 we briefly discuss three types of defectiveness that can be found in verbal paradigms. In section 3 we present the defective verbs that have gaps that correspond to independently established coherent subparts of the paradigm (STEM SLOTS). In section 4 we present the analysis. We briefly sketch the analysis of Spanish verb morphology proposed in Boyé and Cabredo Hofherr (2006). Following Bonami and Boyé (2002), we assume that the morphological information associated with verbs specifies a list of stems that can be suppleted independently. According to this analysis each zone of systematic co-variation in the verbal paradigm corresponds to the forms built on the same stem. Stems are organized by a graph where links between stems represent default implicative relations (Ackerman and Malouf 2009). In regular verbs only one stem needs to be

[1] We would like to thank the participants of the *Defective paradigms* workshop for their comments. We are grateful to Olivier Bonami and Matthew Baerman for detailed comments on an earlier version of this paper. This work is supported in part by the project MorPa (ANR, Toulouse, Fabio Montermini).

specified and the other stems can be deduced from the graph. For irregular verbs more than one stem needs to be specified, since in irregular verbs one or more of the regular correspondences between the different stems do not obtain. We then proceed to show that the zones of defectiveness identified in section 3 coincide with independently established zones of stem suppletion in the analysis of irregular verbs. Further support for our claim that defectiveness is at the level of stems can be found in Spanish, where the defective stems form a connected subgraph of the stem graph. In section 5 we distinguish three distinct scenarios that can lead to stem defectiveness: stem indeterminacy, stem avoidance, and stem gaps.

2. Three Types of Defective Verbs

Defectiveness is not a homogenous phenomenon; at least three types of defectiveness have to be distinguished.

The first type of defectiveness concerns historical vestiges. These are isolated forms of verbs that have disappeared as lexemes with a full paradigm. This is arguably the case of Spanish DESCOLORIDO[2] 'discoloured' which only appears in past participle form[3] and of French APPAROIR 'to appear', which is only used in the 3rd person singular present (*il appert*). This type of paradigm can be understood as the trace of disappearing lexemes where some forms remain used either in a single category (participle/adjective) or in idiomatic expressions.

The second type of defectiveness is semantically motivated. The forms concerned by this type of defectiveness are forms of existing lexemes which give rise to a semantic conflict between the features expressed by a form and the semantic features of the verb. One example of this type is provided by French FALLOIR 'to be necessary that . . .' which only appears in 3rd person singular finite forms, in the past participle, and the infinitive because FALLOIR is an impersonal verb that can only take expletive *il* as its subject:

(1) il faut,   il aurait   fallu,   il faudra
     it is-necessary, it would-have been-necessary, it will-be-necessary

For this verb, speakers do not have a clear intuition what the missing forms should be, even though the existing forms suggest that FALLOIR behaves like

---

[2] We will use small capitals for lexemes, while word-forms are in italics.
[3] The infinitive *descolorir* 'to discolour' is listed in some dictionaries since the infinitive is the traditional citation form, but this form is not acceptable for the informants we consulted, i.e. it would not be used in a sentence requiring an infinitive.

VALOIR 'to be worth': speakers cannot construct a context in which FALLOIR would take a subject other than 3rd person singular expletive *il*.

Semantic defectiveness and morphological defectiveness need not coincide, however. Meteorological verbs like NEIGER 'to snow' (Fr), are overwhelmingly used in the 3rd person singular. In the case of NEIGER, however, which patterns with regular verbs such as MANGER 'to eat', native speakers have no doubts as to the other forms of the verb such as *je neige*, 'I snow', or *nous neigerons*, 'we will snow'.

The imperative of verbs meaning 'can' presents a similar picture: These forms give rise to a conflict between the conditions on the felicitous use of the imperative (that the speaker be able to control whether the action or state required of him takes place) and the lack of such control of the subject of PODER (Sp)/POUVOIR (Fr) 'can'; nevertheless speakers of Spanish and French know that the forms would be *puede/poded* (Sp) and *peux/pouvez* (Fr).

The third type of defectiveness is morphologically motivated; it concerns forms of verbs which are existing lexemes that have lost part of their paradigms or whose paradigms were never fleshed out (Baerman 2008, Baerman and Corbett, this volume).

(2) Examples of morphologically motivated defectiveness
   a. French CLORE 'to close' lacks present tense indicative 1st person plural and 2PL forms and the imperfective is completely absent.
   b. Spanish ABOLIR 'to abolish' lacks present tense indicative singular and 3rd person plural forms, the whole present subjunctive and the singular form of imperative while the rest of its paradigm is full.

In what follows we will concentrate on morphologically motivated defectiveness.

3. Morphologically Defective Verbs in French and Spanish

As pointed out by Morin (1987: 33–5), certain French verbs do not have a complete paradigm for some speakers.[4]

(3) a. je fris,   tu   fris, il frit,   nous ???, vous   ???, ils   ???
       I fry,   you.SG fry, he fries, we   ???, you.PL ???, they ???
    b. je clos,   tu   clos, il clôt,   nous ???, vous   ???, ils   closent
       I close, you.SG close, he closes, we   ???, you.PL ???, they close

Morin (1987: 37) observes that this defectiveness is structured and proposes that the patterns are a reflex of directed default implicative rules that extend stems across the paradigm:

---

[4] This type of defectiveness is variable across speakers: for *frire*, for example, other speakers have a full paradigm, following the pattern of *rire*, 'to laugh'.

(4) Il n'y a pas de verbes qui sont défectifs pour la 3PL mais non pour la 1PL, ni pour la 3SG mais non pour la 3PL de l'Ind. prés. Ceci peut s'interpréter comme la conséquence d'une règle générale de distribution des radicaux qui étend automatiquement à la 3PL le radical de la 1PL et à la 3SG celui de la 3PL.
[There are no verbs that are defective for the 3rd person plural but not for the 1PL, nor verbs that are defective for the 3rd person singular but not for the 3rd person plural of the present indicative. This can be interpreted as the consequence of a general rule of stem distribution that automatically extends the stem of the 1st person plural to the 3rd person plural and the stem of the 3rd person plural to the 3rd person singular.]
(Translation GB and PCH)

The analysis proposed below shares with Morin's approach that the structured distribution of defectiveness is attributed to implicative rules relating different stems.

In what follows we will examine the morphologically defective verbs given by Arrivé (1997):

(5) a. ABSOUDRE 'to absolve', DISSOUDRE 'to dissolve', TRAIRE 'to milk (a cow)' EXTRAIRE 'to extract', DISTRAIRE 'to distract', SOUSTRAIRE 'to subtract': lack simple past, imperfective subjunctive
b. PAÎTRE 'to graze', SEOIR 'to sit': lack simple past, imperfective subjunctive, past participle
c. CLORE 'to close': lacks present indicative 1PL, 2PL, imperfective, simple past, imperfective subjunctive, imperative PL
d. MESSEOIR 'to be unseemly for': lacks past participle, simple past, imperfective subjunctive, present participle
e. DÉCHOIR 'to fall (morally)': lacks imperfective, imperative, present participle[5]
f. BRAIRE 'to bray': lacks present indicative 1PL, 2PL, imperfective, simple past, imperfective subjunctive, imperative PL, present participle, present subjunctive 1PL, 2PL
g. FRIRE 'to fry': lacks present 1PL, 2PL, 3PL, imperfective, simple past, subjunctive imperfective, imperative PL, present participle, present subjunctive (only has present SG, future, conditional, infinitive, past participle)
h. GÉSIR 'to lie (verb of position)': only has present indicative, imperfective, present participle
i. DÉPOURVOIR 'to strip someone of something': only has infinitive, past participle, simple past, subjunctive imperfective
j. CHOIR 'to fall': only has present indicative 3SG, 3PL, simple past 3SG, 3PL, subjunctive imperfective 3SG, infinitive, past participle

For Spanish, the morphologically defective verbs listed in Mateo and Sastre (1995) are the following:[6]

---

[5] DÉCHOIR is not listed as defective for present indicative 12PL by Arrivé (1997) but attested *déchoyons* and *déchoyez* forms are predominantly imperative forms.
[6] SOLER 'to do habitually' is listed as defective for the forms of future, conditional, subjunctive future, imperative, present participle, past participle. We exclude this verb here since the absence

(6) ABOLIR 'to abolish', AGREDIR 'to attack', AGUERRIR 'to inure, harden', ARRECIR 'to get numb with cold', ATERIRSE 'to get numb with cold', BALBUCIR 'to stammer',[7] BLANDIR 'to brandish', COLORIR 'to colour', DESPAVORIR 'to terrify', EMBAÍR 'to swindle, cheat', EMPEDERNIR 'to harden', GARANTIR 'to guarantee', GUARNIR 'to equip sth with sth', MANIR 'to hang (meat)', PRETERIR 'to omit, pass over', PULIR 'to polish', TRANSGREDIR, TRASGREDIR 'to transgress': lack subjunctive present, present SG, 3PL, imperative SG

4. The Analysis

For both French and Spanish, the gap patterns for the type of defectiveness in (5/6) parallel the patterns observed in analyses of suppletion in these languages (see Bonami and Boyé (2002) for French and Boyé and Cabredo Hofherr (2006) for Spanish, and section 4.3 below). We therefore propose to analyse the defectiveness patterns discussed above as defectiveness at the level of verbal stems. Our analysis of defectiveness is couched in a more general analysis of the structure of stem alternations in Romance. This analysis takes as its starting point the observation that stem alternations in Romance are structured in that stem allomorphy does not target random sets of forms (Maiden 1992; Pirrelli and Battista 2000; Bonami and Boyé 2002).

The analysis is presented as follows. We will first motivate the linguistic status of stems in Romance verbal paradigms (section 4.1). We then present the proposal by Bonami and Boyé (2002) that stems are subject to their own organizing principles, namely the default implicative relations observable between the stems of regular verbs. These relations can be modelled as a graph (the STEM GRAPH, section 4.2). In this analysis, suppletion is modelled as lexicalization of a stem, which blocks the application of the default implicative relations between stems. As the type of defectiveness observed in Spanish and French systematically targets the same sets of forms as suppletion, we propose that this type of morphological defectiveness corresponds, in fact, to a gap in the stem space (section 4.3).

4.1. Stems in Romance verb conjugation

In Romance verbal paradigms, the stem very often varies in form. It has long been observed in traditional grammars that these variations in form are

---

of future forms is semantically motivated: the English USED TO shows the same restrictions. The non-finite forms are rare but attested, particularly in the Iberian variants of Spanish in which have replaced the aorist by the periphrastic HABER + PAST PARTICIPLE construction.

[7] According to the dictionary of the Real Academia Española, *balbucir* lacks only subjunctive present and present 1st person singular.

limited by consistent patterns of allomorphy: certain forms in the verbal paradigm co-vary systematically with respect to stem allomorphs. Two well-known examples of co-variation are the following:

(7) a. The future and the conditional in French have the same stem for all verbs.
b. The infinitive and the 2PL imperative share the same stem allomorph for all verbs in Spanish (cf. e.g. Bello 1847).

The example in (7b) already suggests that these patterns of allomorphy do not mark common feature bundles. As shown in Maiden (1992) patterns of allomorphy can be clearly morphomic, in the sense of Aronoff (1994), as evidenced by the common suppletion zone that groups together 1st person singular of the present indicative and all of the present subjunctive in Spanish (see also Maiden and O'Neill, this volume; Anderson, this volume). Maiden further shows that these patterns of stem distribution cannot be simply viewed as historical relics since they are an active force in diachronic change: innovations often do not lead to regularization but either replicate an existing pattern of allomorphy with a novel alternation (Maiden 1992: 297) or even create such a pattern on a previously invariant verb (Maiden 1992: 302).

Pirrelli and Battista (2000) show that the systematic patterning into suppletion zones does not only concern certain subparts of the paradigm. These authors show that the verbal paradigm of Italian can be partitioned into eight zones that share the same stem allomorph even for the most irregular verbs: we call these zones of systematic co-variation of allomorphs STEM SLOTS. Applying Pirrelli and Battista's idea, Bonami and Boyé (2002), and Boyé and Cabredo Hofherr (2006) propose the following partitions of the paradigm for Spanish and French verbs into stem slots:

(8) Partition of the paradigm into stem slots
a. French (Bonami and Boyé 2002)

Present IND 12PL, imperfective IND	S1	Present SBJV SG, 3PL	S7
Present IND 3PL	S2	Present SBJV 12PL	S8
Present IND SG	S3	Infinitive	S9
Present participle	S4	Future, conditional	S10
Imperative 2SG	S5	Simple past, imperfective SBJV	S11
Imperative 12PL	S6	Past participle	S12

b. Spanish (Boyé and Cabredo Hofherr 2006))

Present IND 1SG, Present SBJV	S1	Imperfective IND	S7
Present IND 23SG, Imperative 2SG	S2	Future IND, conditional	S8
Present IND 1PL	S3	Infinitive, imperative 2PL	S9
Present IND 2PL	S4	Present participle	S10
Present IND 3PL	S5	Past participle	S11
Preterite, imperfective 12 SBJV, Future SBJV	S6		

Each stem slot is assigned an arbitrary STEM INDEX that morphological realization rules make reference to. In the tables above these stem indices are of the form S1, ... S12.

4.2. The organization of stems

Bonami and Boyé (2002) argue that the stems corresponding to each zone of the partition should not be conceived of as an unstructured list. They show that the stems entertain default implicative relations and they propose to represent the stems associated to a verb as a graph that takes these relations into account: the STEM GRAPH (see Boyé and Cabredo Hofherr 2006 for discussion and an application to Spanish).

The stem graph contains two types of information:

(9)   a.   The STEM SPACE: A partition of the paradigm into stem slots. Stem slots are zones that share the same allomorph even for the most irregular verbs.
        b.   A network of default implicative relations between stem slots (the stem graph).

The stem graph for Spanish proposed in Boyé and Cabredo Hofherr (2006) is given below:[8]

(10)   Stem graph for Spanish

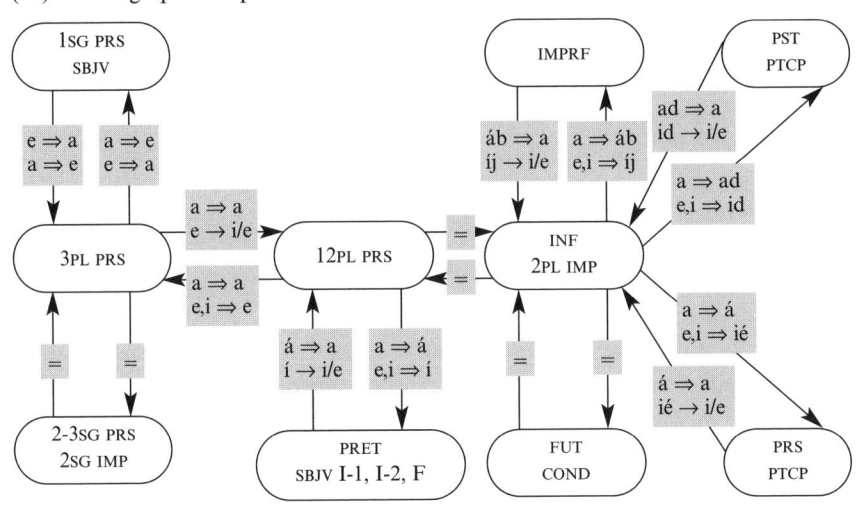

```
┌─────────┐                              ┌───────┐               ┌──────┐
│ 1SG PRS │                              │ IMPRF │               │ PST  │
│  SBJV   │                              │       │               │ PTCP │
└─────────┘                              └───────┘               └──────┘
     ↑                                       ↑                 ad ⇒ a
  e ⇒ a    a ⇒ e                    áb ⇒ a   a ⇒ áb           id → i/e
  a ⇒ e    e ⇒ a                    íj → i/e e,i ⇒ íj
                                                              a ⇒ ad
                                                              e,i ⇒ id
               a ⇒ a                        ┌───────┐
               e → i/e                      │  INF  │
┌─────────┐                  ┌─────────┐    │ 2PL IMP│
│ 3PL PRS │                  │ 12PL PRS│    └───────┘
└─────────┘    a ⇒ a         └─────────┘                        a ⇒ á
               e,i ⇒ e                                          e,i ⇒ ié

                             á ⇒ a   a ⇒ á
                             í → i/e e,i ⇒ í                    á ⇒ a
                                                                ié → i/e
     =          =                       =         =
┌─────────┐                  ┌─────────┐    ┌───────┐          ┌──────┐
│2-3SG PRS│                  │  PRET   │    │  FUT  │          │ PRS  │
│ 2SG IMP │                  │SBJV I-1,│    │ COND  │          │ PTCP │
└─────────┘                  │ I-2, F  │    └───────┘          └──────┘
                             └─────────┘
```

---

[8] As discusssed in Boyé and Cabredo Hofherr (2006), the evidence from suppletion patterns across the verbal paradigm need not uniquely determine a single graph. The graph shown here is one of the possibilities compatible with the evidence.

The boxes represent the suppletion zones that make up the partition of the paradigm; suppletion zones essentially group the verbal forms together that have to share a single allomorph in the language, however irregular the verb.

As stressed by Bonami and Boyé (2002), in this analysis a regular verb does not have an invariant stem across the paradigm;[9] the arrows in the stem graph indicate the regular alternation pattern that regular verbs obey, as illustrated here with the verb AMAR, 'to love':

(11)   Stem graph for Spanish AMAR (= (40) in Boyé and Cabredo Hofherr 2006)

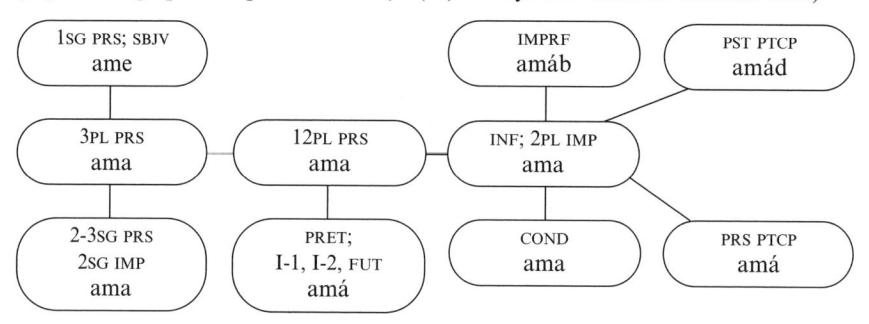

1SG PRS; SBJV		IMPRF	PST PTCP
ame		amáb	amád

3PL PRS	12PL PRS	INF; 2PL IMP	
ama	ama	ama	

2-3SG PRS 2SG IMP	PRET; I-1, I-2, FUT	COND	PRS PTCP
ama	amá	ama	amá

The default implicative rules operate on the final segments of the stem: given the stem AMÁB for the imperfective past, the stem AMA for the infinitive is deduced by the default implicative rule 'áb → a'.

Given one stem of the verb AMAR, all other stems can be deduced using the default implicative relations between stems in the graph in (10). For verbs of the second and third group in Spanish such as COMER 'to eat' or VIVIR 'to live' some forms neutralize the distinction between the two conjugations (e.g. 3rd person plural present indicative *comen/viven*, Preterite *comió/vivió*, the Imperfective past *comía/vivía* and the past participle *comido/vivido*). The default implicative relations leading from these neutralizing stems to stems that distinguish the second and third group are not fully determined: given the nonce past participle *cocorido* the default implicative rules only provide the information that the regular infinitive is either *cocorer* or *cocorir*. In the stem graph in (10) the default implicative rules that give two possible candidates are indicated by a single arrow → while default implicative rules with a single possible output are indicated by a double arrow ⇒.

Notice that the default implicative rules in (10) do not provide an output for every possible stem shape. Consider for example the rule linking the past participle to the infinitive/2nd person plural imperative stem: the default implicative rule is only applicable to participle stems ending in *-ad* or *-id*.

---

[9] In fact, a verb that uses the same stem uniformly may be irregular because this invariance violates default behaviour. This is the case for verbs such as French CONCLURE 'to conclude', RIRE 'to laugh'.

Given an irregular past participle like *puesto*, 'put.PST.PTCP', the default implicative rules do not provide a candidate for the infinitive/2nd person plural imperative stem, which has to be specified independently.

In contrast with regular verbs like *amar*, irregular verbs, such as SER, 'to be', override the implicative relations between stems by lexicalizing more than one stem in the stem graph. The default implicative relations that are respected despite suppletion of the stem form are indicated by links between stems in the graph below.

(12) Stem graph for Spanish SER (= (39) in Boyé and Cabredo Hofherr 2006)

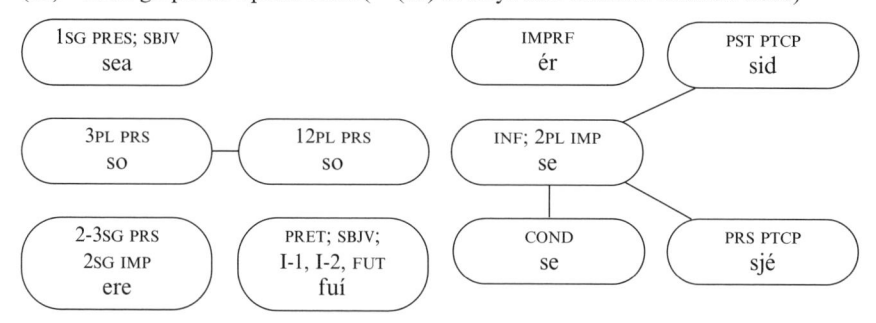

1SG PRES; SBJV sea		IMPRF ér	PST PTCP sid
3PL PRS so	12PL PRS so	INF; 2PL IMP se	
2-3SG PRS 2SG IMP ere	PRET; SBJV; I-1, I-2, FUT fuí	COND se	PRS PTCP sjé

The analysis adopted here takes an inferential-realizational approach (Stump 2001): the verbal forms are calculated by a realization rule making reference to the stem indices given in (8a/b) above and an invariant set of affixes for all verbs (Bonami and Boyé 2002):

(13) Stem-index and affix combinations in French (Bonami and Boyé 2002)

	1SG	2SG	3SG	1PL	2PL	3PL
Present indicative	S3	S3	S3	(S1,-ɔ̃)	(S1,-e)	S2
Present subjunctive	S7	S7	S7	(S8,-jɔ̃)	(S8,-je)	S7
Preterite	(S11,-I)	S11	S11	(S11,-m)	(S11,-t)	(S11,-Ir)
IPFV indicative	(S1,-ɛ)	(S1,-ɛ)	(S1,-ɛ)	(S1,-jɔ̃)	(S1,-je)	(S1,-ɛ)
IPFV subjunctive	(S11,-s)	(S11,-s)	S11	(S11,-sjɔ̃)	(S11,-sje)	(S11,-s)
Future indicative	(S10,-re)	(S10,-ra)	(S10,-ra)	(S10,-rɔ̃)	(S10,-re)	(S10,-rɔ̃)
Conditional	(S10,-rɛ)	(S10,-rɛ)	(S10,-rɛ)	(S10,-rjɔ̃)	(S10,-rje)	S10,-rɛ
Imperative	—	S5	—	(S6,-ɔ̃)	(S6,-e)	—
Infinitive			(S9,-r)			
Present participle			(S4,-ɑ̃)			
Past participle			S12			

(14) Stem-index and affix combinations in Spanish (Boyé and Cabredo Hofherr 2006)

	1SG	2SG	3SG	1PL	2PL	3PL
Present ind.	(S1,-o)	(S2,-s)	S2	(S3,-mos)	(S4, -js)	(S5,-n)
Present subj.	S1	(S1,-s)	S1	(S1,-mos)	(S1,-js)	(S1,-n)
Preterite	S6	(S6,-ste)	(S6,-ó)	(S6,-mos)	(S6,-stejs)	(S6,-ron)

IPEV indicative	(S7,-a)	(S7,-as)	(S7,-a)	(S7,-amos)	(S7,-ajs)	(S7,-an)
IPEV1 subjunctive	(S6,-ra)	(S6,-ras)	(S6,-ra)	(S6,-ramos)	(S6,-rajs)	(S6,-ran)
IPEV2 subjunctive	(S6,-se)	(S6,-ses)	(S6,-se)	(S6,-semos)	(S6,-sejs)	(S6,-sen)
Future indicative	(S8,-re)	(S8,-ras)	(S8,-ra)	(S8,-remos)	(S8,-rejs)	(S8,-ran)
Future subjunctive	(S6,-re)	(S6,-res)	(S6,-re)	(S6,-remos)	(S6,-rejs)	(S6,-ren)
Conditional	(S8,-rija)	(S8,-rijas)	(S8,-rija)	(S8,-rijamos)	(S8,-rijajs)	(S8,-rijan)
Imperative	——	S2	——	——	(S9,-d)	——
Infinitive			(S9,-r)			
Present participle			(S10,-ndo)			
Past participle			(S11,-o)			

The verbal forms are not necessarily derived by concatenation of the stem and the suffix: for some forms the realization-rule includes systematic changes to the stem. As an illustration, we give the realization functions for 1SG present indicative and 2SG present subjunctive of Spanish TENER, 'have, hold', below:[10]

(15) a. TENER, 1SG present indicative:
   S1 → truncate final vowel → add suffix -o
   tenga → teng → teng+o
   b. TENER, 2SG present subjunctive:
   S1 → add suffix -s
   tenga → tenga+s

In our analysis, the 2nd person singular present subjunctive form is built with the unaltered stem, while the 1st person singular present indicative undergoes truncation of the stem final vowel before the suffix is added.[11]

4.3. Defective stem spaces

In the analysis of French and Spanish verbal morphology presented above, the paradigm is partitioned into zones of systematic co-variation, with each zone being represented by a stem that allows prediction of all the co-varying forms. Furthermore, the stems are subject to implicational relations between them that are only overridden by suppletion: stems are organized into a graph.

Now note that the gaps in the paradigms of the French and Spanish verbs in (5)/(6) adhere to the zones established on the basis of suppletion (cf. 8a/b):

---

[10] For details of the affixes and functions assumed, see Bonami and Boyé (2002) for French and Boyé and Cabredo Hofherr (2006) for Spanish.
[11] For an implementation of the analysis of the French verbal forms in Paradigm Function Morphology see Bonami and Boyé (2007).

(16) Defective verbs with their corresponding gaps in the stem space

French verbs — missing stems

a. ABSOUDRE, DISSOUDRE, TRAIRE, EXTRAIRE, DISTRAIRE, SOUSTRAIRE: S11
b. PAÎTRE, SEOIR: S11, S12
c. CLORE: S1, S6, S11
d. MESSEOIR: S4, S11, S12
e. DÉCHOIR: S1, S4, S5, S6
f. BRAIRE: S1, S4, S6, S8, S11
g. FRIRE: S1, S2, S4, S5, S6, S7, S8, S11
h. GÉSIR: S4, S5, S6, S7, S8, S9, S10, S11
i. DÉPOURVOIR: S1, S2, S3, S4, S5, S6, S7, S8, S10
j. CHOIR: S1, S2, S3, S4, S5, S6, S7, S8, S10, S11

Spanish verbs — missing stems

a. ABOLIR, AGREDIR, AGUERRIR, ARRECIR, ATERIR, BALBUCIR, BLANDIR, COLORIR, DESPAVORIR, EMBAÍR, EMPEDERNIR, GARANTIR, GUARNIR, MANIR, PRETERIR, PULIR, TRANSGREDIR/TRASGREDIR: S1, S2, S5
b. BALBUCIR (according to the Real Academia): S1

We propose that the type of defectiveness evidenced by the verbs in (16) above targets objects at the level of the stem space: certain stems are lexicalized as being absent. Given the assumptions of the analysis proposed here, empty stem slots will be filled by default: since the stems are linked by default implicative correspondences, stem slots that have no specific information attached to them would be filled in by the default form predicted by the stem graph. This may lead to more than one possible candidate (e.g. if the cell in question is linked to two different lexicalized cells in the stem graph), but variation is not generally avoided. We therefore have to assume that defective verbs can lexicalize gaps in their stem graph.

As we will show below in section 5, gaps in the stem space can be due to different factors: either speakers do not have a plausible stem for a defective cell (stem indeterminacy) or there are possible stems which are either rejected by speakers for independent reasons (stem conflict) or not used without any discernible synchronic motivation (stem gaps).

In principle, lexicalizing a gap can be distinguished from lexicalization of a null stem in the same way that absence of affixation can be distinguished from zero-affixation. In the case of a gap, there is no linguistic object present. This implies that processes relying on the object that is marked as absent should not be able to take place: if a particular stem is absent, the morphological function calculating the forms of the verbal paradigm dependent on this stem is not applicable. A null stem, on the other hand, is a linguistic entity with a feature matrix that includes morphological information specifying at least the stem index and phonological information.

We will therefore distinguish between the set-theoretical empty set Ø, which indicates a set with no members, and morphological objects with an empty phonological representation which we will indicate by /Ø/. It has to be kept in mind, however, that /Ø/ is a cover-term for a heterogeneous class of morphological objects since an empty phonological form is compatible with further specifications of the feature matrix.

We do not have any examples that would allow us to reliably distinguish between the two possibilities, in particular since auxiliary assumptions as to the morphological behaviour of hypothesized empty stems may vary (e.g.: can empty stems combine with suffixes?). In what follows we will assume that a gap is a set-theoretical empty set Ø.

For Spanish we can now give the following stemgraph for ABOLIR-type defective verbs:

(17) Stem-graph for ABOLIR

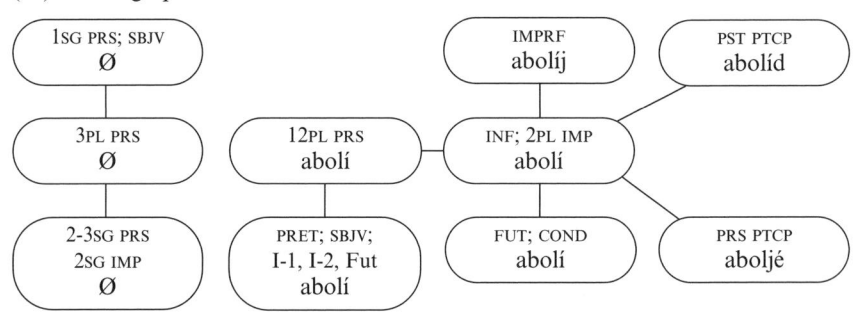

```
┌─────────────┐                          ┌─────────┐    ┌──────────┐
│ 1SG PRS;SBJV│                          │  IMPRF  │    │ PST PTCP │
│      Ø      │                          │  abolíj │    │  abolíd  │
└─────────────┘                          └─────────┘    └──────────┘
┌─────────────┐    ┌─────────┐    ┌─────────────┐
│   3PL PRS   │    │ 12PL PRS│    │ INF; 2PL IMP│
│      Ø      │    │  abolí  │    │    abolí    │
└─────────────┘    └─────────┘    └─────────────┘
┌─────────────┐    ┌──────────┐   ┌─────────────┐   ┌──────────┐
│  2-3SG PRS  │    │PRET; SBJV│   │  FUT; COND  │   │ PRS PTCP │
│   2SG IMP   │    │ I-1, I-2,│   │    abolí    │   │  aboljé  │
│      Ø      │    │ Fut abolí│   │             │   │          │
└─────────────┘    └──────────┘   └─────────────┘   └──────────┘
```

The analysis proposed here is further supported by the fact that, in both Spanish and French, defective stems on the one hand and actual stems on the other hand form connected sub-graphs in the stem space in a way similar to that of suppletive verbs.

5. Three Types of Defectiveness

If morphologically defective verbs in French and Spanish have defective stems as proposed in the previous section, the question of how gaps arise in the stem space and how they can be analysed has to be addressed.

We distinguish two main possibilities that underlie defectiveness:

(18) a. FORM AVOIDANCE:
speakers have a candidate form for the defective form (but do not use it).
b. FORM INDETERMINACY:
speakers do not have a plausible candidate for the defective form.

Within cases of form avoidance we can distinguish two further cases: (i) FORM CONFLICT: the form is avoided for synchronic reasons or (ii) FORM GAPS: a possible form exists and the observed gap (that was possibly due to a process that is no longer synchronically active) is inferred from the fact that other speakers seem to avoid the form (see Daland et al. 2007).

Let us first look at **form indeterminacy**, which arises when the linguistic inference system does not provide a form. With respect to the examples discussed here, in cases of form indeterminacy two things come together: the graph has no output for the stem and there is no information associated to the stem slot. We propose that such an example arises with the simple past of CLORE in French. As the stem graphs in Bonami and Boyé (2002) and Boyé and Cabredo Hofherr (2006) give default implicative relations only between regular stems, the correspondences between stems need not be defined for all stem shapes. Since there are no regular verbs with an infinitive ending in -*re*, the default implicative rules between infinitive and simple past do not have an output for CLORE.

This conclusion converges with the results obtained using Albright's Minimal Generalization Learner (Albright 2002: MGL) which compares pairs of inflected forms and gives a list of rules to derive one from the other. Each rule is associated to a reliability factor depending on the number of its potential targets (scope) and its actual application (hits); the reliability factor is the ratio hits/scope adjusted using confidence limit statistics (Mikheev 1997). To test our proposal, we trained the MGL on French verbs with the 6,370 pairs of <infinitive, simple past 3SG> from the lexical database BDLEX (de Calmès and Pérennou 1998). The resulting rules were then used to generate the simple past of the 6,459 infinitive forms in the BDLEX database. In 98.3 per cent of the cases, the MGL generated the expected form. The MGL gave outputs for most defective verbs for simple past with low reliability factors (*paître* ⇒ *paitit* reliability=0.31, *traire* ⇒ *trut* reliability= 0.235) but none for CLORE or its prefixed forms DÉCLORE, ÉCLORE, ENCLORE, FORCLORE.

We would like to suggest that in this situation speakers can infer that there is a gap from two observations: (i) there is no reliable rule yielding a stem, and (ii) there is no lexicalized form for the stem.

The defective verbs in Spanish and French also provide examples for the two subtypes of **form avoidance**: in these cases potential candidates are available for the defective cells, but speakers reject them as problematic.

We begin with examples of defectivity that we analyse as being due to a synchronic conflict that leads to rejection of all possible candidate forms. The factors giving rise to the rejection of candidates can be of different types. We will discuss two examples: the defective forms of Spanish *abolir*, 'abolish', and the plural of French masculine adjectives ending in -*al*.

The defective forms of Spanish *abolir* appear to be due to a morphological conflict. Speakers have the intuition that there are two potential 1st person singular present indicative forms for this verb: *abolo/abuelo*. None of these forms is perceived as well-formed however.

If the form were *abolo*, then the corresponding infinitive cannot be ABOLIR. The infinitive could either be ABOLAR, since the 1st person singular present indicative is neutral between all conjugations, or ABOLER. A verb ABOLIR with a 1st person singular present indicative *abolo* is excluded since such a verb would have to have a stable mid vowel, and such a verb would violate the vocalic harmony requirement observed across verbs in -*er*/-*ir* in Spanish: the infinitive of verbs in -*er*/-*ir* is part of the sixteen forms in the paradigm that have a morphological well-formedness requirement requiring vocalic harmony between the prethematic vowel and the thematic vowel of the verb (Boyé and Cabredo Hofherr 2004).

If the form were *abuelo*, then ABOLIR would have to have a lexical entry with a diphthongizing vowel, which does not seem to agree with the speakers' intuitions. In particular, as pointed out by Maiden and O'Neill (this volume), if ABOLIR were diphthongizing, it would be expected to pattern with DORMIR. This verb also has an alternation *u/o* in forms such as *durmió*, 'slept.3SG', however, which is not found with ABOLIR: *abolió/*abulió* 'abolished.3SG'.

Notice that form conflict is not simply caused by having more than one possible form: variation on certain forms does not seem to be a problem as such.[12] In cases where form avoidance is observed, other factors lead speakers to avoid all possible forms.

The same reasoning as for *abolo* applies to the other defective forms that have root-stress (present subjunctive singular and 3rd person plural). We would like to propose that the defectiveness of the 1st/2nd person plural in the present subjunctive, which has stress on the suffix, is a consequence of the stemspace: since all seven forms are formed on the same stem, defectiveness for five out of the seven forms spreads to the two forms of the zone of co-variation that do not actually display the morphological conflict that makes the other five defective. The conclusion that the forms with stress on the suffix are equally defective preserves the generalization speakers make over the paradigm that these forms behave as a block.

Another type of conflict is illustrated by the plural of the masculine singular adjectives NASAL, LABIAL, PALATAL, TONAL, 'nasal, labial, palatal, tonal' in French (we know of no parallel example for verbs).[13] These adjectives

---

[12] In this we differ from Albright (2003) who analyses cases such as ABOLIR as lacking a reliable candidate.

[13] Among the four adjectives, two have homophones for their irregular plural form *naseau* 'nose ring' [nazo] and *tonneau* 'barrel' [tono], this could be the source of additional resistance to this

have two potential plural forms: a regular invariant form and an irregular pattern that alternates [-al] with [-o] (orthographic -*aux*): *nasals/nasaux, labials/labiaux, palatals/palataux*.

The invariant forms such as *nasals* [nazal] are a regularization of the pattern *normal/normaux* [nɔrmo]. Such regularization is however perceived to be inappropriate for a word belonging to specialist jargon.

The irregular forms *nasaux* [nazo] follows the robust pattern of words such as *normal/normaux*, but since the word is not part of the frequent vocabulary, the irregular pattern is perceived as pretentious.

In this case, the form conflict seems to be caused by a resistance to regularization for sociolinguistic reasons.

Form gaps. Finally, gaps can also be learnt. Following (Daland et al. 2007) on Russian, we assume that in this case learners are sensitive to the fact that certain forms that seem possible are used by speakers with a frequency far below their expectation, allowing them to identify existing gaps. Using a computer simulation, Sims and Daland (2008) show that by this mechanism gaps that have lost their phonological motivation can plausibly be retained by several generations of speakers.

We propose that the gap for imperfective past and present indicative 1st and 2nd person plural in the paradigms of CLORE and FRIRE in French and the gaps for BALBUCIR and PULIR in Spanish are cases of learnt gaps. The native speakers avoid the forms depending on the concerned stems while they are confident what the forms should be. In French, the native speakers would agree that the present 1st person plural of CLORE would be *closons*, but speakers avoid this form using the synonyms *fermons* or *clôturons*. It seems unlikely that a morphological conflict is at the root of defectiveness for those verbs which can be paired with verbs that inflect the same way for all their existing forms and do not feature these gaps:

(19) a. ENCLORE for CLORE
   b. RIRE for FRIRE

To assess this proposal, we trained the MGL with the 6,396 pairs of 3rd person plural present indicative and imperfective 3rd person singular from the BDLEX database. The MGL gave the expected forms in 93.0% of the cases. For CLORE, it gave *closent* $\Rightarrow$ *closait* with reliability=0.987.

For the rules deriving the 1st person plural present indicative and the 2nd person plural present indicative from the 3rd person plural present indicative, we trained the MGL with 6,390 pairs each. The MGL gave *closent* $\Rightarrow$ *closons* with reliability=0.987 and *closent* $\Rightarrow$ *closez* with reliability=0.987.

---

form as a plural adjective form. Since the other two adjectives LABIAL and PALATAL do not have this additional complication, we will leave this question aside in the following discussion.

The result of the MGL converges with the speakers' intuition that there is a possible well formed candidate. We conclude that in these cases there is no morphological reason for the defectiveness observed: speakers have learnt a gap from the fact that other speakers avoid these forms (as proposed for Modern Greek by Sims and Daland (2008)).

For cases where it is possible to analyse defectiveness as arising from a synchronic conflict it is possible to avoid the assumption that a gap has to be lexicalized.

Two cases suggest, however, that gaps are indeed lexicalized at the stem level. First, as discussed above, the synchronic conflict does not explain the fact that the whole stem is affected by defectiveness, even if some forms do not display the context for the morphological conflict (such as *abolamos, aboláis* discussed above). Second, in the cases discussed as instances of *stem gaps*, we have to assume that speakers have lexicalized an empty cell in the stem graph, since otherwise the stem should be provided by the default implicative rules.

6. Conclusion

We have proposed to analyse morphological defectiveness in French and Spanish exemplified by the verbs in (5) and (6) as defectiveness at the level of the stem space: according to this analysis, these verbs lack certain stems. A representation of defectiveness at the level of the stem space is motivated by the fact that this type of defectiveness follows the same patterns that are observed for stem suppletion.

In the analysis proposed here, empty stems can arise in three different ways. One possibility is that the default implicative rules of the stem graph do not yield a stem form on the basis of the known forms (stem indeterminacy, the case of the simple past of *clore* discussed above). A second possibility is that the available forms for a cell are excluded on independent grounds (stem conflict, the missing forms of ABOLIR, the plural of NASAL, TONAL, PALATAL). A third possibility has to be admitted though, where the default correspondences do yield a form for the defective stem which does not seem to give rise to any further conflict (stem gaps, the case of 1st/2nd person plural present indicative of CLORE). In these cases we have to assume that the absence of content can be specified: the lexical information associated with the cell is then simply that it has no content to fill it.[14]

---

[14] As discussed in section 3.3 this is in principle different from lexicalizing a stem with a phonologically empty form.

The third case of defectiveness shares with suppletion the property that in both cases lexical information specifies that a cell does not obey regular correspondences. In the case of suppletion the cell is associated with an unpredictable morphological object; in the analysis of defectiveness by lexicalization of a gap, the cell is associated with the unpredictable information that it should remain empty.

It is in this sense that some of the cases of morphological defectiveness in French and Spanish illustrated in (5/6) are analysed here as a special case of suppletion.

References

Ackerman, Farrell, James P. Blevins, and Robert Malouf. 2009. Parts and wholes: Implicative patterns in inflectional paradigms. *Analogy in Grammar: Form and Acquisition* ed. by James P. Blevins and Juliette Blevins, 54–82. Oxford: Oxford University Press.

Albright, Adam. 2002. *The identification of bases in morphological paradigms*. Ph.D. thesis, UCLA.

Albright, Adam. 2003. A quantitative study of Spanish paradigm gaps. *West Coast Conference on Formal Linguistics 22 Proceedings*, ed. by G. Garding and M. Tsujimura, 1–14. Somerville, MA: Cascadilla Press.

Anderson, Stephen. This volume. Failing one's obligations: Defectiveness in Rumantsch reflexes of *dēbēre*, 19–34.

Aronoff, Mark. 1994. *Morphology by itself*. Cambridge, Mass.: MIT Press.

Arrivé, Michel. 1997. *La conjugaison pour tous*. Bescherelle. Hatier.

Baerman, Matthew. 2008. Origin and development of defective paradigms. Talk presented at the 13th International Morphology Meeting, Vienna.

Baerman, Matthew and Greville G. Corbett. This volume. Defectiveness: typology and diachrony, 1–18.

Bello, Andrés. 1847. *Gramática de la lengua castellana*. 8th edn. (1970); Buenos Aires: Sopena.

Bonami, Olivier and Gilles Boyé. 2002. Suppletion and dependency in inflectional morphology. *Proceedings of the HPSG-2001 Conference*, ed. by F. van Eynde, L. Hellan, and D. Beermann. Stanford: CSLI Publications.

Bonami, Olivier and Gilles Boyé. 2007. French pronominal clitics and the design of paradigm function morphology. *On-line Proceedings of the Fifth Mediterranean-Morphology Meeting*, ed. by G. Booij, L. Ducceschi, B. Fradin, A. Ralli, E. Guevara, and S. Scalise, 291–322.

Boyé, Gilles and Patricia Cabredo Hofherr. 2004. Étude de la distribution des suffixes -er/-ir dans les infinitifs de l'espagnol à partir d'un corpus exhaustif. *Corpus* 3. 237–60.

Boyé, Gilles and Patricia Cabredo Hofherr. 2006. The structure of allomorphy in Spanish verbal inflection. *Cuadernos de Lingüística del Instituto Universitario Ortega y Gasset* 13. 9–24.

Daland, R., A. D. Sims, and J. Pierrehumbert. 2007. Much ado about nothing: A social network model of Russian paradigmatic gaps. *Proceedings of the 45th Annual Meeting of the Association for Computational Linguistics*, pages 936–43.

de Calmès, Martine and Guy Pérennou. 1998. BDLEX: a lexicon for spoken and written French. *1st International Conference on Language Resources and Evaluation*, 1129–1136. Granada: ELRA.

Maiden, Martin. 1992. Irregularity as a determinant of morphological change. *Journal of Linguistics* 28(2). 285–312.

Maiden, Martin and Paul O'Neill. This volume. On morphomic defectiveness: evidence from the Romance languages of the Iberian peninsula, 103–24.

Mateo, Francis and Antonio J. Rojo Sastre. 1995. *El arte de conjugar en español*. Bescherelle. Hatier.

Mikheev, A. 1997. Automatic rule induction for unknown-word guessing. *Computational Linguistics* 23(3). 405–23.

Morin, Yves-Charles. 1987. Remarques sur l'organisation de la flexion des verbes français. *ITL Review of Applied Linguistics* 77–78: 13–91.

Pirrelli, Vito and Marco Battista. 2000. The paradigmatic dimension of stem allomorphy in Italian verb inflection. *Rivista di linguistica* 2(12). 307–80.

Sims, Andrea and Richard Daland. 2006. Modelling inflectional defectiveness as usage-based probability: Lessons from Modern Greek. Paper presented at the conference 'Defective Paradigms: Missing forms and what they tell us', British Academy, London, April 10–11.

Stump, Greg. This volume. Interactions between defectiveness and syncretism, 181–210.

Stump, Gregory T. 2001. *Inflectional morphology*. Cambridge University Press.

4

Defective Paradigms of Reflexive Nouns and Participles in Latvian

ANDRA KALNAČA AND ILZE LOKMANE

1. Introduction

IN LATVIAN, REFLEXIVENESS OF NOUNS AND VERBS functions as a complex derivational and inflectional system. Reflexive verbs, participles, and nouns were formed via fusion of verbal or noun forms with the enclitic accusative form *si of the reflexive pronoun (Endzelīns and Mīlenbachs 1939: 43):

(1) Verb   *mazgāties* < **mazgātie* + *si* 'to wash [oneself]'
     Noun   *mazgāšanās* < **mazgāšanā* + *si* 'washing [oneself]'
     Participle *mazgājošies* < **mazgājošie* + *si* 'washing [oneself]'
     Participle *mazgājušās* < **mazgājušā* + *si* 'washed [oneself]'

In the Indo-European languages, the synthetic forms of reflexive verbs, nouns and participles have developed in the Baltic and partly in the Slavonic languages. Other languages have analytic forms of reflexive verbs which are called either 'reflexive constructions' or 'reflexive forms' (Gak 1999: 374–9).

Reflexive verbs have full person, tense, and mood paradigms, but reflexive nouns and participles, as opposed to verbs, have defective paradigms in Latvian:

(2) Reflexive noun
     MAZGĀŠANĀS 'washing [oneself]' (feminine)

	singular	plural[1]
NOM	*mazgāšan-ās*	*mazgāšan-ās*
VOC	*mazgāšan-ās*	*mazgāšan-ās*
ACC	*mazgāšan-os*	*mazgāšan-ās*
INS	*(ar) mazgāšan-os*	—

---

[1] Some reflexive nouns are singularia tantum in Latvian, e.g. *atvainošnās* 'apology' or *smiešanās* 'laughing'. However, most reflexive nouns normally are used both in the singular and in the plural.

	DAT	———————	———————
	GEN	*mazgāšan-ās*	*mazgāšan-os*
	LOC	———————	———————

(3) Reflexive participle (present active masc)
    KUSTOŠIES 'moving [oneself]'

	singular	plural
NOM	———————	*kustoš-ies*
VOC	———————	*kustoš-ies*
ACC	*kustoš-os*	*kustoš-os*
INS	*(ar) kustoš-os*	———————
DAT	———————	———————
GEN	———————	*kustoš-os*
LOC	———————	———————

Before we analyse these defective paradigms it is necessary to give some insight into Latvian reflexive verbs. They are the first element in the system of reflexiveness, and therefore the properties of their grammatical and lexical meaning must be clarified.

2. Reflexive Verbs

The standard semantic model of reflexive verbs in modern Latvian is **subject** ↔ **verb**$_{refl}$ where the verb denotes the action that results from the subject and reflects back to the same subject (Veidemane 1972: 429), thus the subject of the action is simultaneously the object of the action. According to Wierzbicka, this model can be related to the prototypical, or primary, meaning of reflexiveness (Wierzbicka 1999: 60–4; a different opinion is held by Holvoet 2001: 187–8), namely, the so-called middle, or neuter meaning in its classical sense. According to Wierzbicka's view, in every language there are verbs encoding this particular meaning (even if there is no dedicated form or construction). The lexical meaning of these verbs is very concrete and describes habitual everyday activities, such as, *mazgāties* 'to wash [oneself]'; *celties* 'to get [oneself] up'; *ķemmēties* 'to comb [one's] hair'; *slaucīties* 'to wipe [oneself] dry'; *ģērbties* 'to dress [oneself]'.

Under the standard model the lexical meaning of the non-reflexive and reflexive verb is the same; the reflexive affix does not change this: *mazgāt/mazgāties, celt/celties*. The difference lies in the syntactic valence. The non-reflexive verb is always transitive and requires a direct object in the accusative, e.g. *ķemmēt matus* 'to comb one's hair', *ģērbt bērnu* 'to dress a child' (for details see Kalnača 2006).

A diachronic view shows that the prototypical meaning has changed after acquiring various semantic shades:

1. Reciprocal reflexive verbs, which indicate reciprocal action and involve at least two subjects and objects (Plungian 2000: 216–17), e.g. *sarunāties* 'to talk', *tikties* 'to meet', *draudzēties* 'to be friends with somebody'.
2. Reflexive verbs in passive or medio-passive meaning, e.g. *nauda glabājas bankā* 'money is kept in the bank'; *svārki šuvās divas nedēļas* 'the jacket was sewn for two weeks'.
3. Reflexive verbs which encode accidental or sudden action (Geniušienė 1983: 45–50; Holvoet 2001: 176–89), e.g. *atvērties* 'to open', *saaukstēties* 'to catch a cold', *sagriezties* 'to twist', *iesāpēties* 'to feel a sudden pain', *iesmelgties* 'to begin aching'.

3. Derivation and Semantics of Reflexive Nouns

In Latvian there are several groups of reflexive nouns derived from reflexive verbs. These nouns have different terminations (derivational suffixes + reflexive endings), such as *-šan-ās, -um-ies, -tāj-ies,* and *-ēj-ies*. Originally, these nouns retained the middle, reciprocal or medio-passive meaning of the motivating verb.

1. The termination *-šanās* expresses middle, medio-passive, or accidental process as the subject, similar to the verbs with *-ing* forms (gerunds) in English:

(4) *mazgāties* 'to wash [oneself]'—*mazgāšanās* 'washing [oneself]'
glabāties 'to keep'—*glabāšanās* 'keeping'
saaukstēties 'to catch a cold'—*saaukstēšanās* 'cold'

2. The termination *-umies* denotes the result of middle action:

(5) *vēlēties* 'to wish [for oneself]'—*vēlējumies* 'a wish [for oneself]'
celties 'to get [oneself] up'—*cēlumies* 'getting [oneself] up'

3. The terminations *-tājies, -ējies* encode the meaning of *nomina agentis* and denote the agents of actions expressed by reciprocal verbs:

(6) *peldēties* 'to swim'—*peldētājies* (MASC), *peldētājās* (FEM) 'a swimmer'
smieties 'to laugh'—*smējējies* (MASC), *smējējās* (FEM) 'the one who laughs'

However, sometimes there is no semantic difference between non-reflexive and reflexive nouns in modern Latvian. If most pairs of non-reflexive and reflexive verbs still retain the opposition of active and middle meaning (e.g. *mazgāt* 'to wash' *mazgāties* 'to wash [oneself]') then pairs of non-reflexive and reflexive nouns (e.g. *mazgāšana* 'washing' *mazgāšanās* 'washing [oneself]') show some semantic overlap. In this case the meaning of the derivational suffix (process or result of action, or *nomen agentis*) is present, but not reflexiveness. Perhaps this is the principal reason for the infrequency of reflexive nouns with terminations *-umies, -ējies, -tājies*. Reflexiveness keeps its semantics and grammatical properties in the the verbal system, but for nouns this distinction has been lost in modern Latvian.

4. Reflexive Participles

There are four different declinable participles in Latvian—two active (present and past) and two passive (present and past) participles. Declinable participles are used mainly in attributive function or as a part of a nominal predicate. Active participles (present active and past active) have reflexive forms with terminations (participle suffixes + reflexive endings) *-oš-ies, -oš-ās, -ies, -us-ies* as well. Originally, these reflexive participles were formed from reflexive verbs with middle, reciprocal, or medio-passive meaning.

(7)   PRESENT ACTIVE
        kustēties 'to move [oneself]'—*kustošies* (M), *kustošās* (F) 'moving [oneself]'
    PAST ACTIVE
        ģērbties 'to dress [oneself]'—*ģērbties* (M), *ģērbusies* (F) 'dressed [oneself]'

Like reflexive nouns, the meaning of reflexive participles reflects the meaning of the suffix (simultaneous or terminate action) rather than reflexiveness in Modern Latvian. The participle *ģērbies,* e.g. expresses perfective action, where the middle meaning is only secondary. As will be discussed later in this paper, in attributive function the opposition between non-reflexive and reflexive participles has become indistinct.

5. Paradigmatic System of Reflexive Nouns and Participles

The paradigmatic system of the finite forms of non-reflexive and reflexive verbs is symmetrical in Latvian. If the verb has a corresponding reflexive the paradigms of person endings in all tense and mood forms are parallel (for details see Kalnača 2004: 54–7). So, full paradigms are fixed both for non-reflexive and reflexive verbs.

(8) Non-reflexive and reflexive verb
Present indefinite
SLAUC-Ī-T 'to wipe' — SLAUCĪ-TIES 'to wipe [oneself] dry'

singular non-reflexive	reflexive	plural non-reflexive	reflexive
1 slauk-u	slauk-os	1 slauk-ām	slauk-āmies
2 slauk-i	slauk-ies	2 slauk-āt	slauk-āties
3 slauk-a	slauk-ās	3 slauk-a	slauk-ās

However, a different situation is observed in the case system of reflexive nouns and participles. While non-reflexive nouns and participles have full paradigms, both reflexive nouns and participles have defective case paradigms in Modern Standard Latvian.

5.1. Paradigms of reflexive nouns

(9) Non-reflexive noun (feminine)
MAZGĀŠANA 'washing' feminine (from MAZGĀT 'to wash')
Reflexive noun
MAZGĀŠANĀS 'washing [oneself]' (feminine) (from MAZGĀTIES 'to wash [oneself]')

	singular	plural	singular	plural
NOM	mazgāšan-a	mazgāšan-as	mazgāšan-ās	mazgāšan-ās
VOC	mazgāšan-a	mazgāšan-as	mazgāšan-ās	mazgāšan-ās
ACC	mazgāšan-u	mazgāšan-as	mazgāšan-os	mazgāšan-ās
INS	(ar) mazgāšan-u	(ar) mazgāšan-ām	(ar) mazgāšan-os	——
DAT	mazgāšan-ai	mazgāšan-ām	——	——
GEN	mazgāšan-as	mazgāšan-u	mazgāšan-ās	mazgāšan-os
LOC	mazgāšan-ā	mazgāšan-ās	——	——

Asymmetry between non-reflexive and reflexive noun paradigms is obvious. Reflexive nouns lack the dative and locative in singular and the dative, instrumental and locative in plural. The formal and semantic causes of this phenomenon are not clear. There are no obvious phonological or semantic reasons for these gaps. Unfortunately, defectiveness of these paradigms has not been investigated in Latvian linguistics so far. Neither basic nor advanced grammar textbooks say anything about the development of defective nominal paradigms. Only some prescriptive rules of correct usage of reflexive nouns and participles have been established in Modern Standard Latvian. These principles without further deep analysis have been repeated unchanged for almost 100 years (see, e.g. Endzelīns and Mīlenbahs 1939: 43; Nītiņa 2001: 20–1; Paegle 2003: 53).

As we can see from the examples reflexive nouns have syncretism of case forms in nominative/vocative/genitive and accusative/instrumental in singular, nominative/vocative/accusative in plural, nominative singular/nominative plural, etc. These forms are historical homonyms; they are the result of regular sound change. Formally, every reflexive noun has only two different endings which can express concrete grammatical meaning depending on context and syntactic function in the utterance.

5.2. Paradigms of reflexive participles

A similar situation to that found with reflexive nouns can also be observed in the asymmetry between full and defective past active participle paradigms in Latvian.

(10) Non-reflexive participle (past active)
  ĢĒRBIS 'dressed' (masculine) (from ĢĒRBT 'to dress')

  Reflexive participle
  ĢĒRBIES 'dressed [oneself]' (masculine) (from ĢĒRBTIES 'to dress [oneself]')

	singular	plural	singular	plural
NOM	ģērb-is	ģērbuš-i	ģērb-ies	ģērbuš-ies
VOC	ģērb-is	ģērbuš-i	ģērb-ies	ģērbuš-ies
ACC	ģērbuš-u	ģērbuš-us	ģērbuš-os	ģērbuš-os
INS	(ar) ģērbuš-u	(ar) ģērbuš-iem	(ar) ģērbuš-os	———
DAT	ģērbuš-am	ģērbuš-iem	———	———
GEN	ģērbuš-a	ģērbuš-u	ģērbuš-ās	ģērbuš-os
LOC	ģērbuš-ā	ģērbuš-os	———	———

(11) ĢĒRBUSI 'dressed' (feminine)
  ĢĒRBUSIES 'dressed [oneself]' (feminine)

	singular	plural	singular	plural
NOM	ģērbus-i	ģērbuš-as	ģērbus-ies	ģērbuš-ās
VOC	ģērbus-i	ģērbuš-as	ģērbus-ies	ģērbuš-ās
ACC	ģērbuš-u	ģērbuš-as	ģērbuš-os	ģērbuš-ās
INS	(ar) ģērbuš-u	(ar) ģērbuš-ām	(ar) ģērbuš-os	———
DAT	ģērbuš-ai	ģērbuš-ām	———	———
GEN	ģērbuš-as	ģērbuš-u	ģērbuš-ās	ģērbuš-os
LOC	ģērbuš-ā	ģērbuš-ās	———	———

In contrast to the previously given reflexive paradigms, active present participles of reflexive verbs lack singular nominative and vocative forms as well. The paradigm of the masculine reflexive participle lacks not only the above mentioned cases, but also the genitive singular.

(12) Non-reflexive participle (present active)
KUSTOŠS 'moving' (masculine) (from KUSTĒT 'to move')

Reflexive participle
KUSTOŠIES 'moving [oneself]' (masculine) (from KUSTĒTIES 'to move [oneself]')

	singular	plural	singular	plural
NOM	kustoš-s	kustoš-i	———	kustoš-ies
VOC	kustoš-s	kustoš-i	———	kustoš-ies
ACC	kustoš-u	kustoš-us	kustoš-os	kustoš-os
INS	(ar) kustoš-u	(ar) kustoš-iem	(ar) kustoš-os	———
DAT	kustoš-am	kustoš-iem	———	———
GEN	kustoš-a	kustoš-u	———	kustoš-os
LOC	kustoš-ā	kustoš-os	———	———

(13) KUSTOŠA 'moving' (feminine)
KUSTOŠĀS 'moving [oneself]' (feminine)

	singular	plural	singular	plural
NOM	kustoš-a	kustoš-as	———	kustoš-ās
VOC	kustoš-a	kustoš-as	———	kustoš-ās
ACC	kustoš-u	kustoš-as	kustoš-os	kustoš-ās
INS	(ar) kustoš-u	(ar) kustoš-ām	(ar) kustoš-os	———
DAT	kustoš-ai	kustoš-ām	———	———
GEN	kustoš-as	kustoš-u	kustoš-ās	kustoš-os
LOC	kustoš-ā	kustoš-ās	———	———

The lack of nominative, vocative, and genitive in the paradigms of the present active reflexive participle is surprising. This 'defectiveness' conflicts with the attributive function of these participles. If we exclude the vocative forms of reflexive nouns and reflexive participles which are syncretic with the nominative in Modern Latvian, we get the following pattern of syncretic case forms, which is not systemic in the inflectional morphology of Latvian:

(14) kustošās—GEN SG F, NOM PL F, ACC PL F
kustošos—ACC SG M, ACC SG F, INS SG M, INS SG F, GEN PL M, GEN PL F, ACC PL M

The form kustošies NOM PL M is the only one which is not syncretic with any other forms. The fact that there is both defectiveness and syncretism in the paradigm complicates the use of reflexive participles, since language users can easily get confused.

6. Functioning of the Paradigms of Reflexive Nouns

Let us examine the use of the reflexive noun tikšanās 'a meeting'. Like all reflexive nouns belonging to this group, it has both singular and plural forms and the corresponding semantics (the paradigm has been shown in (9) for *mazgāšanās* 'washing [oneself]').

The dative and locative singular and plural of the non-reflexive noun TIKŠANA are typically used to fill the gaps in the paradigm, despite the fact that the non-reflexive noun has a totally different meaning in Latvian (*tikšana* 'getting somewhere'). This is shown in bold in the paradigm (17) below. Both the dative and the locative are structurally important case-forms in Modern Latvian, therefore the meaning of the sentence would not be clear without the specific ending of the noun. That is probably why there is no tendency to generalize just one word-form in the paradigm of reflexive nouns.

When using dative forms of a non-reflexive noun, the difference between singular and plural is usually retained (speaking about one meeting or several meetings).

(15)   DAT SG of the non-reflexive noun:
Vienkārši dodiet viņam laiku adaptēties **tikšanai** ar 'citplanētieti'.
'Just give him time to tune himself for the meeting with "an alien".'

DAT PL of the non-reflexive noun:
Labvēlīga diena kontaktiem, radošām **tikšanām**.
'A favourable day for contacts and creative meetings.'

It is different with the locative where the singular form of the non-reflexive noun is used only for singular, whereas the plural form of the non-reflexive noun can have both singular and plural meaning.

(16)   LOC SG of the non-reflexive noun:
Plašsaziņu līdzekļu pārstāvji aicināti piedalīties šajā **tikšanā**.
'Representatives of the mass media are invited to take part in this meeting.'

LOC PL of the non-reflexive noun used as plural:
Kopā jau vairāk kā 200 ģimeņu ir piedalījušies **šajās tikšanās**.
'Altogether more than 200 families have already taken part in these meetings.'

LOC PL of the non-reflexive noun used as singular:
Latvijas izdevējus **šajā tikšanās** pārstāvēs Guntars Līcis.
'Publishers of Latvia in this meeting will be represented by Guntars Līcis.'

The conclusion is that the reflexive noun TIKŠANĀS has a mixed paradigm in Modern Latvian: TIKŠANĀS + TIKŠANA

(17)

	SG F	PL F
NOM	tikšan-ās	tikšan-ās
GEN	tikšan-ās	tikšan-os
DAT	**tikšan-ai (!)**	**tikšan-ām (!)**
ACC	tikšan-os	tikšan-ās
INS	(ar) tikšan-os	(ar) **tikšan-ām (!)**
LOC	**tikšan-ā (!),** tikšan-ās (!)	**tikšan-ās (!)**

It should be pointed out that the mixed paradigm also has syncretic forms (see, e.g. the six places occupied by the form *tikšanās*).

7. Functioning of the Paradigms of Reflexive Participles in Modern Latvian

As it has been mentioned above, the usage of case forms of reflexive participles does not always correspond to the codified norms. Modern Standard Latvian requires use of other participles, subordinate clauses, or periphrastic expressions instead of the missing forms, which is a kind of syntactic compensation. However, in as much as Latvian is rich in synthetic case forms of nouns and word-order is relatively free, synthetic inflectional forms are preferred.

Several types of morphological (paradigmatic) compensation of the missing forms can be found in Modern Latvian. Let us take the reflexive present active participle of the verb *darboties* 'to function, to operate, to act' as an example.

7.1. Construction of non-standard forms

Quite often a non-standard form *darbojošamies* is used. According to the morphemic structure of the form it could possibly be dative singular masculine (although it is not built according to the model of the existing forms of the paradigm as they are the result of fusion of several affixes). The form *DARB-O-J-OŠ-AM-IES* consists of the **participle stem+case ending** (dative singular masculine) **+reflexive element**. Surprisingly, the form *darbojošamies* is used for all the four possible dative forms.

(18) Used as DAT SG M:
Tam jābūt pastāvīgi darbojošamies parlamentam.
'It has to be an independently functioning parliament.'

Used as DAT SG F:
Slēptā kamera ļauj sajusties kā darbojošamies personai notiekošajā.
'The hidden camera lets us feel like the persons acting in the event.'

Used as DAT PL M:
Brauciens uz vienu no darbojošamies vulkāniem.
'A trip to one of the active volcanoes'.

Used as DAT PL F:
Iedarbība uz darbojošamies personām.
'Impact on the acting persons.'

The same pattern is available to any other participle; however, *darbojošamies* is one of the most frequently used lexemes, probably due to the lexical meaning of the verb.

An important question arises: are the language users really aware of the grammatical meanings that each of the affixes contributes to the form? Probably not, as the evidence shows; this word-form is used for all four dative forms to fill a single-cell morphological gap in the defective paradigm. Even more, the *-amies* form is used instead of the other missing forms of the paradigm thus filling a functional gap which is much larger. It is extremely confusing for language users that the nominative singular form does not exist, and the *-amies* form is frequently used to fill the gap.

(19) Used as NOM SG M:
*Aiz viņa nestāv pats nopietnākais—veiksmīgi uzcelts un **darbojošamies** bizness.*
'He lacks the most important thing—a successfully established and functioning business.'

Used as NOM SG F:
*Brīvdabas muzejā ir arī **darbojošamies** pirts.*
'There is a functioning sauna in the open-air museum.'

Used as GEN SG M:
*Ciemā nav centralizēta visu gadu **darbojošamies** ūdensvada.*
'The village does not have a centralized and permanently functioning water-pipe.'

The form *darbojošamies* used as the locative is not attested; however, other lexical items are used in the locative function as well, e.g. the form *tuvojošamies* 'approaching':

(20) *Igauņi tieši to darīs **tuvojošamies** brīvdienās.*
'This is what Estonians will do during the approaching holidays.'

However, the most interesting fact is that this form is also used instead of the normative standard 'correct' forms of the paradigm:

(21) Used instead of the correct form of NOM PL F:
***Darbojošamies** personas gausi slīd pa nejaušību trajektorijām.* [correct—*darbojošās*]
'The acting persons slowly float along accidental trajectories.'

Used instead of the correct form of NOM PL M:
*Ir arī patiesi mākslas darbi, bet vairāk tikai estētiskajā vai emocionālajā līmenī **darbojošamies**.* [correct—*darbojošies*]
'There are real works of art as well, functioning mostly on aesthetic and emotional levels.'

Used instead of the correct form of GEN SG F:
*Nav spēcīgas, **darbojošamies** sociālās partnerības.* [correct—*darbojošās*]
'There is no strong and functioning social partnership.'

Used instead of the correct form of ACC SG M:
*Sakarīgāk laikam par 10 latiem nopirkt **darbojošamies** [fotoaparātu].* [correct—*darbojošos*]
'It would be more sensible to buy a functioning one [= a camera] for 10 lats.'

Used instead of the correct form of ACC PL M:
*... izmantojot maketus un **darbojošamies** mehanizācijas līdzekļus.* [correct—*darbojošos*]
'... using models and functioning mechanical devices.'

It must be stressed that this 'incorrect' use exists side by side with the standard one. Nevertheless, this tendency shows one of the possible ways of dealing with defective paradigms having many syncretic forms—that is to get rid of the paradigm and use just one (indeclinable) form. It is possible because the present active participle is used mostly as an attribute and case semantics is expressed by the noun.

7.2. Use of other forms of the same paradigm to fill the gaps

(22) The form *DARBOJOŠĀS* is quite often used as NOM SG F:
*Par to var ironizēt, ka Mēness ir **darbojošās** persona.*
'One can joke about the Moon being an acting person.'

The same form used as DAT SG F:
*Organizācija pieprasa atsevišķu numuru savai filiālei vai **darbojošās** vienībai.*
'The organization requires a separate number for its branch or other functioning unit.'

This strategy supports the assumption that the language users are confused and would prefer to use just one word-form in all contexts.

7.3. Use of corresponding non-reflexive participle forms

This option is widely used despite the fact that the non-reflexive verb *darbot does not even exist in Modern Latvian. Participles of non-reflexive verbs have the indefinite as well as definite forms (like adjectives). Both of them are used equally often. This option is used both for the dative and the locative, as well as other missing forms.

(23) DAT SG M of the non-reflexive participle:
*Kāpēc **darbojošam** motoram nokrīt apgriezieni?*
'Why does a functioning engine reduce rpm (revolutions per minute)?'

DAT SG F of the non-reflexive participle:
*Tā tiek piemērota katrai **darbojošai** personai (individuāli).*
'It is adapted to each acting person (individually).'

DAT PL M of the non-reflexive participle:
*Mēs vēlamies veidot dialogu ar pagastā **darbojošajiem** uzņēmumiem.*
'We want to create a dialogue with the enterprises functioning in the village.'

DAT PL F of the non-reflexive participle:
*Dialogi starp galvenām **darbojošām** personām ir mazliet savdabīgi.*
'Dialogues between the main acting persons are somewhat peculiar.'

LOC SG M of the non-reflexive participle instead of the required reflexive form:
*Visas iekārtas ir labā **darbojošā** stāvoklī.*
'All devices are in a functioning condition.'

LOC PL M of the non-reflexive participle:
*. . . projektu īpatnības, kas tiek pieļautas **darbojošos** uzņēmumos.*
'. . . specific features of the projects accepted in functioning enterprises.'

LOC SG F of the non-reflexive participle:
*Līdz ar to **darbojošā** baznīcā šāds aizlūgums nav iespējams.*
'Therefore such a commemoration is not possible in a functioning church.'

LOC PL F of the non-reflexive participle:
***Darbojošajās** bioloģiskajās sistēmās nav atkritumu.*
'The functioning biological systems do not produce waste.'

NOM SG M of the non-reflexive participle:
*Pārdodas **darbojošs** kokapstrādes uzņēmums Ikšķilē.*
'A functioning wood-working enterprise in Ikšķilē is on sale.'

NOM SG F of the non-reflexive participle:
*Ir **darbojošā** krāsns, ir vieta kamīnam.*
'There is a functioning oven and place for a fire.'

GEN SG M of the non-reflexive participle:
*Mašīna nelec bez **darbojošā** imobilaizera.*
'The car will not start without a functioning immobilizer.'

Why is it possible to use the above-mentioned non-reflexive forms instead of the reflexive ones? One of the possible answers is the following. The more affixes a word-form includes, the more complicated are the relations between the meanings expressed. The participles analysed in the present study are in fact large semantic complexes:

lexical meaning of the verb + the meanings of the participle affix [adjectivity +tense+activeness] + the meanings of the ending [case semantics+number +gender] + reflexiveness.

All the meanings are not equally important, and reflexiveness seems to be the least important one. As it has been stated before, the meanings of reflexive verbs in Latvian are various, and in some cases the non-reflexive and reflexive verbs do not differ much—it seems that language users do not always have a clear notion about the meaning the reflexive element actually has. Besides, it is difficult to interpret and use such long and complicated word-forms.

We could conclude that as a means of morphological compensation, mixed paradigms of reflexive participles emerge, in that all the above-mentioned strategies exist side by side.

We suggest the following mixed paradigm of the reflexive present active participle of the verb *darboties*:

(24)

	singular masculine	plural masculine
NOM	——————	*darbojoš-ies*
	darbojoš-amies	***darbojoš-amies***
	darbojoš-s (darbojoš-ais)	
ACC	*darbojoš-os*	*darbojoš-os*
	darbojoš-amies	***darbojoš-amies***
INS	*(ar) darbojošos*	——————
	(ar) darbojoš-u (darbojoš-o)	***(ar) darbojoš-iem (darbojoš-ajiem)***
DAT	——————	
	darbojoš-amies	***darbojoš-amies***
	darbojoš-am (darbojoš-ajam)	***darbojoš-iem (darbojoš-ajiem)***
GEN	——————	*darbojoš-os*
	darbojoš-amies	
	darbojoš-a (darbojoš-ā)	
LOC	——————	——————
	darbojoš-ā (darbojoš-ajā)	***darbojoš-os (darbojoš-ajos)***

	singular feminine	plural feminine
NOM	——————	*darbojoš-ās*
	darbojoš-amies	***darbojoš-amies***
	darbojoš-a (darbojoš-ā)	
	darbojoš-ās	
ACC	*darbojoš-os*	*darbojoš-ās*
INS	*(ar) darbojošos*	——————
	(ar) darbojoš-u (darbojoš-o)	***(ar) darbojoš-ām (darbojoš-ajām)***
DAT	——————	
	darbojoš-amies	***darbojoš-amies***
	darbojoš-ai (darbojoš-ajai)	***darbojoš-ām (darbojoš-ajām)***
	darbojoš-ās	
GEN	*darbojoš-ās*	*darbojoš-os*
	darbojoš-amies	
LOC	——————	——————
	darbojoš-ā (darbojoš-ajā)	***darbojoš-ās (darbojoš-ajās)***

The *-amies* form of this particular lexeme is used to fill the gaps except for the locative and the instrumental, possibly because of the lexical meaning of the verb. The corresponding forms of the non-reflexive participle are used to fill all the gaps.

The use of *-amies* form and non-reflexive forms instead of the standard forms still has to be investigated; however, there seem to be no restrictions for extention of this strategy to all functions. (In the table only the attested forms are included.)

The form *darbojošās* can be occasionally used to fill the gaps, too.

In order to get a more complete paradigm of reflexive present active participles other lexemes should be checked as well; however, this is beyond the scope of the present investigation.

8. Conclusions

1. It is difficult to say why the paradigms of reflexive nouns and participles are defective and why the dative and the locative are the missing case-forms. There are neither obvious phonetic reasons, nor any semantic constraints. The only possible reason could be systemic, i.e. competition of several inflectional patterns at some stage of development of reflexive paradigms.

2. There are several types of compensation for defectiveness in Modern Latvian. They are as follows: 1) use of non-standard forms, 2) use of other forms of the paradigm instead of the missing ones, 3) use of the corresponding non-reflexive participle and noun forms. Morphological compensation is preferred to syntactic due to the rich inflectional system of Modern Latvian. All three strategies exist side by side.

3. The choice of the strategy partly depends on the syntactic function of the word-form: case-marking is more important for nouns rather than for declinable participles which are used mostly as attributes.

4. The emerging new paradigms are mixed. Language users very often seem to be confused about the correct use of the existing case-forms.

5. If case-marking is not necessary, one case-form tends to be generalized and used instead of other forms. It could be one step towards the loss of the entire paradigm; however, the structure of Modern Latvian and the rich morphological system as a whole still keeps the paradigm alive (this regards especially the paradigm of reflexive nouns).

References

Endzelīns, Jānis and Mīlenbachs, Kārlis. 1939. *Latviešu valodas mācība.* 13th edition (1st edition Rīga: K. I. Sichmaṇa apgahdiba, 1907). Rīga: Valters un Rapa.

Gak, Vladimir G. 2000. *Teoreticeskaja grammatika francuzskogo jazyka.* Moscow: Dobrosvet.

Geniušienė, Emma. 1983. *Refleksivnye glagoly v baltijskix jazykov i tipologija refleksivov.* Vilnius: Viljnjusskij gosudarstvennij universitet.

Holvoet, Axel. 2001. *Studies in the Latvian Verb.* Kraków: Wydawnictwo universitetu Jagiellońskiego.
Kalnača, Andra. 2004. *Morfēmika un morfonoloģija.* Rīga: LU Akadēmiskais apgāds.
—— 2006. Reflexiveness and transitivity of Latvian verbs. *Humanities and Social Sciences.* 1(47), 92–101. Rīga: University of Latvia.
Nītiņa, Daina. 2001. *Latviešu valodas morfoloģija.* Rīga: Rīgas Tehniskā universitāte.
Paegle, Dzintra. 2003. *Latviešu literārās valodas morfoloģija.* I daļa. Rīga: Zinātne.
Plungian, Vladimir A. 2000. *Obscaja morfologija.* Moscow: Editorial URSS.
Veidemane, Ruta. 1972. Morfēmas—ies vieta latviešu valodas verbu sistēmā. *Veltījums akadēmiķim Jānim Endzelīnam (1873–1973),* 427–42. Rīga: Zinātne.
Wierzbicka, Anna. 1999. *Semanticeskie universalii i opisanie jazykov.* Moscow: Jazyki russkoi kul'tury.

5

Relative Acceptability of Missing Adjective Forms in Swedish

JOHN LÖWENADLER

1. Introduction

THE AIM OF THIS CHAPTER IS TO DISCUSS the implications of an acceptability test designed to measure Swedish native speakers' reluctance to form the neuter gender of certain adjectives, so-called *defective* adjectives. This chapter presents some observations related to a larger paper (Löwenadler, to appear), where it is argued that defectiveness in Swedish adjective paradigms can be explained by a number of interacting constraints that block productivity. In that paper the main aim is to explain why certain adjective forms in Swedish are regarded as ungrammatical by the majority of Swedish speakers.

In this paper, by contrast, the discussion will concern the actual evaluation of the logically possible, but nevertheless unacceptable neuter alternatives. One possibility is that the constraints themselves could be ranked according to their relative strength, or 'impact' on the inflectional process, and that such a ranking correlates with the evaluation of the possible adjective forms. While this will be shown to be a good starting-point, it cannot entirely explain the different evaluations. Thus, I will provide a number of additional factors that interact to produce the judgements found in the acceptability test. While the notion of gradience in acceptability tests has become increasingly important in recent years (for example Bard et al. 1996), I am not aware of any tests specifically aimed at connecting such relative acceptability to the causes of defectiveness. This is the main aim of the present chapter.

2. Background

A well-known and widely discussed phenomenon in Swedish concerns the fact that certain adjectives only occur in the common gender and not in the neuter.[1] For example, while *en lat man* ('a.COM lazy.COM man') is perfectly natural, there is no adjective form that can be used in the phrase *ett *lat barn* ('a.N lazy.N child'), since the noun *barn* 'child' is formally neuter in Swedish. This also indicates that the restriction is not directly semantically motivated, which is also shown by the fact that *det lata barnet* ('the lazy child') and *de lata barnen* ('the lazy children') are perfectly grammatical phrases. While at least thirty adjectives are defective in this sense, they all belong to five different phonological categories, as shown in (1) (Teleman, Hellberg, and Andersson 1999: 210–13):

(1) Defective adjective categories in Swedish
  (i) Most polysyllabic adjectives with final stress and stem ending in a long vowel plus *-d*
    For example: *gravid* [graˈviːd] 'pregnant', *morbid* [mɔrˈbiːd] 'morbid'
  (ii) The two monosyllabic adjectives with short vowels ending in *-d*
    rädd [rɛd] 'afraid', *fadd* [fad] 'stale'
  (iii) Certain monosyllabic adjectives with long vowels ending in *-t*
    For example: *lat* [lɑːt] 'lazy', *flat* [flɑːt] 'flat'
  (iv) Certain monosyllabic adjectives with long vowels ending in *-d*
    For example: *pryd* [pryːd] 'prudish', *vred* [vreːd] 'wrathful'
  (v) Certain adjectives with final stress ending in a vowel
    For example: *disträ* [dɪstˈrɛː] 'absent-minded', *blasé* [blaˈseː] 'jaded'

While the common form of Swedish adjectives is represented by the stem, the neuter is generally formed by adding a *t*-suffix. However, the neuter forms are also affected by two general morphophonological processes known as *dental assimilation* and *vowel shortening*, which also occur in the verbal inflectional system and in adjective-adverb conversion. The result of dental assimilation is that stem final dental plosives are assimilated with the *-t* suffix. The result of vowel shortening is that in adjectives ending in a long stressed vowel, the vowel is shortened when a *-t* suffix is added. Actually, vowel shortening sometimes leads to an additional change of vowel quality, as in the shift between [ɑː] and [a], [oː] and [ɔ] and [eː] and [ɛ].

The explanation in Löwenadler (to appear) is based on the assumption that, in the case of neuter formation, vowel shortening and certain types of dental assimilation block productivity because the changes are less transparent than simple suffixation, and because there is an insufficient number of low-frequency adjective types using those processes. The processes themselves appear in order to avoid the violation of certain generalized constraints, such as a phonotactic rule blocking clusters of same-place plosive

---

[1] For more discussion and analyses that differ from the one presented in Löwenadler (to appear), see, for example, Hellberg (1974) and Pettersson (1990). These other explanations are discussed and evaluated in detail in the above-mentioned article.

consonants, and a morphophonological constraint against long vowels preceding plosive suffixes.[2] The explanation is connected to the notion of *morphotactic transparency* presented in Dressler (1985), and to the discussion in Plag (1999: 38), where it is argued that speakers infer that a process is productive when it is semantically and phonologically transparent and when it has a large proportion of low-frequency types. Thus, although dental assimilation and vowel shortening are very consistent processes in the Swedish morphological system, they are still unproductive in the case of adjectives. In effect, forms that must employ these processes only appear if there is sufficient communicative motivation, in which case the neuter is formed by analogy with similar forms.[3] In this sense, productivity is claimed only to apply when neuter forms of adjectives are perceived as perfectly acceptable regardless of whether they have previously been encountered.[4] By contrast, when neuter forms that can only be formed by analogy with other similar forms are heard or used for the first time, they are perceived as non-existing forms. An important consequence of this line of reasoning is that, even though they are part of a very general pattern, high-frequency neuter forms such as *rött* [rœt] from the stem *röd* [rø:d] 'red', *sött* [sœt] from the stem *söt* [sø:t] 'sweet', and *nytt* [nʏt] from the stem *ny* [ny:] 'new', are not the result of productivity. Therefore, neuter forms of adjectives in these phonological categories must be supported by sufficient positive evidence in the language a speaker encounters, or they will be perceived as defective. Thus, in the present context, frequency is important in two respects. First, the proportion of low-frequency types (referring to the number of *distinct* infrequent adjectives that

---

[2] Thus, the *constraints* specify the type of morphological or phonological structures that are blocked, while the *processes* refer to the actual morphological, phonological, or morphophonological operations used.

[3] As pointed out by an anonymous reviewer, one might wonder whether not all linguistic forms require communicative motivation, and whether there is any measurable difference in the way communicative situations are handled versus a situation where a linguist forces a speaker to generate paradigms. These are important and extremely interesting questions without any simple answers. The issue is discussed in some detail in Löwenadler (to appear), but a short comment might be in place here. First, the question of whether all linguistic forms require communicative motivation depends on whether or not one accepts that a form can be added to the mental lexicon of a speaker without having previously been encountered. In my view, the fact that many unencountered forms are immediately accessible when needed is the essence of productivity. Second, to a lesser degree it actually seems that defective adjectives do become more acceptable for speakers forced to generate a paradigm a sufficient number of times. In that sense there are similarities between such situations and true communicative situations. However, encountering a form in a communicative situation leads to the form being *subconsciously* acquired which is not the case in the experimental situation, and this may very well be a crucial difference.

[4] This definition of productivity is described in detail in Löwenadler (to appear) and is related to earlier discussions of productivity such as the one presented in Baayen and Lieber (1991). See also interesting discussions concerning similar issues in Plag (1999) and Bauer (2001).

use a particular process) partly determines whether a process is productive or not. Second, in the case of unproductive processes, the frequency (or need) of a specific adjective form determines whether it may employ the process by analogy with other forms.

3. Results and Discussion

The present study presents an acceptability judgement test where a number of logically possible neuter forms of ten defective adjectives were introduced to native Swedish speakers. By analogy with neuter forms of non-defective adjectives, the alternatives in the acceptability test represent null suffixation, *t*-suffixation, *t*-suffixation with dental assimilation, *t*-suffixation with vowel shortening, and *t*-suffixation with both dental assimilation and vowel shortening. However, depending on the form of the stem, the actual possibilities range from two to four different neuter forms. More specifically, twenty native Swedish speakers were asked to rate the acceptability of neuter alternatives of the ten adjectives (two from each phonological category) exemplified in (1). When possible, the two adjectives in each category were chosen to represent one relatively frequent and one relatively infrequent stem (see (8)). The scale ranged from 0 per cent (completely unacceptable) to 100 per cent (completely acceptable, on a par with the neuter of non-defective adjectives). The participants were asked to judge the forms in terms of spoken language, and the forms were therefore read out by the experimenter as part of a noun phrase with a semantically and pragmatically suitable head. The order of the forms was randomly determined, but no two forms from the same category were allowed to occur immediately after each other. The participants were also assured that there are no correct or incorrect answers. The mean results of the test are shown in (2) (where the left column shows the relatively more frequent stems and the right column the relatively less frequent stems):

(2) Acceptability of the main neuter alternatives of some defective adjectives[5]

Neuter formation of *distra* [dɪstˈrɛː] and *blasé* [blaˈseː]

null suffixation	[dɪstˈrɛː]	66%	[blaˈseː]	90%
dental assimilation + vowel shortening	[dɪstˈrɛt]	42%	[blaˈsɛt]	9%
t-suffixation	[dɪstˈrɛːt]	21%	[blaˈseːt]	17%

---

[5] Note that in the general case, the neuter of non-defective *t*-final, *d*-final, or vowel-final adjective stems are formed by *t*-suffixation + dental assimilation + vowel shortening (or two of these processes if the stem has no final dental consonant to assimilate or long vowel to shorten). Thus, for non-defective adjectives only one neuter form is grammatical while the other possibilities are completely ungrammatical.

MISSING ADJECTIVE FORMS IN SWEDISH

Neuter formation of *lat* [lɑ:t] and *flat* [flɑ:t]

null suffixation[6]	[lɑ:t]	66%	[flɑ:t]	49%
t-suffix + dental assim + vowel sh	[lat]	3%	[flat]	31%

Neuter formation of *gravid* [graˈvi:d] and *morbid* [mɔrˈbi:d]

t-suffixation	[graˈvi:dt]	51%	[mɔrˈbi:dt]	54%
t-suffix + dental assim + vowel sh	[graˈvɪt]	21%	[mɔrˈbɪt]	37%
dental assimilation	[graˈvi:t]	26%	[mɔrˈbi:t]	44%
null suffixation	[graˈvi:d]	17%	[mɔrˈbi:d]	15%

Neuter formation of *pryd* [pry:d] and *vred* [vre:d]

t-suffixation	[pry:dt]	43%	[vre:dt]	33%
t-suffix + dental assim + vowel sh	[prʏt]	48%	[vrɛt]	62%
dental assimilation	[pry:t]	20%	[vre:t]	29%
null suffixation	[pry:d]	13%	[vre:d]	14%

Neuter formation of *rädd* [rɛd] and *fadd* [fad]

t-suffixation + dental assimilation	[rɛt]	30%	[fat]	49%
t-suffixation	[rɛdt]	33%	[fadt]	39%
null suffixation	[rɛd]	17%	[fad]	23%

First of all, in Löwenadler (to appear) constraints similar to the following are argued to block productivity in Swedish adjective paradigms:

(3) Productivity-blocking structural constraints in Swedish adjective patterns

[*CSP]: Avoid clusters of same-place plosives (*d-t, t-t, g-k, b-p*, etc.)
[*LVS]: Avoid long vowels immediately preceding the suffix
[*ASC]: Avoid assimilation of salient unidentical coda consonants[7]
[*VSP]: Avoid the process of vowel shortening, i.e. vowel shortening in the syllable of the added suffix
[*NSX]: Avoid null suffixation
[*SUP]: Avoid strong and weak suppletion (arbitrary changes not based on any existing processes)

As a first approximation, I will rank the constraints according to their relative impact on the acceptability of the different neuter alternatives. Note that this is not a ranking in the sense of determining which form is grammatical, since all of the alternatives are generally regarded as ungrammatical by Swedish speakers. Furthermore, the constraints interact so that two low-ranked constraints may be stronger than one high-ranked constraint. Given the data and elaborating on the constraints used in (3), the following constraints seem to be needed, ranked as ordered from high to low:

---

[6] Actually, one might argue that this form represents dental assimilation, but for various reasons this approach is not chosen here (see discussion below).

[7] For a definition of salience, see Löwenadler (to appear). For the present purposes it suffices to say that salient consonants are those which are the most important in order for the stem to be perceived as unchanged.

(4) Constraint-ranking determining the acceptability of defective adjective forms

STRONG

[*SUP]: Avoid strong and weak suppletion
[*CIP]: Avoid clusters of identical plosives
[*LVS]: Avoid long vowels immediately preceding the suffix
[*CSP]: Avoid clusters of same-place but unidentical plosives
[*VSP]: Avoid vowel shortening
[*ASC]: Avoid assimilation of salient unidentical coda consonants
[*NSX]: Avoid null suffixation

WEAK

The ranking of the constraints in (4) aims to describe relative analogical efficiency. Thus, the higher a constraint is ranked, the stronger the resistance to analogical formation. Forms which violate one or more constraints cannot appear through productivity, but have to resort to analogical formation requiring communicative motivation and creativity (which in time may lead to conventionalization).

In comparison with (3), the constraint [*CIP] has been separated from the related [*CSP] in order to account for the (intuitively reasonable) fact that while speakers are generally reluctant to allow *d-t* clusters, there is an even stronger resistance to non-assimilated *t-t* clusters. However, since neuter forms that violate the two strongest constraints [*SUP] and [*CIP] are so completely unacceptable for speakers (confirmed by my own intuition as well as many informal interviews), such forms were not even included as possible alternatives in the acceptability judgement test. Thus, if the relevant constraints are introduced, the following patterns emerge:

(5) Constraints and acceptability of defective adjectives in the neuter

Neuter formation of *disträ* [dɪstˈrɛː] and *blasé* [blaˈseː]

Forms	Mean %	*CIP	*LVS	*CSP	*VSP	*ASC	*NSX
[dɪstˈrɛːt], [blaˈseːt]	21/17		X				
[dɪstˈrɛt], [blaˈsɛt]	42/9				X		
[dɪstˈrɛː], [blaˈseː]	66/90						X

Neuter formation of *lat* [lɑːt] and *flat* [flɑːt]

Forms	Mean %	*CIP	*LVS	*CSP	*VSP	*ASC	*NSX
[lɑːtt], [flɑːtt]	—	X					
[lɑːt], [flɑːt]	?		X				
[lat], [flat]	3/31				X		
[lɑːt], [flɑːt]	66/49						X

Neuter formation of *gravid* [graˈviːd] and *morbid* [mɔrˈbiːd]

Forms	Mean %	*CIP	*LVS	*CSP	*VSP	*ASC	*NSX
[graˈviːt], [mɔrˈbiːt]	26/44		X			X	
[graˈvɪt], [mɔrˈbɪt]	21/37				X	X	
[graˈviːdt], [mɔrˈbiːdt]	51/54			X			
[graˈviːd], [mɔrˈbiːd]	17/15						X

Neuter formation of *pryd* [pryːd] and *vred* [vreːd]

Forms	Mean %	*CIP	*LVS	*CSP	*VSP	*ASC	*NSX
[pryːt], [vreːt]	20/29	X				X	
[pryːdt], [vreːdt]	43/33		X				
[prʏt], [vrɛt]	48/62				X	X	
[pryːd], [vreːd]	13/14						X

Neuter formation of *rädd* [rɛd] and *fadd* [fad]

Forms	Mean %	*CIP	*LVS	*CSP	*VSP	*ASC	*NSX
[rɛdt], [fadt]	33/39			X			
[rɛt], [fat]	30/49					X	
[rɛd], [fad]	17/23						X

Studying the data in (5), we find that in many respects the violations of the constraints correlate quite well with the acceptability judgements in the test, although this is not always the case. The main exception is *d*-final neuter adjectives formed by null suffixation, which receive unexpectedly low ratings (see (6)). Although it would be possible to define [*NSX] as a high-ranked constraint, a low-ranked (weak) constraint seems more appropriate in view of factors that will be discussed below.

Note also that [lɑːt] may be interpreted in two different ways, depending on whether the form is regarded as a result of identical consonant assimilation or null suffixation. In the former case, the form violates the constraint against long vowels immediately preceding the suffix, [*LVS], and following the pattern of *pryd*, *gravid* and *disträ*, this should lead to a form which has a low potential for analogical formation. In the case of null suffixation, however, the suffix is simply not added to the stem, and therefore there is no violation of [*LVS]. In effect, this might explain why a form identical to the common form seems to be preferred by speakers.[8] This kind of reasoning also helps to explain why [distˈrɛːt] seems to be less acceptable than [lɑːt] in the neuter—a fact that would be unexplained if [lɑːt] is only analysed as a suffixed form.

---

[8] Still, there is no clear way to determine whether speakers interpret the word-final *t* as a neuter suffix or as part of the stem. Since the latter option is more consistent with the theory presented here, until evidence is presented that the *t* is in fact interpreted as a suffix, I will assume that suffixation is not taking place.

The constraints are best regarded as motivating factors of different strength which lead speakers to prefer certain forms to others in a quite consistent way, as illustrated by (5). Still, as pointed out above, there are a number of forms which receive unexpected evaluations if only these constraints are taken into account. (6–9) show the most marked differences found in the result of the acceptability tests:[9]

(6) Cross-categorial differences in need of explanation: null suffixation

[dɪstˈrɛː]	66%	[blaˈseː]	90%
[lɑːt]	66%	[flɑːt]	49%
[graˈviːd]	17%	[mɔrˈbiːd]	15%
[pryːd]	13%	[vreːd]	14%
[rɛd]	17%	[fad]	23%

The data in (6) suggest a particularly strong resistance to null suffixation in *d*-final adjectives. Note that null suffixation is not generally a productive process in Swedish, as long as productivity is defined as a process which leads to neuter forms automatically appearing in the mental lexicon (see Löwenadler, to appear). In the theory presented here, this means that many additional factors come into play when speakers judge the possibility of using certain non-conventionalized forms. Thus, an important fact may be that generally a word-final -*d* phoneme is a clear indication of common gender in Swedish. For example, in adjectival uses of verb participles, there is a *d/t* distinction depending on whether the modified nouns are common or neuter, as in *en öppna-d väska* ('an opened-COM bag') versus *ett öppna-t paket* ('an opened-N package') derived from the verb stem *öppna* ('open.INF'), or *en måla-d dörr* ('a painted-COM door') versus *ett måla-t hus* ('a painted-N house') derived from the verb stem *måla* ('paint.INF'). Possibly, this influence leads speakers to reject *d*-final neuter forms to a greater extent than other forms. While such a constraint might not be particularly likely to block productivity as such, it may explain differences between 10–20 per cent and 50–60 per cent acceptability in forms that are not the result of productivity. In the case of the high (90 per cent) acceptability of [blaˈseː], this might be due to the fact that, for the majority of the participants in the experiment, this adjective is not defective at all. Thus, twelve out of twenty subjects marked [blaˈseː] as fully acceptable, on a par with other 'existing' words in Swedish. As argued in detail in Löwenadler (to appear), if there is sufficient communicative motivation such conventionalization may always occur in potentially defective adjectives. However, conventionalization is much more likely to take place if the process only requires violation of a weak productivity-blocking constraint. This is

---

[9] Note again that the percentages refer to the mean acceptability of a certain form, where 0 per cent represents a completely unacceptable and 100 per cent represents a fully acceptable form.

therefore another reason to analyse the constraint against null suffixation as a weak constraint, and this could partly explain the high acceptability of a form such as [blaˈseː]. An additional factor likely to support the high acceptance of null suffixation in the neuter of *blasé* is the very obvious foreign nature of the word, as evidenced by its very unorthodox stressed final [eː] phoneme, requiring an acute accent in the spelling, otherwise very rare in Swedish.

Next, consider a few differences *within* the five phonological categories, i.e. differences between the two words in each pair used in the acceptability test:

(7) Intra-categorial differences in need of explanation

[dɪstˈrɛt]	42%	[blaˈsɛt]	9%
[lat]	3%	[flat]	31%
[graˈvɪt]	21%	[mɔrˈbɪt]	37%
[rɛt]	30%	[fat]	49%

In the case of the great difference in acceptability between [dɪstˈrɛt] and [blaˈsɛt], there are at least two different factors that may be involved. First, it is probably important that while the vowel shortening process producing the form [dɪstˈrɛt] does not change the vowel quality, the vowel shortening in [blaˈsɛt] does (remember that the stems are [dɪstˈrɛː] and [blaˈseː] respectively). Second, it is possible that the obvious foreignness of *blasé* leads speakers to prefer null suffixation to the standard (but unproductive) inflectional principles of Swedish adjectives.

The fact that [lat] is much less accepted than [flat], [graˈvɪt] less accepted than [mɔrˈbɪt], and [rɛt] less accepted than [fat] is another striking matter in need of explanation. As in the case of [blaˈsɛt] above, the vowel shortening process giving rise to [lat] and [flat] requires change of vowel quality, which might explain their low mean acceptability in comparison with the other two categories where no such change is required. However, it seems likely that the main factor determining the acceptability of these forms is the degree of *entrenchment* (Tomasello 2003: 178ff.). Thus, it may be that the degree of (common gender) entrenchment of a certain form could negatively affect the analogical formation potential of a certain process, in the sense that the less entrenched a word is, the more acceptable an inflected form might be.[10] Compare this with experimental findings that there is a distinction between word pairs like *disappear* and *vanish* as regards the potential for being used transitively (Brooks et al. 1999). Thus, it seems that children are less prone to generalize transitive patterns to frequently used forms such as *disappear* (*John disappeared the doll*) than to more unusual forms such as *vanish* (*John*

---

[10] By contrast, in the case of true productivity, the degree of entrenchment is irrelevant (following the hypothesis presented in Löwenadler, to appear).

vanished the dog). The statistics in (8) from the 100 million word corpus of *Språkbanken* support the claim that entrenchment is involved:

(8)　Common gender entrenchment: Token frequency per 100 million words[11]
　　　lat: 343　　　*flat*: 118
　　　gravid: 807　*morbid*: 28
　　　rädd: 8256　 *fadd*: 93

As seen in (8) the intra-categorial differences in acceptability in the three word pairs correlate with differences in common gender entrenchment. Thus, the neuter form [flat] is more acceptable than [lat], [mɔrˈbɪt] is more acceptable than [graˈvɪt] and [fat] is more acceptable than [rɛt], presumably because the latter form in each pair is more entrenched in its common form.

Furthermore, in a comparison between two similar but distinct categories, we see that in the case of the polysyllabic *gravid* ('pregnant') a *d-t* cluster is preferred to the form employing dental assimilation and vowel shortening. By contrast, in the case of the monosyllabic *vred* ('wrathful') it is the other way around:

(9)　Polysyllabic versus monosyllabic *d*-final adjectives
　　　[graˈviːdt]　51%　　　　[graˈvɪt]　21%
　　　[vreːdt]　　33%　　　　[vrɛt]　　62%

Besides an explanation related to entrenchment,[12] there might be an additional explanation for this fact. One issue concerns the fact that while dental clustering is used in the most acceptable neuter form of *gravid*, the conventionalized neuter form of a similar but non-defective adjective such as *solid* [sʊˈliːd] 'solid' is the result of vowel shortening ([sʊˈlɪt]). Presumably, sequences of dental plosives are only possible as marginal alternatives, since they violate a 'hard' phonotactic constraint in Swedish. That is, except in compounds, forms that violate the constraints [*CIP] and [*CSP] are never possible as fully acceptable forms. Thus, when a new form enters the lexicon it takes the form which is the most likely *phonotactically acceptable* word. Yet, a phonotactically unacceptable form may be the most transparent one and therefore the form speakers select when they are forced to choose from 'unacceptable' forms. Then, the reason why speakers tend to prefer [vrɛt] to [vreːdt], but not [graˈvɪt] to [graˈviːdt] could simply be that a neuter form of

---

[11] The frequencies of the other four forms are *disträ* (70), *blasé* (58), *pryd* (52) and *vred* (50).
[12] Thus, it is clear that the stem *vred* is a much less entrenched form than the corresponding form *gravid*, since in the 100 million word corpus of *Språkbanken*, the adjective *gravid* occurs 807 times while the adjective *vred* occurs only 50 times. Therefore it is possible that the judgements simply reflect the fact that speakers prefer stem changes with a less entrenched word. In this sense, differences in the judgements as regards dental clustering should be seen as a word-internal relative value.

vred is closer to becoming conventionalized, as seen in the fact that several speakers regard [vrɛt] as a fully acceptable form.

4. Conclusions

We have thus seen that while the acceptability judgements to some extent can be explained by ranking productivity-blocking constraints, the actual evaluation seems to be very complicated and dependent on many different factors. A few such possible factors are those presented in (10), of which some have been discussed above:

(10) Possible non-morphophonological factors determining relative acceptability

Factors affecting whole phonological categories:
    Association of word final *-t* with neuter and *-d* with common gender

Factors affecting individual words:
    Entrenchment of adjective stems
    Vowel quality alteration
    Availability of patterns on which to build analogies, i.e. type frequency
    Competition between different neuter alternatives
    'Foreignness' of adjective stems
    Degree of conventionalization[13]

In connection with the hypothesis presented in Löwenadler (to appear) it seems plausible, for example, that potentially defective adjectives with a high degree of common gender entrenchment, vowel quality change and lack of patterns on which to build analogies require a lot of communicative motivation to avoid defectiveness. That is, a low rating on the acceptability judgement test indicates that a neuter form is far from being conventionalized and part of the norm.

It is clear that the interaction between structural (morphophonological) constraints and other factors is extremely complex and therefore very difficult to quantify. For example, it is very unclear how the violation of two low-ranked constraints measures up against a single violation of a more highly ranked constraint. Yet, by including the only additional factor that affects categories as a whole (i.e. not connected to individual words) we arrive at a result which actually quite well correlates with the observed acceptability judgements.

---

[13] Such conventionalization, in turn, is connected to the degree of communicative motivation in each individual case. For a lengthy discussion of the role of communicative motivation, see Löwenadler (to appear).

(11) Combined category-internal acceptability
[*IGA]: Avoid incorrect gender association (as in -*t* with common gender and -*d* with neuter gender)

Neuter formation of *disträ* [dɪstˈrɛː] and *blasé* [blaˈseː]

Forms	Mean %	*CIP	*IGA	*LVS	*CSP	*VSP	*ASC	*NSX
[dɪstˈrɛːt], [blaˈseːt]	19		X					
[dɪstˈrɛt], [blaˈsɛt]	26				X			
[dɪstˈrɛː], [blaˈseː]	78							X

Neuter formation of *lat* [lɑːt] and *flat* [flɑːt]

Forms	Mean %	*CIP	*IGA	*LVS	*CSP	*VSP	*ASC	*NSX
[lat], [flat]	17				X			
[lɑːt], [flɑːt]	58							X

Neuter formation of *gravid* [graˈviːd] and *morbid* [mɔrˈbiːd]

Forms	Mean %	*CIP	*IGA	*LVS	*CSP	*VSP	*ASC	*NSX
[graˈviːd], [mɔrˈbiːd]	16		X					X
[graˈviːt], [mɔrˈbiːt]	35			X			X	
[graˈvɪt], [mɔrˈbɪt]	29					X	X	
[graˈviːdt], [mɔrˈbiːdt]	53				X			

Neuter formation of *pryd* [pryːd] and *vred* [vreːd]

Forms	Mean %	*CIP	*IGA	*LVS	*CSP	*VSP	*ASC	*NSX
[pryːd], [vreːd]	14		X					X
[pryːt], [vreːt]	25			X			X	
[pryːdt], [vreːdt]	38				X			
[prʏt], [vrɛt]	55						X	X

Neuter formation of *rädd* [rɛd] and *fadd* [fad]

Forms	Mean %	*CIP	*IGA	*LVS	*CSP	*VSP	*ASC	*NSX
[rɛd], [fad]	20		X					X
[rɛdt], [fadt]	36				X			
[rɛt], [fat]	40						X	

As shown by the patterns of violations in the tables, low acceptability judgements seem to correlate with violations of high-ranked constraints, while high acceptability judgements seem to correlate with violations of low-ranked constraints. Thus, even though the ranking itself is directly determined by the result of the test and not for any independent reasons,[14] the way the different

---

[14] One possibility is to relate the constraints to their effect on transparency and to how many existing types there are in that category. For example, a form violating [*CSP] is very transparent but belongs to a category with no existing types at all, while a form violating [*VSP] or [*ASC] lack transparency but belongs to a category with many existing types. It is very unclear, however, how these factors could be weighted, other than by looking at the result of an acceptability judgement test.

phonological categories react to the constraints is quite consistent. Furthermore, the constraints themselves are not arbitrary stipulations, but based on functional, intuitively natural considerations (see the discussion in Löwenadler, to appear). In fact, a more formalized way to describe the result of the acceptability test would be to assign a 'strength value' to each constraint, showing the actual impact on speaker judgements. In that sense, values could potentially be added up to give the total resistance to the various forms.[15] However, the problem of such a formalization is that the exact impact of individual constraints is not constant among the five phonological categories, since the additional factors shown in (10) affect the constraints differently depending on word form. What does seem to be fairly stable is the actual ranking of the constraints, which is why a straightforward graphic approach has been chosen here.

In (11), certain results in particular illustrate the complexities. In the category containing the adjectives *gravid* and *morbid*, the forms using vowel shortening, i.e. [graˈvɪt] and [mɔrˈbɪt], receive slightly lower ratings than expected. I take this to be an effect of the fact that, due to lack of communicative motivation, practically all words in Swedish in that phonological category are defective. Thus, the analogy must be made with monosyllabic words, which presumably is slightly more difficult.[16] In view of these results, one may wonder whether all of the acceptability judgements could in fact be directly connected to the number of forms on which to build analogies, i.e. on type frequency. However, what is at stake here is whether one believes that word forms other than those previously encountered can be said to 'exist' for an individual speaker. That is, are there unencountered word forms that are perceived as fully natural and immediately accessible? If there are such words, speakers must somehow distinguish them from words that are not immediately accessible. However, if this distinction is defined in relative notions such as type frequency, speakers must be able to define the category to which the types belong. For example, imagine that a speaker finds himself in a situation where he needs to express the neuter of *disträ* [dɪstˈrɛː]. Since the neuter of almost all adjectives in Swedish is formed by adding a *t*-suffix (i.e. a very high type frequency), speakers should simply consider [dɪstˈrɛːt] to be a perfectly acceptable form. Of course, as we have seen, this form only receives a score of 21 per cent in the acceptability judgement test. Since many other novel adjectives are immediately accessible in the neuter, this means that speakers intuitively know that there is something special about the adjective *disträ* that

---

[15] This was suggested by an anonymous reviewer.
[16] This indicates that in a more precise description of the correlation between the constraint-ranking and the acceptability test, constraints such as [*VSP] and [*ASC] might be separate for monosyllabic and polysyllabic adjectives. This is justified as long as speakers (in part) connect type frequency to the two categories individually.

distinguishes it from non-defective adjectives. Such defining properties, in this case the long final vowel, are exactly what the constraints express. In other words, the constraints express the way speakers have organized their categories of word forms, and type frequencies can only be defined within these categories. In this sense, the constraints are needed to express the domains of the categories in which type frequency plays a role. While the acceptability is therefore affected by the type frequency of a particular subcategory, the constraints used in this paper are generalizations of a number of sub-constraints with the unifying property that they block productivity. Thus, although the constraint against vowel shortening may not have the exact same impact on polysyllabic and monosyllabic forms in terms of relative acceptability, it blocks productivity in both cases.

In conclusion, this paper is mainly meant to show the range of factors that seem to affect how speakers judge the acceptability of defective forms. Still, while the paper only presents a broad outline of the interaction between such factors, it is clear that such acceptability judgements are far from random and the patterns that appear provide an interesting area for future research on defectiveness.

References

Baayen, R. Harald and Rochelle Lieber. 1991. Productivity and English derivation: A corpus-based study. *Linguistics* 29. 801–43.

Bard, Ellen Gurman, Dan Robertson, and Antonella Sorace. 1996. Magnitude estimation of linguistic acceptability. *Language* 72. 32–68.

Bauer, Laurie. 2001. *Morphological productivity*. Cambridge: Cambridge University Press.

Brooks, Patricia, Michael Tomasello, Lawrence Lewis, and Kelly Dodson. 1999. Young children's overgeneralization of fixed transitivity verbs: The entrenchment hypothesis. *Child Development* 70. 1325–37.

Dressler, Wolfgang. 1985. On the predictiveness of natural morphology. *Journal of Linguistics* 21. 321–37.

Hellberg, Staffer. 1974. *Graphonomic rules in phonology. Studies in the expression component of Swedish*. Göteborg: Acta Universitatis Gothoburgensis.

Löwenadler, John. To appear. Restrictions on productivity: Defectiveness in Swedish adjective paradigms. *Morphology*.

Pettersson, Thore. 1990. Varför barnet inte kan vara latt. *Svenskans beskrivning 17. Åbo den 18–19 maj 1989*, ed. by E. Andersson and M. Sundman, 293–302. Åbo: Åbo Academy Press.

Plag, Iingo. 1999. *Morphological productivity. Structural constraints in English derivation*. Berlin: Mouton de Gruyter.

Teleman, Ulf, Staffan Hellberg, and Erik Andersson. 1999. *Svenska Akademiens Grammatik, Band 2*. Stockholm: Svenska Akademien.

Tomasello, Michael. 2003. *Constructing a language*. Cambridge, Mass.: Harvard University Press.

6

Defective Verbal Paradigms in Hungarian—Description and Experimental Study

ÁGNES LUKÁCS, PÉTER REBRUS,
AND MIKLÓS TÖRKENCZY

1. Introduction

THIS PAPER CONSISTS OF TWO MAIN PARTS. In section 1 we give an overview of defectiveness in Hungarian, focussing on the systematic, phonotactically motivated defectiveness of the paradigms of some verbal stems (the class of 'defective stems'). In this section our aim is to be as theoretically neutral and descriptive as possible in order to facilitate comparison with other instances or types of defectiveness in other languages.[1] In section 2 we report on the results of experiments we ran targeting various aspects of defectiveness in the verbal paradigm. We have tested (i) *gap locations*, i.e. correlations between the occurrence of forms in some designated cell(s) of the verbal paradigm and the occurrence and variation of forms in other designated cells; and (ii) *gap properties*: the variation in the classification of specific verb stems into different stem-classes, and the range of variation displayed by the forms that native speakers accept as fill-ins for the gaps that occur in the paradigms of defective verbs.

---

[1] Accordingly, we shall not discuss the problems that defectiveness, in general, or Hungarian defective verbs, in particular, pose for various theoretical models; see Hetzron 1975; Iverson 1981; Rebrus and Törkenczy 1999; Rebrus 2000; Siptár and Törkenczy 2000; Prince and Smolensky 1993; Orgun and Sprouse 1999; Raffelsiefen 2004; Rice 2005; McCarthy and Wolf forthcoming, Rebrus and Törkenczy forthcoming, etc.

2. Defectiveness in the Paradigm of Hungarian Verbs

Verbs that belong to the class of defective stems have defective paradigms in that they systematically lack certain forms that other verbs systematically[2] *do* have. Consider the following examples:

(1)[3] a. Az én mókusom ide **ugrik**, a magáé csak **ugorjon** oda.
   'My squirrel **jumps** here, **yours should jump** over there.'
   b. Az én kígyóm itt **vedlik**, a magáé csak ***vedeljen** ott.
   'My snake **sloughs** here, yours **should slough** over there.'
   c. Az én tyúkom majd itt **kotlik**, magáé csak ***?kotoljon** ott.
   'My hen **broods** here, yours **should brood** over there.'

As can be seen in (1) certain forms (e.g. **vedel-jen* slough-3SG.INDEFINITE. SUBJUNCTIVE/IMPERATIVE) of a defective verb like *vedl-ik* 'slough' are missing while paradigmatically equivalent forms (e.g. *ugor-jon* jump-3SG.INDEFINITE. SUBJUNCTIVE/IMPERATIVE) of a non-defective verb like *ugr-ik* 'jump' are perfectly well-formed. There is simply no way to say (1b) with the verb *vedl-ik* in a non-periphrastic way even though the suffixes involved are fully productive. (1c) is included to show that with some verbs (like *kotl-ik* 'brood') there is variation across speakers: for some speakers they are defective; for others they are non-defective.

There are about sixty-five verb stems in the defective class. Defective verbs can have a wide range of meanings, and they can be intransitive (e.g. *csukl-ik* 'hiccup', *sikl-ik* 'glide', *ízl-ik* 'taste good', *patakz-ik* 'gush', *habz-ik* 'foam', *burjánz-ik* 'proliferate' etc.), optionally transitive (e.g. *vedl-ik* 'shed skin', *háml-ik* 'peel') or obligatorily transitive (*sínyl-i* 'suffer', *kétl-i* 'doubt', etc.). They can belong to either of the two morphological classes of verbs: typically they belong to the '*ik*-class', but there are two 'non-*ik*' defective verbs (*sínyl-* 'suffer',

---

[2] There are sporadic examples of defectiveness that involve verbs (and also some non-verbs) that do not belong to the class of defective stems, e.g. in standard Hungarian, the (auxiliary) verb *szok-* 'perform/carry out often/regularly' only has forms that are morphologically (though not necessarily semantically) past: *szok-t-am* 1SG.PAST, but **szok-om* 1SG.PRESENT, etc. These instances of defectiveness, however, are isolated and unsystematic in the sense that the stems involved do not behave in the same way (as opposed to members of the class of defective stems, which all lack the same forms).

[3] Note on spelling: Hungarian consonant letters typically have the transparent phonetic values except <*sz*> [s], <*s*> [ʃ], <*zs*> [ʒ], <*cs*> [tʃ], <*c*> [ts], <*ny*> [ɲ], <*ty*> [c], <*gy*> [ɟ], <*j*> [j]. The doubling of a consonant letter or the first letter of a consonant digraph indicates a geminate consonant: <*tt*> [tː], <*ggy*> [ɟː]. A single or a double acute accent above a vowel letter means length and not stress (which is always on the first syllable of the word). Non-transparent vowel letters: <*í*> [iː], <*ü*> [y], <*ű*> [yː], <*ú*> [uː], <*ö*> [ø], <*ő*> [øː], <*ó*> [oː], <*e*> [ɛ], <*é*> [eː], <*a*> [ɒ], <*á*> [aː]. The hyphens that appear in some of the forms we cite are there to help the reader identify stem/suffix alternants, and are not present in normal spelling.

kétl- 'doubt').[4] Defective stems[5] are phonologically characterizable: all defective verb stems (in all their allomorphs) end in a two-term consonant cluster whose second consonant is either /l/ or /z/.[6] The stem-final consonant cluster is typically one that cannot occur finally in a phonotactically well-formed verb (e.g. /kl/ *sikl-ik* 'slide', /ml/ *háml-ik* 'peel', /bz/ *habz-ik* 'foam', etc.), but there are a few defective verbs that end in a cluster that does occur word-finally in a verb: e.g. /nz/ *burjánz-ik* 'proliferate' (compare the non-defective verb *vonz* 'attract'). This suggests that while the defectiveness of Hungarian defective verbs is phonotactically motivated, it is also lexical.[7]

Defective verbs have gaps in some designated cells in their paradigms, i.e. where they should be expected to combine with certain suffixes. The set of suffixes that induce paradigm gaps when combined with defective verbs cannot be identified on the basis of the meanings or morphosyntactic dimensions/values the suffixes realize. The reason is that the gap inducing set includes such wildly different suffixes as the Subjunctive/Imperative, the Modal, the Adverbial Participle or some Definite Person/Number suffixes, and furthermore, crucially, one allomorph of a particular suffix may induce a gap while another allomorph of the same suffix does not (e.g. 3SG.DEFINITE suffix, see the discussion below). Gaps are not limited to the inflectional paradigm of defective stems since the same pattern also manifests itself in their derivational forms.

Nevertheless, gap locations are predictable on the basis of the *morphophonological* class membership of the stems and suffixes involved.

According to the stem-final CV pattern of their allomorphs and the distribution of these allomorphs in their paradigms there are five morphophonological classes of verb stems in Hungarian.

Stable VC-stems always end in a VC string and stable CC-stems and defective stems always end in a CC string. Epenthetic[8] non-*ik* stems and epenthetic *ik*-stems alternate: some of their allomorphs are VC-final, others are CC-final (the former occur before consonant-initial suffix allomorphs, the latter before vowel-initial ones). This is shown in (2) below:

---

[4] In present-day colloquial Hungarian the essential difference between the paradigms of *ik*-class verbs and non-*ik* class verbs is in 3SG.INDEFINITE.PRESENT, where the former have the suffix -*ik* and the latter have zero: e.g. *isz-ik* 'drink', *ér-ik* 'ripen' vs. *hisz*, 'believe', *kér* 'ask'.

[5] Throughout the paper we shall use the term 'defective stem' to refer to a stem which is a member of the defective stem class.

[6] This property does not uniquely identify a stem as a member of the defective class since there are Cl and Cz final stems in some of the other morphophonological stem classes as well.

[7] Note, however, that the defective verbs that end in a well-formed final cluster are non-defective for many speakers.

[8] We use 'epenthetic' as a convenient traditional label to refer to these verbs and make no claim about the phonological status of the vowel that alternates with zero.

(2) Morphophonological stem classes (CV patterns)

	3SG.INDEF.INDIC.PRES	1SG/1PL.INDEF.INDIC.PRES VS. SUBJUNCTIVE/ MODAL/ADV.PART
i.	**stable VC**-stem (stable):	always **VC**-
	e.g.: *rámol* 'rearrange'	*rámol-ok, rámol-unk* vs. *rámol-jon, rámol-hat, rámol-va*
ii.	**epenthetic**, non-*ik* (alternating):	<u>CC</u>- ~ **VC**-
	e.g.: *söpör* 'sweep'	*söp<u>r</u>-ök, söp<u>r</u>-ünk* vs. *söpör-jön, söpör-het, söpör-ve*
iii.	**epenthetic** *ik*-stem (alternating):	<u>CC</u>- ~ **VC**-
	e.g.: *o<u>ml</u>-ik* 'collapse'	*o<u>ml</u>-ok, o<u>ml</u>-unk* vs. *omol-jon, omol-hat, omol-va*
iv.	**defective** (CC-)stem (stable):	always **CC**-
	e.g.: *há<u>ml</u>-ik* 'peel'	*há<u>ml</u>-ok, há<u>ml</u>-unk* vs. **hám(o)l-jon, *hám(o)l-hat, *hám(o)l-va*
v.	**stable CC**-stem (stable):	always **CC**-
	e.g.: *ho<u>rd</u>* 'wear'	*ho<u>rd</u>-ok, ho<u>rd</u>-unk* vs. *ho<u>rd</u>-jon, ho<u>rd</u>-hat, ho<u>rd</u>-va*

The difference between epenthetic non-*ik* stems vs. epenthetic *ik*-stems (both have CC-final and VC-final allomorphs) and defective stems vs. stable CC-stems (both have CC-final allomorphs only) is in the way the allomorphs are distributed among the cells in the paradigms of these stem-classes (depending on the type of suffix the given stem combines with in the cell).

Verbal suffixes fall into three morphophonological classes[9] in Hungarian according to the suffix-initial CV pattern. Synthetic suffixes are always vowel-initial,[10] analytic suffixes are always consonant-initial and quasi-analytic suffixes alternate (they have vowel-initial and consonant-initial allomorphs). Traditionally, suffixes of the last type are assumed to begin with a 'linking vowel' which is present in one allomorph (which appears after consonant cluster final stems) but is missing from the other (which appears after stems ending in a single consonant). The three morphophonological classes of affixes are shown in (3):

---

[9] For the sake of simplicity we disregard the past tense suffix, whose classification as synthetic or quasi-analytic is a problematic issue (see Rebrus 2000; Siptár and Törkenczy 2000; Trón and Rebrus 2005). Since the past suffix is clearly non-analytic, this problem has no bearing on the analysis of defectiveness.

[10] Pre-suffix (relative and absolute) verb-stems end in a consonant except when they contain the conditional suffix -*(V)na/ne/ná/né*, which ends in a vowel. Synthetic suffixes lose their initial vowel after the conditional suffix: e.g. *ül*$_{root}$-*né*$_{conditional}$-*k*$_{synthetic}$ suffix 'sit' 1SG.INDEF.COND.

(3) Morphophonological affix classes (CV patterns)
   a. **synthetic** (stable): always -VC...
      e.g. *-ik* (3SF.INDEF.INDIC.PRES), *-ok/ek/ök* (1SG.INDEF.), *-unk/ünk* (1PL.INDEF.), *-i* (3SG.DEF), etc.
   b. **quasi-analytic** (alternating): -VC... ~ -C...
      e.g. *-(V)nak/nek* (3PL.INDEF), *-(V)na/ne* (COND), *-(V)ni* (INF), *-(V)tok/tek/tök* (2PL.INDEF), etc.
   c. **analytic** (stable): always -C...
      e.g. *-j-* (SUBJUNCTIVE), *-hat/-het,* (MODAL), *-va/ve* (ADVERBIAL.PARTICIPLE), etc.

Epenthetic non-*ik* stems vs. epenthetic *ik*-stems differ in that the latter display systematic optionality with quasi-analytic suffixes such that in the relevant cells of the paradigm a form with a CC-final stem allomorph (and a V-initial suffix alternant) and a form with a VC-final stem allomorph (and a C-initial suffix alternant) are both possible e.g. *omlik*: *omol-nak* or *oml-anak* 'collapse' 3PL.INDEFINITE.PRESENT. By contrast, epenthetic non-*ik* stems only permit a VC-final stem allomorph in the corresponding cells of their paradigm (e.g. *söpör*: *söpör-nek* but *söpr-enek 'sweep' 3PL.INDEF.IND.PRESENT).

Defective CC-stems differ from stable CC-stems in that they lack forms with analytic suffixes. This is summarized in (4):[11]

(4) Morphophonological stem classes × suffix classes

stem classes:	suffix types: a. **synthetic**	b. **quasi-analytic**	c. **analytic**
i. **stable VC**	rámolok	rámolnak	rámolhat
ii. **epenthetic** non-*ik*	söprök	söpörnek	söpörhet
iii. **epenthetic** -*ik*	omlok	omlanak/omolnak	omolhat
iv. **defective**	hámlok	hámlanak	
v. **stable CC**	hordok	hordanak	hordhat

As can be seen, defectiveness occurs when a defective CC-stem (iv) and an analytic suffix (c) combine (shaded in (4)). Thus, gap locations within the paradigm are independent of morphosyntactic categories, dimensions, and values. Since affix category is determined at the level of allomorphs, and one and the same affix morpheme may have allomorphs that belong to different morphophonological classes, the same suffix may cause defectiveness with some defective stems, but not with others. For example, some Definite Person/Number suffixes induce a gap only with back-vowel defective stems because the *j*-initial suffix allomorph that back-vowel stems require is analytic as opposed to the *i*-initial one required by front-vowel stems, which is synthetic:[12]

---

[11] Glosses: *rámol* 'arrange', *söpör* 'sweep', *oml(ik)* 'collapse', *háml(ik)* 'peel', *hord* 'wear'
[12] Glosses: *csukl-* 'hiccup', *háml-* 'peel', *vedl-* 'slough', *sínyl-* 'suffer'.

(5) Affix category is determined at the level of allomorphs

	back-vowel stem	front-vowel stem
3SG.DEFINITE	*csuk(o)l-ja	vedl-i
	*hám(o)l-ja	sínyl-i

The behaviour of defective stems is also phonologically motivated since the gaps occur where suffixation would result in a phonotactically ill-formed cluster:

(6) *...C1C2+C...
    where C1C2C is phonotactically ill-formed[13]

The gaps in the paradigms of defective verbs are not *only* due to phonotactics since in principle the ill-formed clusters could be repaired by epenthesis:[14] (i) C1C2C → C1VC2C or (ii) C1C2C → C1C2VC. This, however is not possible because (a) defective verb stems do not alternate (as opposed to epenthetic stems) and (b) analytic suffixes never have an initial (linking) vowel (as opposed to synthetic and quasi-analytic suffixes). Thus, the gaps in the paradigms of defective verbs are the result of an interplay of phonotactic and paradigmatic (lexical) factors. The causes of defectiveness are summarized in (7) below:

(7) háml+hat 'may peel'   *há<u>ml-h</u>at   *hám<u>o</u>l-hat   *háml-<u>o</u>hat
                 cause: **phonotactics**   **stem paradigm (a)**   **suffix paradigm (b)**

Since paradigmatic defectiveness is a functionally disadvantageous state of affairs, speakers sometimes 'fill' the gaps in the paradigms of defective verbs. This forced repair (reclassification) is unsystematic,[15] but crucially, it is confined to the 'paradigmatic space' defined by the morphophonologically licit stem classes (paradigm types) given in (2), see Rebrus and Törkenczy (forthcoming).

Since most of what we have discussed above (and in general, what is known about the nature of paradigm gaps) is essentially based on the authors' intuition (and that of other authors who have written on the subject),

---

[13] More precisely: where C_1C_2 is phonotactically ill-formed in the environment _C or _#, since there are two non-*ik* defective verb stems (*kétl-* 'doubt' and *sínyl-* 'suffer'), which also have gaps in 3SG.INDEF.PRES, where non-*ik* verbs have no overt suffix. Recall that (for some speakers) there are a few stems which are defective although their stem final cluster is well-formed. The defectiveness of these stems is phonotactically unmotivated.

[14] Consonant deletion is another conceivable repair strategy—consonant deletion, however, does not occur in the phonology of Hungarian (except post-lexically as a fast-speech phenomenon), see Siptár and Törkenczy (2000).

[15] Speakers when forced to come up with forms that fill the gaps tend to be uncomfortable with the result and generally choose to express the meaning of the missing forms in some periphrastic way.

and since defectiveness seems to be a fuzzy (gradual) and therefore elusive phenomenon, we think it is especially important to study defectiveness experimentally.

3. The Experiment

We tested the hypotheses/assumptions and gap properties discussed in section 1 in a psycholinguistic experiment in which participants had to decide for the string appearing on the screen (in this case for each alternant) whether it is an existing word of the Hungarian language or not, and press a button accordingly as fast as possible. Since this experiment contained an extremely large number of items, the experiment was divided into ten sessions by pauses. The length of the pause was determined by the participant.[16]

The task was to make lexical decisions about twelve forms of 120 verbs adding up to 1,440 items (presented in random order), in the following design (examples are given in (8) below)

- 26 epenthetic *ik*-stems (E)
- 34 defective stems (D)
- 60 stable -CC control stems matched individually on frequency to the defective and epenthetic stems (CD, CE).

Results for the last two groups of items (CD, CE), although they are expected to behave the same way since they belong to the same class, are shown separately, to allow for defective-control and epenthetic-control comparisons that are matched on frequency and are not distorted by the number of items tested. From Figure 1 to Figure 7, results for defective stems will be shown in black, epenthetic stems will be plotted in grey, and results for stable CC stems (CD and CE) will be given in white columns. For each stem, VC and CC alternants were generated with four quasi-analytic suffixes (Q1: *-tOk* 2PL.INDEF; Q2: *-nAk* 3PL.INDEF; Q3: *-nA* CONDITIONAL, Q4: *-ni* INFINITIVE) and two analytic suffixes (A: *-hAt* MODAL, *-vA* ADVERBIAL.PARTICIPLE, i.e. altogether 12 alternants.[17] We predicted differences in response patterns to different alternants (VC vs. CC) according to stem class and suffix type, as outlined in the hypotheses below.

---

[16] 100 adult Hungarian native speakers participated in the experiment (62 males and 38 females, mean age: 27.4 years; age range: 19.2–44.8 years).
[17] Capital letters in suffixes indicate that the suffix harmonizes: *A=ale; O=olelö*.

(8) Examples of stimuli for each stem class × suffix × stem alternant combinations. Unshaded cells contain forms that are, according to the authors' intuition, legitimate words in Hungarian; shaded cells contain nonwords.[18]

		Defective (D)		Epenthetic (E)		Stable CC (CD, CE)	
		-CC	-VC	-CC	-VC	-CC	-VC
-tOk	Q1	hámlotok	*hámoltok	ugrotok	ugortok	toldotok	*tolodtok
-nAk	Q2	hámlanak	*hámolnak	ugranak	ugornak	toldanak	*tolodnak
-nA	Q3	hámlana	*hámolna	ugrana	ugorna	toldana	*tolodna
-ni	Q4	hámlani	*hámolni	ugrani	ugorni	toldani	*tolodni
-hAt	A1	*hámlhat	*hámolhat	*ugrhat	ugorhat	toldhat	*tolodhat
-vA	A2	*hámlva	*hámolva	*ugrva	ugorva	toldva	*tolodva

We can think of the responses of a particular participant to the stimuli that are generated from one particular verb (see (8)) as a series that consists of twelve yes/no answers. We shall represent this series by a Boolean vector consisting of 0s and 1s. These numbers encode whether the participant rejects (0) or accepts (1) a given form of a particular verb. We shall call these vectors *response vectors*. The complete data set of the experiment consists of 12,000 response vectors, each twelve digits long, which represent the well-formedness judgements by 100 participants about forms generated from 120 verb stems.

Within a given response vector the order of positions is the following: every odd-numbered position (i.e. the 1st, 3rd, 5th, 7th, 9th and 11th) shows a response given to a form containing a CC stem alternant, and every even-numbered position (i.e. the 2nd, 4th, 6th, 8th, 10th and 12th) shows a response given to a form containing a VC stem alternant. The first eight positions (1–8) show responses given to forms that contain the four quasi-analytic suffixes examined (Q1, Q2, Q3 and Q4—see (8)), and the last four positions (9–12) show responses given to forms that contain the two analytic suffixes examined (A1 and A2—see (8)). This is summarized in (9) below.

(9) The structure of response vectors

	CC	VC
Q1	1	2
Q2	3	4
Q3	5	6
Q4	7	8
A1	9	10
A2	11	12

The 12-tuples described above are useful in examining the differences between verb stems on the one hand, and differences in the well-formedness

---

[18] In these examples the word-forms are based on the following stems: defective: *háml-* 'peel', epenthetic *ugr-/ugor* 'jump', and stable CC *told* 'extend'.

judgements by the participants on the other. We hypothesize that the verbs examined fall into three classes according to the stem alternants that appear before the suffixes examined: (i) stable CC-stems (which only have CC stem alternants), (ii) epenthetic *ik*-stems (which have both CC and VC stem alternants before Q-suffixes, and only VC stem alternants before A-suffixes), and (iii) defective stems (which only have CC stem alternants before Q-suffixes, and neither CC nor VC stem alternants before A-suffixes). Specific response vectors correspond to these stem classes—henceforward, we shall refer to these as *canonical vectors*. The three canonical vectors are the following:

(10) Canonical vectors

(i) defective	CC	VC		(ii) epenthetic	CC	VC		(iii) stable CC	CC	VC
Q1	1	0		Q1	1	1		Q1	1	0
Q2	1	0		Q2	1	1		Q2	1	0
Q3	1	0		Q3	1	1		Q3	1	0
Q4	1	0		Q4	1	1		Q4	1	0
A1	0	0		A1	0	1		A1	1	0
A2	0	0		A2	0	1		A2	1	0

In what follows we shall analyse the differences between the 12,000 response vectors gained from the experiment and the three expected canonical vectors.

We also introduce the notion of Hamming distance, which is defined for strings of equal length, and gives the number of positions where the two strings differ, e.g. the string 1110 is within a Hamming distance of 1 from the string 1111, the string 1010 is within a Hamming distance of 2 from the same string, etc. We will measure deviation of participants' response pattern from canonical vectors by the response patterns' Hamming distance from a given vector. Notice that the three canonical vectors are not equidistant from each other: the canonical vectors representing E and stable -CC are at a Hamming distance of 8 from one another, the Hamming distance between D and E is 6, while the distance between the canonical vectors representing D and C is only 2.

4. Hypotheses

Several predictions follow from the analysis in Rebrus and Törkenczy (forthcoming) about the *classification*, *uncertainty*, and *forced repair* of defective stems:

1. There is no stem class that would fall outside the paradigmatic space defined by the five stem classes and the three suffix classes described above (see (4)).

2. Assignment of stems into classes by participants shows differing degrees of *uncertainty* (stable CC < E < D). We expect greater variability for stem classes with smaller family size (the number of stems belonging to a class increases from D (~65) through E (~280) to CC (~350)). Greater uncertainty would be manifest in (i) *longer reaction times* and (ii) *greater variability* in response patterns.
3. We also expect *larger variation* in stem classes with a functionally disadvantageous behaviour. We consider optionality a functionally disadvantageous state of affairs, and defectiveness even more so. This functional 'handicap' manifests itself in greater variability in responses, as speakers are expected to show individual variation in repair strategies and in what stems they select as targets of forced repair. *Forced repair* of D-stems would be manifest in (i) *more 'accept' answers* than expected in class D and (ii) the direction of repair depends on stem shape (*sonority relations*).

5. Results

We present the results for each hypothesis separately.

Hypothesis 1
There is no stem class that would fall outside the paradigmatic space defined by the three canonical vectors.

We expect that this hypothesis is borne out if the majority of response vectors correspond to either of the three canonical vectors given above, and there is no other vector outside these three that has an outstanding frequency among response vectors. The analysis of response pattern frequencies shows that the three canonical vectors have the highest frequencies of occurrence (percentages including vectors within a Hamming distance of 1 for each vector are given in parentheses): CC: 29.1 per cent (42.1 per cent); E: 5.5 per cent (11.6 per cent); D: 4.4 per cent (9.76 per cent); the three canonical vectors together cover 39 per cent of response patterns (summing the frequencies for 0+1 Hamming distance (given in parentheses) would give a misleadingly large percentage; a subset of vectors within a Hamming distance of 1 are overlapping for D and CC stems, which are at a distance of 2 from each other).

Figure 1 below shows the mean percentages of canonical answers[19] by stem type. The thirty most frequent vectors (those with a relative frequency

---

[19] More precisely: answers whose distance from the canonical vectors is ≤1, i.e. we disregarded a distance of 1 from the canonical vectors.

> 0.5 per cent) are within a Hamming distance of 1 from canonical vectors.[20] There were no other vectors with relative frequencies larger than 0.5 per cent, so no answer patterns fell outside the paradigmatic space defined by the five morphophonological stem classes.

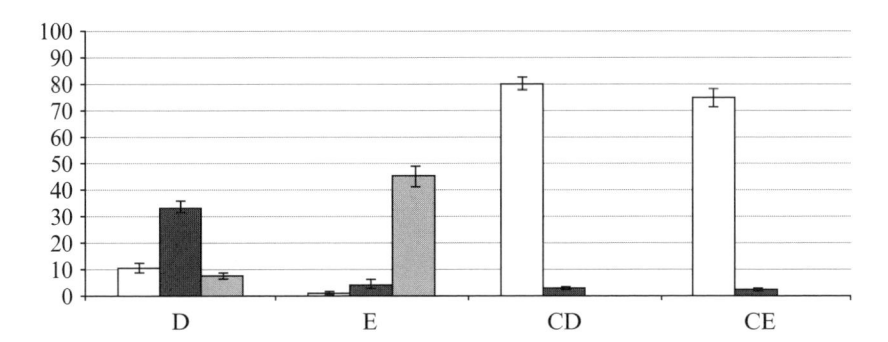

Figure 1. Mean percentage of canonical answers (+0/1) by stem type. (Standard errors are also shown.)

As Figure 1 shows, participants' response patterns confirm our classification of stems: for each stem type, mean percentage of canonical answers is highest for its own canonical vector (black column for D, grey for E and white columns for CD and CE stems). For epenthetic and stable CC (CD and CE) stems, participants did not reclassify stems, i.e. there were very few answers matching the other two canonical patterns. With defective stems, the percentages were higher for the E and C canonical vectors, but percentages were nevertheless highest for the D vector. Importantly, percentages of corresponding canonical answers were highest for stable CC stems, followed by the E class, and ratios were lowest for D stems.

* * *

[20] With the exception of the following five vectors (which were among the thirty most frequent ones although more distant than 1): (a) total rejection: ⟨00.00.00.00 | 00.00⟩; (b) total acceptance: ⟨11.11.11.11 | 11.11⟩; (c) only VC stem alternants: ⟨01.01.01.01 | 01.01⟩; (d) only CC stem alternants with Q-suffixes: ⟨10.10.10.10 | 01.01⟩ and (e) variation with only one Q-suffix, otherwise same as c): ⟨11.01.01.01 | 01.01⟩. We suggest that this is due to (i) the rarity of some of the stems involved in the case of (a) and (b) (i.e. total rejection and total acceptance of all the generated forms of some stems is due to the fact that some of the participants simply did not know the stems in question); (ii) dispreference for variation in the paradigm of epenthetic -*ik* stems in the case of (c), (d) (i.e. some participants accepted only VC alternants (c) or only CC alternants (d) in the quasi-analytic forms of these stems) and (e) (i.e. some participants only accepted variation—*both* VC and CC alternants—in *some* of the quasi-analytic forms of these stems (-*nAk* in the case of (e)). In the experiment we did not examine differences of behaviour between suffixes belonging to the *same* morphophonological class.).

Hypothesis 2
Assignment of stems into classes by participants shows differing degrees of uncertainty (stable CC < E < D). Greater uncertainty would be manifest in: (i) longer reaction times and (ii) greater variability in response patterns.

Reaction times are taken to reflect the time required for mental operations in a task; in a lexical decision experiment, RT shows the duration of lexical retrieval of an item which increases with the difficulty of retrieval. Lexical decision times are longer for less frequent and longer words than for frequent and short words, but there are many other factors influencing lexical retrieval; we hypothesized that optionality and defectiveness, as factors of uncertainty, are among them.

A one-way ANOVA on reaction times (only on medians of correct answers) showed a significant main effect of stem type.[21] Post hoc tests revealed that reaction times for defective stems were significantly longer than reaction times for either epenthetic or stable CC stems ($p<0.001$). E differed from CD at $p<0.05$, while the difference between the two control groups approached, but did not reach significance (CD>CE at $p=0.07$). Mean reaction times for each stem class are shown in Figure 2. Since we did our best to control for frequency across stem types, we did not expect frequency to explain differences between stem types (indeed, frequency showed only a significant but very marginal correlation with RTs: $r=-0.063$; $p<0.01$). Length is also a potential confound in measuring reaction times, and length showed a very strong and significant correlation with RT: $r=0.687$; $p<0.001$. Including length in character as a covariate showed a significant main effect of length,[22] but it did not eliminate the main effect of stem type,[23] which this way proved

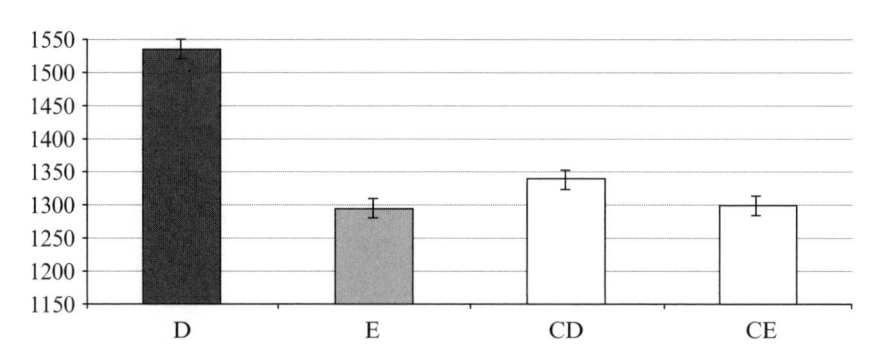

Figure 2. Reaction time (in ms) by stem type (only 'correct' answers; averaged over medians, standard errors are also shown).

[21] $F(3,1676)=56.29$; $p<0.001$.
[22] $F(1,1676)=0505.03$; $p<0.001$.
[23] $F(3,1676)=58.6$; $p<0.001$.

to be an independent factor in explaining RT differences (D was matched to CD, and E to CE on length, but on average, D and CD were one character longer than E and CE. This difference is statistically significant, which might explain the marginally significant difference between CD and CE).

In summary, as we expected, deciding whether a string seen on the screen is an existing word in Hungarian or not took much longer with items belonging to the defective stem class than with items in any other class. Contrary to our expectations, decisions on epenthetic items were not longer than controls: optionality did not make lexical retrieval more difficult. The length of the items, as in all lexical decision tasks, was an important factor influencing decision times, but it did not eliminate the effects of stem type.

* * *

Besides reaction times, we had other measures of uncertainty reflecting variability of responses in different stem types. The simplest measure of variability was the number of 'correct' answers in each stem class (a correct answer was taken to be one that agreed with our classification of a stem into a particular stem type and the behaviour predicted by that classification). A one-way ANOVA showed a significant main effect for stem type, again.[24] Posthoc LSD tests showed all differences except the difference between CD and CE to be significant at $p<0.001$: as shown by Figure 3 below, participants gave most correct answers about control stems (the missing percentages are probably random errors), they agreed with our expectations less for epenthetic stems, and showed the largest deviation in responses to defective stems, conforming to the expected order of uncertainty in responses to items in different stem types.

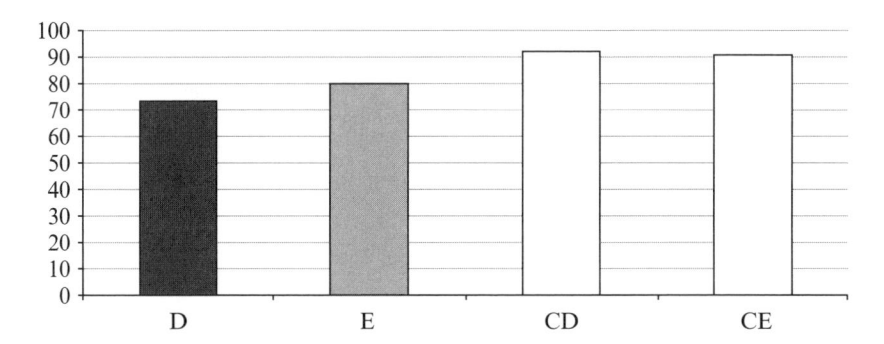

Figure 3. Percentage of 'correct' answer by stem type (averaged over accuracy scores for words, max=100).

[24] $F(3,1676)=145.21; p<0.001$.

The next measure of uncertainty we calculated was the average Hamming distance of answers from canonical vectors (i.e. from expected class behaviour). Figure 4 shows the average Hamming distance of answers from the three canonical vectors by stem type. For each stem type, only the distance from its own canonical vector is shown (although not shown, we calculated average distances of answers from all three canonical vectors for each stem type, and in each stem type, the distance from its own canonical vector was the smallest). The predictions for uncertainty are borne out by this measure as well: the two control groups display a very small distance from their expected behaviour (represented by the CC canonical vector) as stable CC-stems, and this deviation is probably the result of *random errors*. Group E shows a *greater distance* from the expected behaviour; there is greater variation between items. Group D's distance from the expected behaviour is *much greater* than that of the other three groups (CE, CD, and E). Individual D-items also show *great variation*.

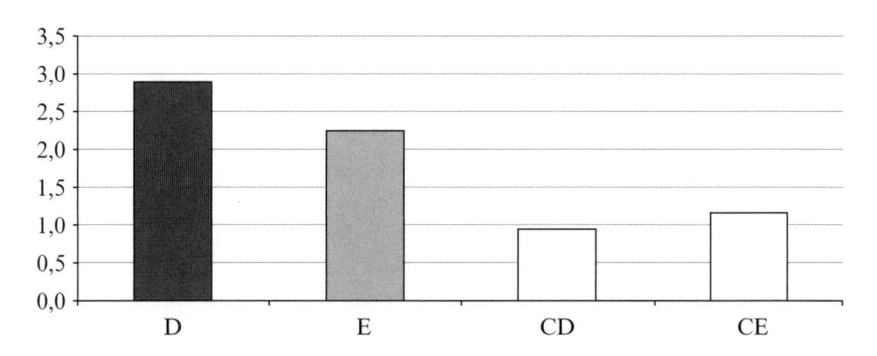

Figure 4. Average Hamming distance of answers from canonical vectors.

A third, more direct measure of variability is the average number of different vectors participants gave for stems (shown in Figure 5 for each stem type).

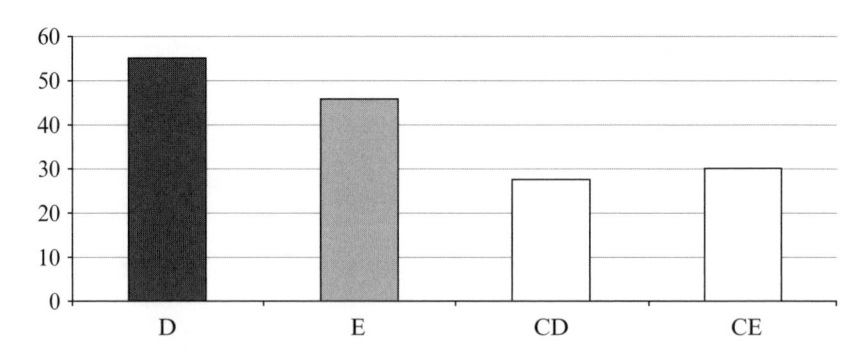

Figure 5. Average number of different vectors by stem type.

Participants answered with a larger number of different vectors for defective and epenthetic stems and were significantly more consistent with control stems (D and E comparisons are not relevant here because of the different number of stems in the two classes).

* * *

The fourth measure of uncertainty was the entropy of answers calculated for each stem type. Entropy is a measure that shows the number of bits required to encode the information in answer patterns (it gives the minimum number of questions you would need on average to guess with many trials).

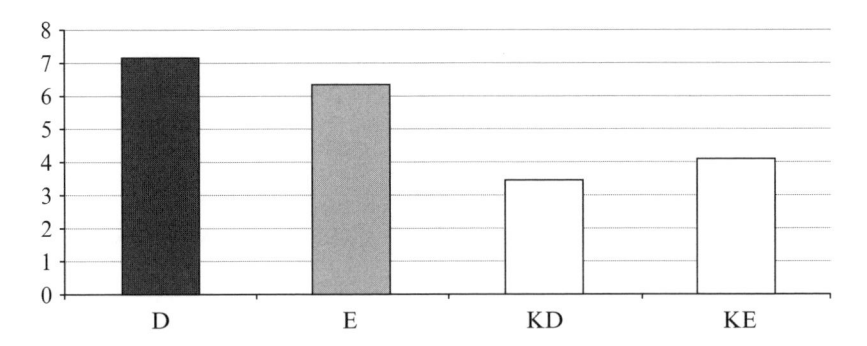

Figure 6. Entropy by stem type.

Figure 7 below shows the percentage of 'accept' answers for each stem type. Horizontal lines show the percentages of 'accept' answers (1s) in the canonical vector of the corresponding stem type, i.e. the percentage of 'accept' answers we would expect if participants were strictly following our classification of stems and their predicted behaviour. With stable CC-stems (CD and CE), forms with -VC stem alternants are illicit, which makes the expected distribution of accept and refuse answers 50-50 per cent. Participants very closely follow this expected pattern with this stem class. With epenthetic stems allowing for the optionality with quasi-analytic suffixes, the canonical answer pattern predicts that 83.3 per cent of answers should be 'accept' answers. The actual average ratio of 'accept' answers was 66.2 per cent in the E class. Since (as we hypothesized) optionality is functionally disadvantageous, this ratio is indicative of participants' tendency to move away from optionality towards stability (50 per cent), by not accepting optionality with every item where it *is* a possibility in principle. The behaviour of defective stems deviates from expectations in the opposite direction: participants accepted 45.12 per cent of strings in this class while the percentage predicted by the canonical vector is 33.3 per cent. This shows that with defective stems, too, participants worked against a functionally disadvantageous state (defectiveness), and again, towards stability

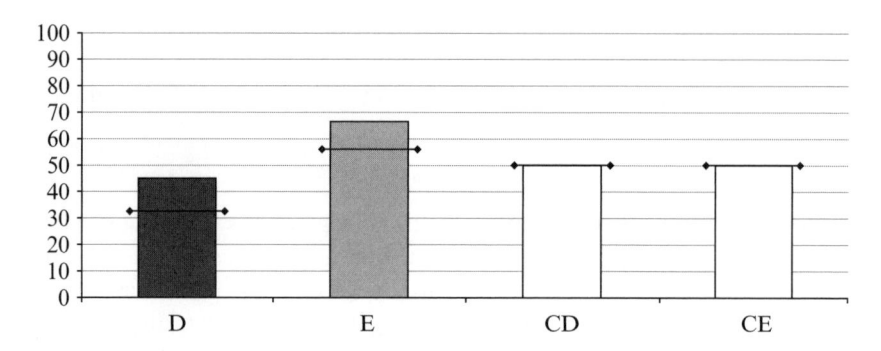

Figure 7. Mean percentage of 'accept' answers by stem type (horizontal lines indicate the percentage of 'accept' values in canonical vectors).

(50 per cent), but this time by accepting strings that are ungrammatical by our prediction for defective stems. Although with both defective and epenthetic stems, the tendency to repair the functionally disadvantageous state is clear and percentages in both classes regress towards stability, this repair is non-systematic and shows great variation across individuals and individual stems too.

* * *

Forced repair: C1C2 phonotactics and defectiveness

Hypothesis 3
The greater the sonority 'downstep' in the stem-final CC of a defective stem, the greater the (marginal) acceptability of the form in which the defective stem combines with an analytic suffix.

As we saw in the previous section, speakers are motivated to repair functionally disadvantageous states, but this repair is speaker and stem dependent. We predicted that repair of defective forms will partly depend on the phonotactics of the stem-final CC cluster such that the more well-formed the final cluster of the D-stem is, the more tempted speakers are to accept (canonically defective) forms with analytic suffixes. To create a measure for phonotactic well-formedness, we established a tentative sonority scale given in (11), and we calculated sonority slope values for stem-final CC clusters by subtracting the sonority value of C1 from the sonority value of C2. The greater the sonority slope value, the more well-formed a cluster is; examples are given in (12).

(11)   Tentative sonority scale

glide	> homorganic nasals	> liquids	> non-homorganic nasals	> fricatives	> plosives
j	nt nd nk ng	l r	m ny	s sz z zs	t d k g b p
0	0.5	1	2	3	4

(12) Sonority slope value = C2−C1

e.g. *csukl-*: **−3**, *fesl-*: **−2**, *háml-*: **−1**, *habz-*: **−1**
  porl-: **0**, *morajl-*: **1**, *párz-*: **2**, *burjánz-*: **2.5**

We correlated the number of 'accept' answers (only with CC-alternants) with sonority slope values for defective stem+analytic suffix combinations and found that they were highly correlated (sonority × number of accept answers, Pearson correlation, Defective stems + Analytic suffixes: $r=0.693$; $p<0.001$). Speakers had a greater tendency to accept defective -CC alternants that are more well-formed.

6. Conclusion

Gap locations in the Hungarian verbal paradigm are independent of morpho-syntactic categories, dimensions and values, and are predictable on the basis of the *morphophonological* class membership of the stems and suffixes involved: defectiveness occurs when a defective CC-stem and an analytic suffix combine. After giving a descriptive overview of phonotactically motivated defectiveness in the Hungarian verbal paradigm, we presented results from an experiment testing gap locations and gap properties. Analysing frequencies of participants' response patterns, we confirmed that there is no stem class that would fall outside the paradigmatic space defined by the canonical vectors. As expected, we observed longest reaction times, greatest distance of response patterns from expected behaviour and greatest variation in responses with defective stems, explained by the smallest family size of the class and by individual variation in speakers' strategies to repair a functionally disadvantageous state of affairs like defectiveness. We predicted that repair of defective forms will partly depend on the phonotactics of the stem-final CC cluster: stem final CC clusters with a greater sonority downstep are more well-formed and speakers had a greater tendency to accept defective CC alternants that are more well-formed. Great variation between stems warrants further investigation of responses to individual stems to determine factors other than phonotactic well-formedness that influence repair.

References

Hetzron, Robert. 1975. Where the grammar fails. *Language* 51:4. 859–72.
Iverson, Gregory. 1981. Rules, constraints, and paradigmatic lacunae. *Glossa* 15:1. 136–44.

McCarthy, John J. and Matthew Wolf. Forthcoming. Less than zero: Correspondence and the null output. *Modeling ungrammaticality in optimality theory*, ed. by Curt Rice. London: Equinox Publishing.

Orgun, Cemil Orhan and Ronald L. Sprouse. 1999. From MPARSE to CONTROL: deriving ungrammaticality. *Phonology* 16. 191–224.

Prince, Alan and Paul Smolensky. 1993/2004. *Optimality theory: Constraint interaction in generative grammar*. Ms. Rutgers University, New Brunswick, and University of Colorado, Boulder (Published by Oxford: Blackwell, 2004).

Raffelsiefen, Renate. 2004. Absolute ill-formedness and other morphophonological effects. *Phonology* 21. 91–142.

Rebrus, Péter. 2000. Morfofonológiai jelenségek. *Strukturális magyar nyelvtan, 3. kötet: Morfológia*, ed. by Ferenc Kiefer, 763–949. Budapest: Akadémiai Kiadó.

Rebrus, Péter and Miklós Törkenczy. 1999. Defectivity. Talk delivered at the Budapest Phonology Circle and Linguistic Discussion Group (BuPhoC), Budapest on 28 April 1999.

Rebrus, Péter and Miklós Törkenczy. Forthcoming. *Modeling ungrammaticality in optimality theory*, ed. by Sylvia Blaho and Curt Rice, London: Equinox Publishing.

Rice, Curtis. 2005. Optimal gaps in optimal paradigms. *Catalan Journal of Linguistics* 4. 155–70

Siptár, Péter and Miklós Törkenczy. 2000. *The phonology of Hungarian. The phonology of the world's languages*. Oxford: Clarendon Press/Oxford University Press.

Trón, Viktor and Péter Rebrus. 2005. Re-presenting the past: Contrast and uniformity in Hungarian past tense suffixation. *Approaches to Hungarian 9. Papers from the Düsseldorf Conference,* ed. by István Kenesei, Christopher Piñón and Péter Siptár, 303–27. Budapest: Akadémiai Kiadó.

7

On Morphomic Defectiveness: Evidence from the Romance Languages of the Iberian Peninsula[1]

MARTIN MAIDEN AND PAUL O'NEILL

1. Introduction

DEFECTIVENESS IN ROMANCE LANGUAGES HAS RECEIVED little theoretical attention, a notable exception being Albright (2003), who closely examines 'arbitrary lexical paradigm gaps' in modern Spanish verbs[2]—concluding that they arise through a combination of unfamiliarity of the lexical item, and *uncertainty* over which of a range of possible 'morphophonological' alternation patterns should apply to those verbs. We revisit the Spanish data from a historical and comparative perspective, considering also defectiveness in a closely related language, Portuguese, and our interpretation of the facts is in interesting ways complementary to Albright's. We share the insight of Boyé and Hofherr (this volume)[3] that paradigm gaps are determined not only by lexical rarity but also by 'morphomic' patterning in the sense of Aronoff (1994). 'Low speaker confidence' in the realization of a particular cell of a paradigm, unquestionably a major source of defectiveness, turns out to be neither a necessary nor a sufficient condition. That it is not necessary will be shown from a number of verbs (e.g. Spanish *blandir* 'to brandish') which present no potential morphological difficulties whatever, yet are still defective.

---

[1] Derived from comparative work on our project in *Autonomous morphology in diachrony: comparative evidence from the Romance languages* based at Oxford University funded by AHRC research grant *AH/D503396/1*. http://www.ling-phil.ox.ac.uk/romance-linguistics.
[2] That is, gaps that are not determined by pragmatic/semantic (or phonological) factors. If a verb like Spanish *llover* 'to rain' lacks plural, and first and second person, forms, this is trivially a product of the semantics of the verb. In fact it is likely that given an appropriate scenario (an animate subject somehow capable of 'raining'), speakers would be able to produce the entire paradigm without hesitation.
[3] Cf. also Boyé (2000).

That it is not sufficient will be shown from verbs like *abolir* ('to abolish'), parts of whose paradigm are defective yet none the less highly predictable.

Our perspective is to consider the overall paradigmatic distribution of gaps. Ibero-Romance paradigm gaps replicate a characteristic and recurrent Romance 'morphomic' pattern (in origin phonologically determined, but long exclusively morphological in character—cf. Maiden 2005) such that, in non-first conjugation verbs, the first person singular present indicative and the whole of the present subjunctive nearly always share the same stem and, more importantly, that the same set of cells is often the locus for distinctive and idiosyncratic allomorphy. In verbs which show defectiveness along these lines, a second type of defectiveness is also sometimes present, replicating another major Romance morpheme which unites the singular and third person stems of the present as the locus of certain types of allomorphy.

These data offer an insight into at least one way in which 'morphomic defectiveness', a phenomenon to which Aronoff (1994: 54ff.) briefly alludes for Latin, may come into being. What we find in Ibero-Romance complements Maiden's findings (2004a) on the role of morphomic patterning in suppletion. In the latter case, speakers react to lexical superabundance by accommodating synonymous, semantically basic and highly frequent lexemes into a suppletive paradigm according to morphomic patterns of distribution. In defectiveness, speakers leave unfilled a 'morphomically' defined array of cells.

Before embarking on our analysis of Spanish and Portuguese defectiveness, we need briefly to address an objection which we will answer in greater detail later. A good many of our examples will draw on prescriptive grammarians' accounts of defectiveness in what are often fairly recondite verbs: yet Albright, for one, has shown that speaker usage is often a good deal more 'fuzzy' than the rigid prescriptions of grammarians. The suspicion is bound to arise at some points below that what we are discussing is not really the linguistic usage of ordinary speakers, but little more than grammarians' pipedreams. In some cases we shall see that this suspicion is not far from the truth. Pending our more detailed discussion of this issue later, suffice it to say for the moment that the grammarians we cite are native speakers, too, and that in fact their idealizations of the facts may actually tell us more about native speakers' knowledge of the organization of inflectional paradigms in their language than we could learn from observation of their spontaneous usage.

2. The Determinants of Defectiveness

Two classic examples of defectiveness in Spanish are the verbs *abolir* 'to abolish' and *pacer* 'to graze [of an animal]'. *Abolir* has a full paradigm (with the root *abol-*), except that there are no forms in the whole of the present subjunctive nor in the singular and third person forms of the present indicative. Likewise *pacer*, except that the domain of defectiveness is the whole of the present subjunctive and just the first person singular present indicative (1).

(1) The defective verbs *abolir* and *pacer*

Infinitive	*abolir*
Gerund	*aboliendo*
Past participle	*abolido*

present indicative	present subjunctive	imperfect indicative	future	conditional	preterite	imperfect subjunctive
———	———	*abolía*	*aboliré*	*aboliría*	*abolí*	*aboliese*
———	———	*abolías*	*abolirás*	*abolirías*	*aboliste*	*abolieses*
———	———	*abolía*	*abolirá*	*aboliría*	*abolió*	*aboliese*
abolimos	———	*abolíamos*	*aboliremos*	*aboliríamos*	*abolimos*	*aboliésemos*
abolís	———	*abolíais*	*aboliréis*	*aboliríais*	*abolisteis*	*abolieseis*
———	———	*abolían*	*abolirán*	*abolirían*	*abolieron*	*aboliesen*

Infinitive	*pacer*
Gerund	*paciendo*
Past participle	*pacido*

present indicative	present subjunctive	imperfect indicative	future	conditional	preterite	imperfect subjunctive
———	———	*pacía*	*paceré*	*pacería*	*pací*	*paciese*
paces	———	*pacías*	*pacerás*	*pacerías*	*paciste*	*pacieses*
pace	———	*pacía*	*pacerá*	*pacería*	*pació*	*paciese*
pacemos	———	*pacíamos*	*paceremos*	*paceríamos*	*pacimos*	*paciésemos*
pacéis	———	*pacíais*	*paceréis*	*paceríais*	*pacisteis*	*pacieseis*
pacen	———	*pacían*	*pacerán*	*pacerían*	*pacieron*	*paciesen*

Nothing in the semantics of these verbs explains why, for example, one should be able to say 'I abolished' but not 'I abolish', or 'we abolish' in the present indicative, but not 'we abolish' in the present subjunctive, or why one should be able to say 'I grazed' (however pragmatically unlikely, given that only animals graze, but animals do not talk), but not 'I graze'; or 'it grazes' in the present indicative, but not in the present subjunctive. Moreover, there is no phonological explanation of why the missing forms are missing: in the 1SG present indicative and present subjunctive of *abolir*, for example, we might expect respectively *abolo* or *abuelo* and *abola* or *abuela*, and for *pacer*, *pazco* or *pazo*, *pazca* or *paza*: the fact that there are two possibilities in each case is highly significant, as we shall see, but the point here is that any of these possibilities is wholly unexceptionable in Spanish phonology.[4]

---

[4] In fact, *abuelo* and *abuela(s)* happen to be real Spanish words, meaning 'grandfather' and 'grandmother(s)'. In most varieties of Spanish, *pazo* and *paza* would be homophonous with words meaning 'I pass' and 'he passes'. We concur entirely with Albright (2003: 7f.) that

Albright (2003, 2006) argues that the major determinant of defectiveness is speaker uncertainty in deciding whether possible morphophonological alternations should apply to some input, in words which are typically low frequency and unfamiliar. For example, some verbs with *o* in their root show a diphthong *ue* in most present tense forms, while others have *o* everywhere; and some verbs in *-cer* have root-final *-zc-* in the first person singular present indicative and throughout the present subjunctive, while others have just *z/c* (*z* and *c* are, in the relevant forms, merely orthographic variants of the same sound). The gaps that are listed in grammars emerge not just because speakers are unsure whether to apply alternation or not, but (Albright 2003: 13) because they

> lie at just one extreme of a gradient range of uncertainty that speakers feel when deciding whether or not to apply morphophonological alternations. This uncertainty is strongest when two factors collide: first the word must be relatively infrequent or unfamiliar, so that the speaker is forced to synthesize a form. In addition, the lexicon must contain conflicting evidence about whether or not the alternation should apply.

Defectiveness occurs when speakers know (Albright 2006: 2) that 'an inflected form must stand in a certain relation to another inflected form, but the language does not provide enough data to be certain of what that relation should be.' Arbitrary gaps occur (2006: 19) in:

> just those cases where there is too little data to be sure about any of the available generalizations. Concretely, there is no *o* → *ó* rule that would map *abolír* to 3SG *abóle* [. . .], while the *o* → *ué* rule that would map *abolír* to *abuéle* is supported by really just two verbs (*dormir* 'sleep', *morir* 'die' [. . .]).

While we do not deny the role that low speaker certainty plays in generating defectiveness, there are significant aspects of defectiveness in Spanish, and even more so in the closely parallel patterns of Portuguese, which cannot be so determined. That defectiveness can persist independently of 'low speaker confidence' regarding the possible application of alternation has been recently demonstrated, for example, by Daland, Sims, and Pierrehumbert (2007) for Russian, or by Sims (2008) for Greek. Our data point in the same direction, with the important difference that in many of our cases there is not, and never was, any possibility at all of 'morphological competition' or 'speaker uncertainty', with regard to alternation in the specific lexemes affected. Given a low frequency rare lexeme, defectiveness can come into

---

a homophonic clash of this kind is most unlikely to have any role in determining defectiveness. In most defective verbs there is no such potential homophony and, where there is, the defectiveness of this verb would be even harder to explain in terms of speaker uncertainty, since 'clash avoidance' ought clearly to favour the option *abolo and *abola(*s*).

being, and persist, for absolutely no reason discernible in the morphological or phonological structure of the lexeme itself. We shall argue, ultimately, that there is in fact a sense in which one may speak of 'uncertainty', but that this resides at an extremely abstract—'morphomic'—level of knowledge about the structure of paradigms in Spanish and Portuguese.

3. Defectiveness in Spanish and Portuguese

The stock example of defectiveness in both these languages is *abolir* 'to abolish' (see (1)). It is typical of defective verbs in belonging to the third conjugation with infinitive in *-ir* (the continuant of the Latin fourth conjugation in -IRE, to which a good many, but by no means all, loan words from classical and other foreign languages have been assigned), and in appearing relatively late in the history of both languages.[5] It is not in fact a direct borrowing from Classical Latin, since the Latin verb ABOLĒRE belonged to the second conjugation. Nonetheless, in Italian, French, Spanish and Portuguese it appears in the form *abolir(e)*, and the consensus in the etymological dictionaries of these languages is that it is a learnèd neologism whose basis is continuants of the Latin verbal noun ABOLITIO 'abolition', which has the vowel /i/. The word has a 'cosmopolitan' air, belonging to the realm of 'international', intellectual vocabulary, rather than to everyday usage. Where it first arose, and how it came subsequently to be diffused among the Romance languages of western Europe (and English), is unclear: the earliest attestation in French is from the beginning of the fifteenth century and in Spanish and Italian from the first half of the sixteenth century, but there is no attestation in Portuguese before the late seventeenth.

The main domain of defectiveness is, as we have seen, the singular and third person plural forms of the present indicative and of the present subjunctive, plus the first and second person plural forms of the present subjunctive.[6] There is no doubt that speakers as well as grammarians overwhelmingly reject any

---

[5] For Portuguese, from Machado (1967) it appears that none of the Portuguese defective verbs are attested earlier than the fourteenth century, and most are not attested before the sixteenth. Many of them have clear phonological signs of late borrowing from outside Portuguese, such as retention of intervocalic /l/ in *demolir* 'demolish' (first attested in the seventeenth century), or retention of the diphthong /au/ in *exaurir* 'exhaust' (nineteenth century). To take some examples from Spanish, according to Corominas and Pascual (1991), *blandir* is a loan from French, attested from the fourteenth century, *abolir* is not found before the sixteenth, and *agredir* is first recorded in the nineteenth.

[6] Drawing principally on the Academy grammar (cf. Elvira 1998: 98–100), one obtains a list for Spanish of: *abolir agredir aguerrir arrecirse aterirse balbucir blandir colorir compungir desabrir descolorir desmarrirse despavorir embair empedernir fallir garantir manir preterir transgredir*.

forms for any of the blank cells in (1), even if the behaviour of speakers (as observed and tested by Albright 2003) shows that the sharp boundaries established in prescriptive grammars correspond to a rather more 'fuzzy' linguistic reality, with speakers sometimes producing, albeit in a hesitant and contradictory way, 3SG present indicative forms such as *abuele* or *abole*. Unpredictability and speaker uncertainty about what the 'missing' forms should be undoubtedly play a role in determining defectiveness in the present indicative and present subjunctive. The principal reason for this is that Spanish verbs with unstressed /o/ in the root fall into two, erratic and wholly unpredictable, classes, according to whether in the singular and third person forms of the present indicative and present subjunctive (where stress falls on the root), the vowel is /o/ or the diphthong /we/. In the third conjugation there is simply insufficient evidence from other verbs to indicate whether the diphthongized or non-diphthongized form is to be expected.

What equally deserve our attention, however, are not only the defective parts of this verb and others like it, but also the *non-defective* parts. What occurs here is unusual, yet has generally gone unremarked. These are parts of the verb about which neither grammarians nor (it seems) ordinary speakers have the slightest hesitation, but the fact is that they are downright *aberrant*, contradicting an otherwise general[7] principle of Spanish morphology. Observe in *abolir* the preterite third person forms, the two varieties of imperfect subjunctive, and the gerund: it is true of all[8] other Spanish verbs in -*ir* that if they contain a back vowel in the root, they will display /u/ in at least these parts of the paradigm, but always there. In most cases, /u/ appears throughout the paradigm (e.g. *cubrir* 'to cover', *conducir* 'to drive', *aludir* 'to allude'), but even *morir* 'to die' and *dormir* 'to sleep', which exceptionally show /o/ in their root, duly display /u/ in the third person preterite, the imperfect subjunctive and the gerund (e.g. preterite *durmió, durmieron*; imperfect subjunctive *durmiese*; gerund *durmiendo*).

The position described for defective -*ir* verbs containing /o/ in the root is broadly matched by those containing /e/ in the root. Such verbs (e.g. *agredir* 'to attack') show unexpected /e/ in the preterite third person, the imperfect subjunctives and the gerund, and are defective in the whole of the present subjunctive and in the singular and third person forms of the present indica-

---

[7] To the extent that there are exceptions to these general principles, these comprise verbs which have the same status as *abolir*—namely that they are relatively late, learnèd, loans from Latin or French. For example *colorir*, *demolir*, *agredir*. There are also some non-defective verbs which 'aberrantly' display /e/ where /i/ would be expected in the preterite and imperfect subjunctives, such as *cernir/concernir/discernir* and *divergir/convergir/sumergir*. But these verbs too are of learnèd origin and relatively recent arrivals in the language.

[8] Except *oír* 'hear', which is additionally exceptional in a number of respects, including displaying a diphthongal root /oj/ in the relevant parts of the paradigm.

tive. With the exception of a few such other verbs in *-ir* which are also learnèd borrowings, such verbs systematically show /i/ at least in the third person preterite, the imperfect subjunctive, and the gerund. For example *sentir* 'to feel': preterite *sintió, sintieron*; imperfect subjunctive *sintiese*; gerund *sintiendo*.

The co-occurrence of defectiveness and aberrant failure of overwhelmingly predictable allomorphy in the same lexemes is surely not accidental, and it points to a major generalization which is true for all Spanish and Portuguese defective verbs: *defective verbs of learnèd origin*[9] *never show any kind of allomorphy*. In fact it is true of all Spanish defective verbs that they never display allomorphy in the root. It is also overwhelmingly the case that verbs lacking expected root allomorphy in the preterite and imperfect subjunctives display defectiveness in the present subjunctive and indicative. The motivation is surely the preservation of the input in its clearly identifiable etymological form. Wherever allomorphy *could* occur, it is avoided — either by the overriding of general principles of paradigmatic structure or, quite simply, by avoiding the potentially troublesome form altogether.

That speakers should adopt such radically different strategies to ensure the same result may seem paradoxical but, at least as far as a verb like *abolir* is concerned, it could be seen as lending weight to Albright's view. Forms such as *abolió* are not a matter of 'uncertainty': speakers actually have to *override* what is otherwise certain. And in so far as the /we/—/o/ alternation is usually one between the singular and third person forms of the present, on the one hand, and the rest of the paradigm, on the other, the form for 'the rest of the paradigm' is already given in the etymological input, *abolir*, whereas the other alternant is not given. In contrast, a form such as **abole* is perfectly possible, but speakers have no indication whether it, or the equally possible **abuele*, is to be used.

Yet there is a crucial aspect to Spanish defectiveness which remains unexplained by anything we have said so far, and it concerns the first and second persons plural present subjunctive. If a Spanish verb is defective, these cells of the paradigm are always among the defective ones. Yet it is otherwise true of all Spanish *-ir* verbs containing a back vowel in the root, and all but one[10]

---

[9] This proviso is occasioned by just one Portuguese verb, *reaver* 'to recuperate, have back', which is not obviously learnèd in origin and is in any case derived by prefixation from the non-learnèd *haver* which, in Old Portuguese, meant 'to have' (see Vázquez and Mendes 1971: 94ff.). It shares with *haver* an idiosyncratic allomorph in the preterite and some other tense forms (cf. 1SG preterite *houve, rehouve*), but it does not share with it the suppletive forms singular and third person present indicative forms *hei, has, há*, and *hão*, or any of the (also suppletive) forms of the present subjunctive (*haja*, etc.). In effect, it allows vocalic allomorphy, but not consonantal allomorphy (the root-final consonant must always be /v/).
[10] The exception is *venir* 'to come', which has present subjunctive *vengamos vengáis* but imperfect subjunctive *viniese*, etc.

verbs with a front vowel, that their root in the first and second person plural present subjunctive is identical to that of the third person preterite, the imperfect subjunctives and the gerund. For example, preterite *durmió, durmieron*; imperfect subjunctive *durmiese*; gerund *durmiendo*; 1PL present subjunctive *durmamos*, 2PL present subjunctive *durmáis*; preterite *sintió, sintieron*; imperfect subjunctive *sintiese*; gerund *sintiendo*; 1PL present subjunctive *sintamos*, 2PL present subjunctive *sintáis*. Now if, as we have seen, the third person preterite (etc.) of *abolir* and *agredir* is *abolió*, etc., and *agredió*, etc., surely the first and second persons plural of the present subjunctive should, unproblematically, be not a gaping hole but *abolamos *aboláis, and *agredamos *agredáis?

The case of the first and second persons plural present subjunctive shows that there are aspects of defectiveness which are not explicable in terms of 'uncertainty'. This observation becomes even more significant when we are confronted with a set of Spanish defective verbs *none* of whose defective parts could be subject to any kind of allomorphy. The missing forms are infallibly predictable, but they do not occur. These are verbs whose root vowel is /a/, such are *garantir* 'guarantee', *blandir* 'brandish', *desmarrirse* 'become abject, listless'. There is nothing in Spanish morphology to suggest that *blandir*, etc., could have any root other than *bland-* throughout its paradigm, yet grammars[11] give the paradigm as defective in exactly the same way as *abolir*.

The role of 'uncertainty' in determining the paradigmatic distribution of defectiveness dwindles yet further if we turn our attention to Portuguese. Virtually all (alleged) defectiveness in Portuguese involves forms which are infallibly predictable, either because the nature of the allomorph is certain, or because no allomorph is possible. All grammarians describing defectiveness concur that 1SG present indicative and the whole of the present subjunctive is involved; they tend to differ as to whether 2SG and 3SG present indicative is also affected. The following verbs in *-ir* are claimed by many grammarians to be defective: *abolir* 'abolish', *agir* 'act', *banir* 'banish', *brandir* 'brandish', *brunir* 'polish', *carpir* 'carp', *coagir* 'coerce', *colorir* 'colour', *combalir* 'weaken', *delir* 'erase', *demolir* 'demolish', *embair* 'impose upon', *emergir* 'emerge', *escapulir* 'slip from', *exaurir* 'drain', *falir* 'go bankrupt', *fremir* 'tremble', 'roar', *fulgir* 'shine', *imergir* 'immerse', *latir* 'bark', *munir* 'provide', *polir* 'polish', *punir* 'punish', *reagir* 'react', *renhir* 'scold', *ungir* 'anoint', also a second conjugation verb *precaver*[12] 'guard against'. For example (2):

---

[11] Some use of third person present indicative *blande*; *blanden* is mentioned by more modern grammars.

[12] This verb is claimed to be defective only in 1SG and present subjunctive. It is, by the way, unusual in being a second conjugation verb, in *-er*. But like most other defective verbs, it is a late (and learnèd) borrowing, from Latin PRAECAUERE.

(2) The Portuguese defective verbs *abolir*, *delir*, and *carpir*

PRS IND	PRS SBJV	IMPRF IND	FUT	PRET	IMPRF SBJV	PLUPRF	FUT SBJV
——	——	abolia	abolirei	aboli	abolisse	abolira	abolir
——	——	abolias	abolirás	aboliste	abolisses	aboliras	abolires
——	——	abolia	abolirá	aboliu	abolisse	abolira	abolir
abolimos	——	abolíamos	aboliremos	abolimos	abolíssemos	abolíramos	abolirmos
abolis	——	abolíeis	abolireis	abolistes	abolísseis	abolíreis	abolirdes
——	——	aboliam	abolirão	aboliram	abolissem	aboliram	abolirem

PRS IND	PRS SBJV	IMPRF IND	FUT	PRET	IMPRF SBJV	PLUPRF	FUT SBJV
——	——	delia	delirei	deli	delisse	delira	delir
——	——	delias	delirás	deliste	delisses	deliras	delires
——	——	delia	delirá	deliu	delisse	delira	delir
delimos	——	delíamos	deliremos	delimos	delíssemos	delíramos	delirmos
delis	——	delíeis	delireis	delistes	delísseis	delíreis	delirdes
——	——	deliam	delirão	deliram	delissem	deliram	delirem

PRS IND	PRS SBJV	IMPRF IND	FUT	PRET	IMPRF SBJV	PLUPRF	FUT SBJV
——	——	carpia	carpirei	carpi	carpisse	carpira	carpir
——	——	carpias	carpirás	carpiste	carpisses	carpiras	carpires
——	——	carpia	carpirá	carpiu	carpisse	carpira	carpir
carpimos	——	carpíamos	carpiremos	carpimos	carpíssemos	carpíramos	carpirmos
carpis	——	carpíeis	carpireis	carpistes	carpísseis	carpíreis	carpirdes
——	——	carpiam	carpirão	carpiram	carpissem	carpiram	carpirem

In contrast to at least some of the Spanish data, the *potential* formation of the missing forms of virtually all Portuguese defective verbs simply poses no problems to Portuguese speakers. Witness the rather wayward pronouncements of the Brazilian grammarian De Sá Nogueira, who repeatedly makes the following type of claim (e.g. De Sá Nogueira 1945: 8): 'This verb [here *abolir*] is generally deemed defective, and claimed to lack the forms of the first, second and third person singular and the third person plural of the present indicative, and all the forms of the present subjunctive. I hold this judgement to be unjustifiable and therefore groundless' [our translation]. De Sá Nogueira says this of nearly all the allegedly defective verbs in Portuguese, indeed he even says it of forms such as the imperative of *poder* 'be able', whose defectiveness is actually indisputable (certainly no other Romance language has an *imperative* of this verb) and is clearly pragmatically motivated. For De Sá Nogueira the missing forms of, for example, the verbs in (2) are *abulo, abula* (etc.), *dilo, dila* (etc.), *carpo, carpa* (etc.). The justification for his confident defiance of his fellow grammarians is, precisely, that the missing forms really are infallibly predictable.

Most defective verbs in Portuguese belong to the third conjugation with infinitives in *-ir*. Verbs of this class whose root does not contain an /a/ almost always show a high vowel /u/ or /i/ *at least* in 1SG present and throughout the present subjunctive (see examples), and often throughout the whole verb. Verbs that contain /a/, such as *abrir* 'to open' show only low-level phonetic alternation according to stress. The sole exceptions are *medir* 'measure' and *pedir* 'ask', which have the root allomorphs *meç-* and *peç-* in these parts of the paradigm.[13] Paradoxically, while there is general assent that certain Portuguese verbs are defective in cells whose forms are infallibly predictable, the domain in which there really is some potential unpredictability is precisely that domain in which not all grammarians (or native speakers) acknowledge defectiveness, namely the 2SG and 3SG present indicative of verbs having (orthographic) *o* and *e* in the root. Orthographic *o* is generally pronounced /u/, and verbs with root /u/ sometimes and unpredictably show /ɔ/ in those parts of the paradigm (e.g. *subir* 'go up', 3SG.PRS.IND *sobe*; *dormir* 'sleep', 3SG.PRS.IND *dorme* but *instruir* 'instruct', 3SG.PRS.IND *instrui*). And some verbs with /e/ in the root (e.g. *agredir* 'to attack') show /i/ in the singular and third person forms of the present indicative.

In sum, to a notable extent in Spanish, and overwhelmingly in Portuguese, defectiveness in any given lexical verb does not seem to be correlated with possible speaker uncertainty about the missing forms. In addition, defectiveness is overwhelmingly correlated with lack of root allomorphy.

4. The 'Shape' of Defectiveness

Defectiveness in both languages has a strikingly familiar 'shape'. If a verb is defective, it will be so in the first person present indicative and throughout the present subjunctive. Some verbs may additionally be defective in the second person singular and third person present indicative, but this latter domain of defectiveness always presupposes the former.

The major domain of defectiveness (present subjunctive and 1SG present indicative) seems, and is, irreducibly arbitrary if one seeks a motivation outside the morphological system itself. Many linguists might consider 'present

---

[13] Since the forms of *medir* and *pedir* clearly have to be learnt as lexical exceptions, one might even want to say that 100 per cent of Portuguese third conjugation verbs that lack root /a/ or consonantal allomorphy have /i/ or /u/ in the root of the 1SG present indicative and the whole of the subjunctive.

subjunctive' as in some sense constituting a 'natural class',[14] but any attempt to discern a distinctive and coherent class of features in 'present subjunctive + 1SG present indicative' is futile. None the less, this combination of cells is a very familiar one, which appears over and over again in the history of the Romance languages. Its remote origin is phonological (arising in not one but two sets of sound change involving different kinds of palatalization, which—coincidentally—had identical paradigmatic effects). It has long lost any trace of phonological motivation (see Maiden 2005 and, especially, Maiden 2001b), and the set of alternants associated with this pattern is phonologically quite heterogeneous (see below). It is the 'morphomic' pattern which Maiden (e.g. 2005) has dubbed the 'L-pattern'. The second domain of defectiveness, in which the 2SG and third person forms of the present indicative are also affected, is in fact recognisable as the *union* of the L-pattern with one of the other major morphomic patterns encountered in nearly all Romance languages, the so-called 'N-pattern',[15] in which the singular and third person cells of the present indicative and present subjunctive, with the 2SG imperative, often share an allomorph, in distinction to all other parts of the paradigm. The N-pattern was originally the product of the fact that Latin stress fell (for purely phonological reasons) on the lexical root in those parts of the paradigm, but usually fell on the endings everywhere else. In early Romance, vowels undergo considerable differentiation according to whether they are unstressed or stressed, producing root allomorphy which is rapidly morphologized/lexicalized. The position of stress itself also becomes morphologized. In general, the L-pattern and the N-pattern constitute both a 'bond', and a 'boundary', in the sense that allomorphs associated with them tend to be identical throughout the relevant domains, and different from what occurs elsewhere in the paradigm. Our purpose in (3) to (6) is merely to illustrate the sheer range of alternations organized in these ways, rather than to analyse their history. Suffice it to say that very few of them are, in fact, the direct historical products of sound change, and most of them involve historical replication and extension of the original patterns (cf. Maiden 2005, 2007):

---

[14] A view not necessarily shared by us. Simply because some combination of features finds recurrent morphological expression in some language or group of languages (nearly all Romance languages have a present subjunctive), and is therefore somehow 'familiar', should not blind us to the actually heterogeneous nature of some tense and mood combinations. This is not, however, an issue we intend to pursue here.

[15] Because, as the paradigm is conventionally set out, the array of cells affected has the shape of a letter 'L' (rotated through 180 degrees). The 'N-pattern' is so-called because as conventionally set out, and appropriately rotated, it vaguely resembles an 'N' in Morse Code.

(3)   Examples of 'L-pattern' allomorphy in Spanish
       hacer 'do'

present indicative	present subjunctive	imperfect indicative	future	preterite	imperfect subjunctive
hago	*haga*	*hacía*	*haré*	*hice*	*hiciese*
haces	*hagas*	*hacías*	*harás*	*hiciste*	*hicieses*
hace	*haga*	*hacía*	*hará*	*hizo*	*hiciese*
hacemos	*hagamos*	*hacíamos*	*haremos*	*hicimos*	*hiciésemos*
hacéis	*hagáis*	*hacíais*	*haréis*	*hicisteis*	*hicieseis*
hacen	*hagan*	*hacían*	*harán*	*hicieron*	*hiciesen*

tener 'have'

present indicative	present subjunctive	imperfect indicative	future	preterite	imperfect subjunctive
tengo	*tenga*	*tenía*	*tendré*	*tuve*	*tuviese*
tienes	*tengas*	*tenías*	*tendrás*	*tuviste*	*tuvieses*
tiene	*tenga*	*tenía*	*tendrá*	*tuvo*	*tuviese*
tenemos	*tengamos*	*teníamos*	*tendremos*	*tuvimos*	*tuviésemos*
tenéis	*tengáis*	*teníais*	*tendréis*	*tuvisteis*	*tuvieseis*
tienen	*tengan*	*tenían*	*tendrán*	*tuvieron*	*tuviesen*

caber 'fit, be room for'

present indicative	present subjunctive	imperfect indicative	future	preterite	imperfect subjunctive
quepo	*quepa*	*cabía*	*cabré*	*cupe*	*cupiese*
cabes	*quepas*	*cabías*	*cabrás*	*cupiste*	*cupieses*
cabe	*quepa*	*cabía*	*cabrá*	*cupo*	*cupiese*
cabemos	*quepamos*	*cabíamos*	*cabremos*	*cupimos*	*cupiésemos*
cabéis	*quepáis*	*cabíais*	*cabréis*	*cupisteis*	*cupieseis*
caben	*quepan*	*cabían*	*cabrán*	*cupieron*	*cupiesen*

(4)   Examples of 'N-pattern' allomorphy in Spanish
       contar 'count'

present indicative	present subjunctive	imperfect indicative	future	preterite	imperfect subjunctive
cuento	*cuente*	*contaba*	*contaré*	*conté*	*contase*
cuentas	*cuentes*	*contabas*	*contarás*	*contaste*	*contases*
imp. *cuenta*					
cuenta	*cuente*	*contaba*	*contará*	*contó*	*contase*
contamos	*contemos*	*contábamos*	*contaremos*	*contamos*	*contásemos*
contáis	*contéis*	*contabais*	*contaréis*	*contasteis*	*contaseis*
cuentan	*cuenten*	*contaban*	*contarán*	*contaron*	*contasen*

perder 'lose'

present indicative	present subjunctive	imperfect indicative	future	preterite	imperfect subjunctive
pierdo	*pierda*	*perdía*	*perderé*	*perdí*	*perdiese*
pierdes	*pierdas*	*perdías*	*perderás*	*perdiste*	*perdieses*
imp. *pierde*					
pierde	*pierda*	*perdía*	*perderá*	*perdió*	*perdiese*
perdemos	*perdamos*	*perdíamos*	*perderemos*	*perdimos*	*perdiésemos*
perdéis	*perdáis*	*perdíais*	*perderéis*	*perdisteis*	*perdieseis*
pierden	*pierdan*	*perdían*	*perderán*	*perdieron*	*perdiesen*

(5) Examples of 'L-pattern' allomorphy in Portuguese

fazer 'do'

present indicative	present subjunctive	imperfect indicative	future	preterite	imperfect subjunctive
faço	*faça*	*fazia*	*farei*	*fiz*	*fizesse*
fazes	*faças*	*fazias*	*farás*	*fizeste*	*fizesses*
faz	*faça*	*fazia*	*fará*	*fez*	*fizesse*
fazemos	*façamos*	*fazíamos*	*faremos*	*fizemos*	*fizéssemos*
fazeis	*façais*	*fazíais*	*fareis*	*fizestes*	*fizésseis*
fazem	*façam*	*faziam*	*farão*	*fizeram*	*fizessem*

ter 'have'

present indicative	present subjunctive	imperfect indicative	future	preterite	imperfect subjunctive
tenho	*tenha*	*tinha*	*terei*	*tive*	*tivesse*
tens	*tenhas*	*tinhas*	*terás*	*tiveste*	*tivesses*
tem	*tenha*	*tinha*	*terá*	*teve*	*tivesse*
temos	*tenhamos*	*tínhamos*	*teremos*	*tivemos*	*tivéssemos*
tendes	*tenhais*	*tinhais*	*tereis*	*tivestes*	*tivésseis*
têem	*tenham*	*tinham*	*terão*	*tiveram*	*tivessem*

poder 'be able'

present indicative	present subjunctive	imperfect indicative	future	preterite	imperfect subjunctive
posso	*possa*	*podia*	*poderei*	*pude*	*pudesse*
podes	*possas*	*podias*	*poderás*	*pudeste*	*pudesses*
pode	*possa*	*podia*	*poderá*	*pôde*	*pudesse*
podemos	*possamos*	*podiamos*	*poderemos*	*pudemos*	*pudéssemos*
podeis	*possais*	*podiais*	*podereis*	*pudestes*	*pudésseis*
podem	*possam*	*podiam*	*poderão*	*puderam*	*pudessem*

Some other Portuguese verbs displaying similarly distributed allomorphy are: *dizer* 'to say' (*dig-*, *diz-*); *perder* 'to lose' (*perc-*, *perd-*); *medir* 'to measure' (*meç-*, *med-*); *ouvir* 'to hear' (*ouç-*, *ouv-*); *caber* 'to fit' (*caib-*, *cab-*). Verbs such as *ferir* 'to wound' and *polir* 'to polish', with infinitives in *-ir* and a mid vowel in the root, systematically show *i* and *u* respectively as the root vowel in L-pattern alternation distribution. Verbs such as *beber* 'to drink' and *mover* 'to move', with infinitives in *-er* and a mid vowel in the root, systematically show /e/ and /o/ respectively as the root vowel in L-pattern cells. alternating with /ɛ/ and /ɔ/ in other stressed cells. Verbs such as *beber* and *mover* also display N-pattern allomorphy (overlapping with the L-pattern) in that while /ɛ/ or /e/ and /ɔ/ or /o/ appear in the N-pattern cells, they alternate respectively with /ə/ and /u/ elsewhere in the paradigm. In first conjugation verbs (those in *-ar*) the alternation is typically just between /ɛ/ or /ɔ/ and /ə/ and /u/ (6):

(6) Examples of 'N-pattern' allomorphy in Portuguese

jogar 'play'

present indicative	present subjunctive	imperfect indicative	future	preterite	imperfect subjunctive
j/ɔ/go	j/ɔ/gue	j/u/gava	j/u/garei	j/u/guei	j/u/gasse
j/ɔ/gas imp. j/ɔ/ga	j/ɔ/gues	j/u/gavas	j/u/garás	j/u/gaste	j/u/gasses
j/ɔ/ga	j/ɔ/gue	j/u/gava	j/u/gará	j/u/gou	j/u/gasse
j/u/gamos	j/u/guemos	j/u/gávamos	j/u/garemos	j/u/gamos	j/u/gássemos
j/u/gais	j/u/gueis	j/u/gávais	j/u/gareis	j/u/gastes	j/u/gásseis
j/ɔ/gam	j/ɔ/guem	j/u/gavam	j/u/garão	j/u/garam	j/u/gassem

To describe (Spanish) L-pattern defectiveness as 'anti-egotistic', as Albright does (2003: 6, 9) really does not do justice to the phenomenon (although the label was surely intended as no more than a convenient shorthand). First, it implicitly neglects the present subjunctive, which appears as a mere 'appendage' to the 1SG present indicative. In reality, there are absolutely no grounds particularly to foreground the 1SG, or to imply[16] that the latter is somehow more basic than the subjunctive. Second, it rather obscures the morphomic nature of the distributional pattern within the paradigm.[17] Albright's terminology regarding N-pattern defectiveness also strikes us as ill-chosen: he describes it as a matter of 'anti-stress' gaps, because the singular and third person forms of the present indicative and present subjunctive

---

[16] Albright's use of the term is actually borrowed from Halle's description (1973) of a Russian paradigm gap, where solely the 1SG is involved.

[17] In the specific case of a Spanish defective verb like *pacer* 'graze', treating the defectiveness as 'anti-egotistic' makes it look as if it has a pragmatic motivation (cf. Albright 2003: 7): 'grazing' is something done by animals—but animals do not talk, as mentioned earlier. No such motivation can apply to the non-first person forms of the present subjunctive, which are equally defective.

are cells where stress falls on the root, rather than on the ending. But stress is itself just one of a series of heterogeneous phonological features sensitive to the distributional pattern. What speakers are apparently avoiding is not 'stress', which could not be more predictable, but the problem of knowing whether to apply an alternation whose domain is the same as that of stress placement.

The 'unification' of the L-pattern and N-pattern is not, by the way, something that only occurs in respect of defectiveness. Sundry Spanish dialects achieve stem-identity throughout the present subjunctive by generalizing the N-pattern stem, complete with stress, through the whole of the present subjunctive (e.g. Cano González 1981:143f.;153f. for the dialect of Somiedo; Espinosa 1946 for New Mexico Spanish). Portuguese has a few verbs (for example *agredir*, which interestingly is reported as defective in Spanish) where an L-pattern vocalic alternant /i/ has been extended into the 2SG and third person forms of the present indicative (7):

(7)   Portuguese *agredir* 'to attack'

present indicative	present subjunctive
agrido	agrida
agrides	agridas
agride	agrida
agredimos	agridamos
agredis	agridais
agridem	agridam

The set of cells 'first person singular present indicative + all forms of the present subjunctive' is, of course, the 'L-pattern' described earlier. It is the domain occupied by various types of allomorphy, both vocalic and consonantal. If we add to this domain the second person singular and third person plural present indicative, we have the union of the L-pattern with the N-pattern (the latter being defined over the singular and third person forms of the present indicative and present subjunctive).

The rather secondary place of N-pattern defectiveness is especially apparent in Portuguese. Portuguese grammarians generally concur that certain verbs have (in our terms) L-pattern defectiveness, but tend to disagree over whether they also have N-pattern defectiveness. Botelho de Amaral (1938) and Perini (2002) say *abolir* is L-pattern defective; De Figueiredo (1961) and Mendes de Almeida (1969) say that it is L+N-pattern defective. Similarly, *carpir* is L-pattern defective according to De Figueiredo (1961), Cunha and Lindley Cintra (1984), but L+N-pattern defective for Mendes de Almeida (1969). For Spanish grammarians, L+N-pattern defectiveness seems generally agreed on, except for those cases which involve clear indeterminacy specifically associated with the root-final consonant of the 1SG present indicative and the present subjunctive, such as *pacer* or *asir*, with regard to the root-final consonant. Even here there can be some revealing inconsistencies. The verb *balbucir* 'to stammer' presents indeterminacy just in the aforementioned cells (should it be *balbuzo or *balbuzco, *balbuza or balbuzca, etc.?), while the 2SG and third person present indicative in principle present no difficulties (*balbuces, balbuce, balbucen*).[18] But while Seco (1986:67f.) accordingly declares this verb to be (in our terminology) L-pattern defective, Seco et al. (1999) say that it is L/N-pattern defective. What appears to have happened (at least in the mind of this grammarian) is that a more general abstract pattern of defectiveness has been projected on to parts of the verb where it is not otherwise motivated.

The prevalence in both languages, and especially in Portuguese, of the L-pattern over the N-pattern is probably linked to the type of alternation associated with them. The L-pattern may well have greater salience than the N-pattern because it involves both vocalic and consonantal alternation, the latter (especially in Portuguese) involving a wide range of quite unpredictable alternants. The N-pattern, in contrast, is a matter only of vocalic alternation, in Spanish principally between monophthongal and diphthongal alternants of mid vowels, while in Portuguese (unlike Spanish) the incidence of alternation for mid vowels is often just a matter of predictable differences of aperture. Whatever the reason for the primacy of the L-pattern, it helps to explain something that would otherwise pose a problem, namely the limitation of defectiveness to non-first conjugation verbs. This restriction may be explicable just as long as what is involved really is a matter of potential speaker 'uncertainty': thus Albright (2006: 17–20) is able persuasively to appeal to the greater predictability of vocalic alternation (or rather, of its absence) in the first conjugation than in third conjugation verbs like *abolir*. But we have been at pains to point out that defectiveness can occur in verbs of the third (and second) conjugation where there is no scope whatever for uncertainty, and in this case we have no explanation of why defectiveness should also fail to appear in the first, where there is, precisely, equally little scope for uncertainty. However, if the domain of defectiveness is linked to the L-pattern, and given that L-pattern allomorphy is only discernible in non-first conjugation verbs, then we have a complete, and entirely 'morphomic', explanation of why defectiveness never occurs in the first conjugation.

---

[18] The distinction between the letters *c* and *z* is, here, purely orthographic: they are phonologically identical.

5. Is Defectiveness 'Real'?

We have still left unanswered a fundamental question posed at the start of this study. What exactly are we describing? The usage (and implicit morphological knowledge) of native speakers, or merely the prescriptions of grammarians? The answer is 'probably rather more the latter than the former' and, perhaps surprisingly, we believe that this enhances, rather than detracts from, the significance of our findings.

Albright (2003) shows that the paradigmatic domain of defectiveness is often 'fuzzier' in actual usage than grammars tend to suggest, with forms such as *abuele* and *abole* really being produced. Moreover, the grammarians and lexicographers we have consulted sometimes disagree as to whether a given verb is defective at all or, if they agree that it is defective, they dissent over what pattern of defectiveness it shows. To take Portuguese, the situation may be briefly exemplified as follows: Cunha and Lindley Cintra (1984) identify thirty-two defective verbs, Vázquez and Mendes (1971) twenty-three, Perini (2002) five, and De Sá Nogueira (1945) just one. Perini and Cunha and Lindley Cintra maintain that *abolir* is defective only in the present subjunctive and first person singular present indicative, whilst Vázquez and Mendes hold that it is defective in the second and third person singular, and the third person plural of the present indicative, as well. In Spanish, *garantir* is generally agreed to be L/N-pattern defective, but some dictionaries and grammars do not even list this verb (*Gran Diccionario, Diccionario Salamanca*, Seco 1986), while Seco et al. (1999) mention it as 'rare', but not as defective. Corominas and Pascual (1980–1991, s.v. 'garante') come very close to acknowledging that the alleged defectiveness of this verb (whose missing parts are supposedly supplied by the regular *garantizar*) is a fiction promulgated by grammarians and purists on both sides of the Atlantic, because in reality the verb is scarcely used in Spain, while in Argentina, where it really is used, it is regular and not defective at all—'despite the efforts of many grammarians'. Given all this, we are bound to ask whether data of this kind on defectiveness deserve any serious attention at all.

Normative grammarians and lexicographers of course tend to idealize and 'tidy up' linguistic reality. That there is something artificial in their prescriptions regarding defectiveness is evident from the very fact that they disagree with each other. But for the most part they are also *native speakers*. In fact, it is not too far-fetched to claim that they are native speakers who are involuntarily subjecting themselves to a kind of psycholinguistic experiment. Their task is to impose order on a reality which may be fluid and elusive, but in which it is at least generally agreed that certain verbs are somehow defective. It is most striking that in setting the intraparadigmatic boundaries of defectiveness they almost never 'take the easy way out', by seeking to anchor the missing, or the occurring, forms in any one morphosyntactic property, or in any coherent bundle of such properties, such as 'present indicative', or 'present subjunctive'. Rather, they invariably make defectiveness conform to one of the recurrent morphomic patterns of stem allomorphy in the verb system in their native tongue, despite the apparent messiness of aligning defectiveness with an essentially *incoherent* array of paradigmatic cells, rather than with some feature of bundle of features that 'make sense'.[19] In their very artificiality, the prescriptions of grammarians may be extremely revealing of native speaker knowledge of patterns of paradigmatic organization.

What the grammarians say is not, of course, *completely* artificial and divorced from ordinary speakers' usage.[20] We are not aware of any evidence for grammarians' claims for the distribution of defectiveness in any given verb being totally orthogonal to the 'defective' behaviour of speakers, so that speakers would make paradigms gaps in one set of cells, and grammarians in another, completely different set.[21] In fact there is a substantial measure of common ground between grammar books and ordinary usage. Thus, in the Spanish and Portuguese cases, if ordinary speakers and grammarians agree that there is defectiveness in some verb, then on all the available evidence they at least agree that defectiveness does not occur outside the present indicative and present subjunctive, or in the 1PL and 2PL present indicative.[22]

6. Conclusions

Our observations on Spanish and Portuguese defectiveness place us in a distinctive, but not necessarily contradictory, position with regard to other

---

[19] Indeed, grammarians might be expected to align defectiveness with some category which has a conventional, established, grammatical 'name'. Entities such as the L-pattern have no name (whence the need for the invention of fanciful labels such as 'L-pattern') and are never discussed in traditional grammars.

[20] The fact that our examples of defectiveness are, in some degree, the invention of grammarians and quite possibly perpetuated through grammar books, to some extent absolves us from having to answer the question raised by Daland et al. (2007), and Sims (2008), about how speakers learn lexicalized gaps that are not motivated synchronically by morphological competition. To the extent that our defectiveness is real for ordinary speakers, and not learnt out of a book, it may well be that the mechanism proposed by those scholars for learning of gaps via implicit negative evidence, through Bayesian estimation over the paradigm, is also at work. But the pattern of defectiveness is surely also supported by speakers' knowledge of morphomic patterning.

[21] There may, of course, be discrepancies regarding which verbs are defective and which not, but that is a matter of lexical, rather than paradigmatic, distribution of defectiveness.

[22] Indeed, a statistical study currently in progress, by O'Neill, of Portuguese defective verbs, using the *CETEMPúblico* corpus (180 million words), is suggesting that a majority of the fifty-five verbs alleged in grammars to be defective actually show at least a significantly low frequency in the L-pattern (and N-pattern) parts of the paradigm.

recent descriptions of defective phenomena. Like Albright, we find that the locus of defectiveness is unfamiliar, infrequent vocabulary. But our findings are complementary to his, and rather closer to those of Sims (2008), in that we discern defectiveness in verbs where considerations of low 'speaker confidence' play no role. Sims' examples from Greek genitive plurals, in contrast to ours, involve familiar everyday vocabulary, and demonstrate that defectiveness can be 'lexicalized' independently of the synchronic factors of morphological competition which gave rise to it, but they still suggest that morphological competition is necessary for defectiveness to arise in the first place. Our findings suggest that no such competition is required for defectiveness to emerge or, rather, that no such competition is required for defectiveness to appear in any given lexeme.

Our interpretation of the Spanish and Portuguese data is that the primary motivation for defectiveness in them is likely to be preservation of the unique stem present in the etymological input of what are overwhelmingly loan words, for the most part restricted to learnèd vocabulary, to educated speakers and to elevated registers. Speakers and/or grammarians are effectively protecting such relatively 'foreign' forms from idiosyncratic patterns of stem allomorphy indigenous to, and characteristic of, the host languages. What we observe is actually closer to Albright's interpretation of defectiveness than might at first appear. Albright is discussing specific lexemes for which speakers have reasonable grounds to 'lack confidence'. The behaviour we are describing suggests not so much 'lack of confidence' as 'paranoia': the avoidance of allomorphy even where there are no 'reasonable grounds' to expect allomorphy to occur. What prompts such behaviour at least in part, and what such behaviour presupposes, is speakers' sensitivity, at a level more abstract than any specific alternation in any particular lexeme, to a major distributional pattern of root allomorphy in Spanish and Portuguese, one which in particular marks out the first person singular present indicative together with all persons and numbers of the present subjunctive, in non-first conjugation verbs, as potentially possessing a shared, distinct, root allomorph. At the base of this is a type of abductive reasoning such that the existence of allomorphy within the relevant set of paradigmatic cells for *some* non-first conjugation verbs is reanalysed as a virtual property of all such verbs. With indigenous, familiar, vocabulary, the diachronic result of this kind of analysis has quite often been the creation of novel allomorphy where there was none before (see Maiden 1992, 2001b, 2007). We have shown in this study that exactly the same type of knowledge underpins the deployment of defectiveness as a strategy for ensuring stem-invariance in a certain portion of the Ibero-Romance lexicon.[23]

---

[23] A recently published and important article bearing on some of the issues considered in this study, and particularly the stems of modern Spanish *agredir*, is Pons and Araceli (2007).

References

Alameda, J. R. and F. Cuetos. 1991. *Diccionario de frecuencias de las unidades lingüísticas del castellano.* Oviedo: Universidad de Oviedo.

Albright, Adam. 2003. A quantitative study of Spanish paradigm gaps. *West Coast Conference on Formal Linguistics 22 Proceedings*, ed. by G. Garding and M. Tsujimura, 1–14, Somerville: Cascadilla.

—— 2006. Lexical and morphological conditioning of paradigm gaps [draft ms].

Arnal Purroy, M. 1998. *El habla de la Baja Ribagorzana occidental.* Zaragoza: CSIC.

Aronoff, Mark. 1994. *Morphology By Itself.* Cambridge, Mass./London: MIT Press.

Bello, Andrés and R. Cuervo. 1954. *Gramática de la lengua castellana.* Buenos Aires: Sopena.

Botelho de Amaral, Vasco. 1938. *Dicionário de dificuldades da língua portuguesa.* Porto: Educação Nacional.

Boyé, Gilles. 2000. *Problèmes de morpho-phonologie verbale en français, espagnol et italien.* Doctoral thesis: Université de Paris 7.

Boyé, Gilles and Patricia Cabredo Hofherr. This volume. Defectiveness as stem suppletion in French and Spanish verbs, 35–52.

Cano González, Ana M. 1981. *El habla de Somiedo (Occidente de Asturias).* Santiago: Universidad de Santiago.

Corominas, Juan and J. Pascual. 1980–1991. *Diccionario crítico etimológico castellano e hispánico.* Madrid: Gredos.

Cunha, Celso and Lindley Cintra, Luís. 1984. *Nova gramática do português contemporâneo.* Lisbon: da Costa.

Daland, Robert, Andrea Sims, and Janet Pierrehumbert. 2007. Much ado about nothing: a social network model of Russian paradigmatic gaps. *Proceedings of the 45th Annual Meeting of the Association for Computational Linguistics*, ed. by A. Zaenen and A. van den Bosch, 936–43. Prague: Association for Computational Linguistics.

De Figueiredo, Cândido. 1961. *Gramática sintética da língua portuguesa.* Lisbon: Livraria Clássica.

De Sá Nogueira, R. 1945. *Dicionário de verbos portugueses conjugados.* Lisbon: Livraria clássica.

Diccionario de la lengua española. 2001. Madrid: Real Academia Española.

Diccionario Salamanca de la lengua española. 1996. Madrid: Santillana.

Diccionario Sopena de dudas y dificultades del idioma. 1981. Barcelona: Sopena.

Dworkin, Stephen. 1985 From *-ir* to *-ecer* in Spanish: the loss of OSp. de-adjectival *-ir* verbs. *Hispanic Review* 13. 295–305.

Elvira, Javier. 1993. Verbos defectivos en español. *Actas do XXIX Congreso de Lingüística e Filoloxía Románicas* 5. 573–80. La Coruña: Fundación Pedro Barrié de la Maza, Conde Fenosa.

—— 1998. *El cambio analógico.* Madrid: Gredos.

Espinosa, A. 1946. *Estudios sobre el español de Nuevo Méjico II. Morfología. Notas de morfología dialectal.* Buenos Aires: Universidad de Buenos Aires.

Gran diccionario de uso del español actual. 2001. Madrid: Sociedad General Española.

Halle, Morris. 1973. Prolegomena to a theory of word formation. *Linguistic Inquiry* 4. 3–16.

Harris-Northall, Ray. 1999. Morphological shift in Old Spanish: the paradigmatic relationship between *-ecer* and *-ir* verbs. *Essays in Hispanic Linguistics Dedicated to Paul M. Lloyd*, ed. by R. Blake, D. Ranson, R. Wright, 111–23. Newark: Juan de la Cuesta.

Juilland, Alphonse and E. Chang-Rodriguez. 1964. *Frequency dictionary of Spanish words*. London/The Hague/Paris: Mouton.

Machado, J. P. 1967. *Dicionário etimológico da língua portuguesa* (2nd ed.). Lisbon: Confluência.

Maiden, Martin. 1992. Irregularity as a determinant of morphological change. *Journal of Linguistics* 28. 285–312.

—— 2000. Di un cambiamento intramorfologico: origini del tipo *dissi dicesti*, ecc., nell'italoromanzo. *Archivio glottologico italiano* 85. 3–37.

—— 2001a. A strange affinity: perfecto y tiempos afines. *Bulletin of Hispanic Studies* 58. 441–64.

—— 2001b. Di nuovo sulle alternanze velari nel verbo italiano e spagnolo. *Cuadernos de filología italiana* 8. 39–61.

—— 2004a. When lexemes become allomorphs: on the genesis of suppletion. *Folia Linguistica* 38. 227–56.

—— 2004b. Verb augments and meaninglessness in Romance morphology. *Studi di grammatica italiana* 22. 1–61.

—— 2005. Morphological autonomy and diachrony. *Yearbook of Morphology 2004*, 137–75.

—— 2006. Accommodating synonymy. How some Italo-Romance verbs react to lexical and morphological borrowings. *Rethinking languages in contact: the case of Italian*, ed. by A.Tosi and A-L. Lepschy, 87–98. Oxford: Legenda.

—— 2007. La linguistica romanza alla ricerca dell'arbitrario. *Actes du XXIVe Congrès International de Linguistique et de Philologie Romanes II*, ed. by D. Trotter, 506–18. Tübingen: Niemeyer.

—— Forthcoming. Morphophonological innovation. *The Cambridge history of the Romance languages*, ed. by Adam Ledgeway, Martin Maiden, and John Charles Smith. Cambridge: Cambridge University Press.

Mendes de Almeida, Napoleão. 1969. *Gramática metódica da língua portuguesa*. São Paulo: Saraiva.

Menéndez Pidal, Ramón. 1958. *Manual de gramática histórica española*. Madrid: Espasa-Calpe.

Penny, Ralph. 1972. Verb class as a determiner of stem vowel in the historical morphology of Spanish verbs. *Revue de linguistique romane* 36. 343–59.

—— 2002. *A history of the Spanish language,* 2nd ed. Cambridge: Cambridge University Press.

Perini, Maria A. 2002. *Modern Portuguese. A reference grammar*. New Haven/London: Yale University Press.

Pirrelli, Vito. 2000. *Paradigmi in morfologia. Un approccio interdisciplinare alla flessione verbale dell'italiano*. Pisa-Roma: Istituti editoriali e poligrafici internazionali.

Pons, Rodríguez L. and Serena Araceli López, 2007. Un episodo de la morfología história del español: la pérdida de la defectividad verbal en cos medios, las gramáticas y el uso. *Boletín de la Real Academia Española* 87. 59–95.

Seco, Manuel. 1986. *Dicionario de dudas y dificultades de la lengua española.* Madrid: Espasa-Calpe.
Seco, Manuel, O. and Andrés, G. Ramos. 1999. *Diccionario del español actual.* Madrid: Santillana.
Sims, Andrea. 2008. Why defective paradigms are, and aren't, the result of competing morphological patterns. *Proceedings of the 43rd Annual Meeting of the Chicago Linguistic Society.*
Vázquez Cuesta, Pilar and M. A. Mendes da Luz. 1971. *Gramática portuguesa. II Morfología.* Madrid: Gredos.

8

The Search for Regularity in Irregularity: Defectiveness and its Implications for our Knowledge of Words

MARIANNE MITHUN

A LONGSTANDING ISSUE IN MORPHOLOGICAL THEORY has been the status of inflected forms in memory. Irregular forms are generally assumed to be learned, stored, and retrieved for use. In some models of morphology, such as that of Pinker and associates (Pinker and Prince 1988; Prasada et al. 1990; Kim et al. 1991), all regular forms are assumed to be assembled online by rule from stored stems. Formation by rule accounts both for the regularity itself and for productivity, the capacity of speakers to create inflected forms they have never before encountered. In other models, such as those of Butterworth 1983, Bybee 1985, 1988, 1995, 2001, Stemberger and MacWhinney 1988, and Hare, Ford, and Marslen-Wilson 2001, generalizations are similarly seen as a basis for productivity, but they do not preclude storage of the forms produced. Views vary on the nature of the storage of regular forms. For some, all inflected forms are stored. For others, storage is not homogeneous; frequently-occurring forms are more likely to be stored and retrieved for use, while rarer forms are more likely to be assembled by rule or by analogy to stored forms.

Patterns of defectiveness have the potential to shed some light on the issue of storage. If regular inflected forms are not stored, there should be no gaps in inflectional paradigms: speakers should never feel that a particular possible, meaningful form simply does not exist.

The investigation of inflectional gaps presents both methodological and analytic challenges. On the methodological side, defectiveness can be more difficult to discover than regularity, particularly in languages without long lexicographic traditions or language academies. We seldom witness defectiveness in speech: the forms we hear are by definition existing forms. Defectiveness more often comes to light during the elicitation of paradigms. But paradigm recitation is not a natural use of language, and, particularly in languages with extensive inflection, results can be unclear, as speakers hesitate, stumble, and find themselves racked with uncertainty. Individual speakers vary in their responses at crucial points in paradigms. On the analytic side, a goal of most research is the discovery of generalizations. In its initial stages, the search for defectiveness seems to be the antithesis of normal work: a quest for the failure of generalizations. As outlined by Baerman and Corbett (this volume, also Baerman 2009) generalizations must be sought at a different level: in the types of gaps that occur and the reasons behind them. Such generalizations can in turn further our understanding of what speakers know about their languages.

Languages with particularly rich inflectional systems are sometimes cited as the strongest evidence for inflection by rule. Speakers could not possibly memorize the hundreds of thousands of possible forms. Such languages might even be expected to display less defectiveness than those with limited inflection. At the same time, the existence of larger and more numerous paradigms in a language should provide the potential for more gaps. In what follows, defectiveness will be investigated in two unrelated polysynthetic languages with extensive but regular inflectional paradigms: Central Alaskan Yup'ik, an Eskimo-Aleut language of southwestern Alaska, and Mohawk, an Iroquoian language of northeastern North America. Patterns of defectiveness in each provide evidence that at least some regular inflected forms are stored, and that, along the lines proposed by Bybee and others, the robustness of stored forms is affected by their frequency of occurrence.

1. Central Alaskan Yup'ik Noun Inflection

Nouns in Central Alaskan Yup'ik, as in all Eskimoan languages, are inflected by fused endings indicating number, case, and, where pertinent, possessor. There are no gender distinctions.

(1) Central Alaskan Yup'ik noun
     angya**gemtenek**
     angya-gemtenek
     boat-1PL/3DU.ABL
     '**from our two** boats'

Possession is indicated by transitive suffixes which mark a combination of possessor and possessed. Four persons are distinguished for possessors: first (1), second (2), third (3), and coreferential third (3R). (Coreferential forms are used when the possessor is coreferential with the subject of that clause or a higher clause, as in 'She took out **her own** boat'.) Possessions are always third person. Three numbers are distinguished for both possessors and possessions: singular, dual, and plural. There are seven cases: absolutive, ergative, locative, ablative, allative, vialis ('through'), and aequalis ('as, like'). Absolutive forms carry no overt case marking. The inflectional suffix complexes show extensive but regular phonologically-based allomorphy, reducible to thirteen basic patterns. The inflectional paradigm for the noun *nuna* 'land, village, country' is in Table 1.

Table 1. Central Alaskan Yup'ik noun inflection *nuna* 'land, village, country'

	POSSESSED→	SG	DU	PL
ABSOLUTIVE	POSSESSOR↓	*nuna*	*nunak*	*nunat*
	1SG	*nunaka*	*nunagka*	*nunanka*
	2SG	*nunan*	*nunagken*	*nunaten*
	3SG	*nunii*	*nunak*	*nunai*
	3RSG	*nunani*	*nunagni*	*nunani*
	1DU	*nunavuk*	*nunagpuk*	*nunapuk*
	2DU	*nunasek*	*nunagtek*	*nunatek*
	3DU	*nunangak*	*nunagkek*	*nunakek*
	3RDU	*nunasek*	*nunagtek*	*nunatek*
	1PL	*nunavut*	*nunagput*	*nunaput*
	2PL	*nunasi*	*nunagci*	*nunaci*
	3PL	*nunangat*	*nunagket*	*nunait*
	3RPL	*nunaseng*	*nunagteng*	*nunateng*
ERGATIVE		*nunam*	*nunak*	*nunat*
	1SG	*nunama*	*nunagma*	*nunama*
	2SG	*nunavet*	*nunagpet*	*nunavet*
	3SG	*nunaan*	*nunagken*	*nunain*
	3RSG	*nunami*	*nunagmi*	*nunami*
	1DU	*nunamegnuk*	*nunagmegnuk*	*nunamegnuk*
	2DU	*nunavtek*	*nunagpetek*	*nunavtek*
	3DU	*nunaagnek*	*nunagkenka*	*nunakenka*
	3RDU	*nunamek*	*nunagmek*	*nunamek*
	1PL	*nunamta*	*nunagemta*	*nunamta*
	2PL	*nunavci*	*nunagpeci*	*nunavci*
	3PL	*nunaata*	*nunagketa*	*nunaita*
	3RPL	*nunameng*	*nunagmeng*	*nunameng*
LOCATIVE		*nunami*	*nunagni*	*nunani*
	1SG	*nunamni*	*nunagemni*	*nunamni*
	2SG	*nunavni*	*nunagemni*	*nunavni*
	3SG	*nunaani*	*nunagkeni*	*nunaini*
	3RSG	*nunamni*	*nunagmini*	*nunamni*
	1DU	*nunamegni*	*nunagemegni*	*nunamegni*
	2DU	*nunavtegni*	*nunagpetegni*	*nunavtegni*
	3DU	*nunaagni*	*nunagkegni*	*nunakegni*
	3RDU	*nunamegni*	*nunagmegni*	*nunamegni*
	1PL	*nunamteni*	*nunagemteni*	*nunamteni*
	2PL	*nunavceni*	*nunagpeceni*	*nunavceni*
	3PL	*nunaatni*	*nunagketni*	*nunaitni*
	3RPL	*nunameggni*	*nunagmeggni*	*nunameggni*

Table 1. *Cont.*

	POSSESSED→	SG	DU	PL
ABLATIVE		*nunamnek*	*nunagnek*	*nunanek*
	1SG	*nunamnek*	*nunagemnek*	*nunamnek*
	2SG	*nunavnek*	*nunagemnek*	*nunavcenek*
	3SG	*nunaanek*	*nunagkenek*	*nunainek*
	3RSG	*nunamnek*	*nunagminek*	*nunamnek*
	1DU	*nunamegnek*	*nunagmegnek*	*nunamegnek*
	2DU	*nunavtegnek*	*nunagpetegnek*	*nunavtegnek*
	3DU	*nunaagnek*	*nunagkegnek*	*nunakegnek*
	3RDU	*nunamegnek*	*nunagmegnek*	*nunamegnek*
	1PL	*nunametenek*	*nunagmtenek*	*nunamtenek*
	2PL	*nunavcenek*	*nunagpecenek*	*nunavcenek*
	3PL	*nunaatnek*	*nunagketnek*	*nunaitnek*
	3RPL	*nunameggnek*	*nunagmeggnek*	*nunameggnek*
TERMINALIS		*nunamun*	*nunagnun*	*nunanun*
	1SG	*nunamnun*	*nunagemnun*	*nunamnun*
	2SG	*nunavnun*	*nunagemnun*	*nunavcenun*
	3SG	*nunaanun*	*nunagkenun*	*nunainun*
	3RSG	*nunamnun*	*nunagminun*	*nunamnun*
	1DU	*nunamegnun*	*nunagmegnun*	*nunamegnun*
	2DU	*nunavtegnun*	*nunagpetegnun*	*nunavtegnun*
	3DU	*nunaagnun*	*nunagkegnun*	*nunakegnun*
	3RDU	*nunamegnun*	*nunagmegnun*	*nunamegnun*
	1PL	*nunametenun*	*nunagmtenun*	*nunamtenun*
	2PL	*nunavcenun*	*nunagpecenun*	*nunavcenin*
	3PL	*nunaatnun*	*nunagketnun*	*nunaitnun*
	3RPL	*nunameggnun*	*nunagmeggnun*	*nunameggnun*
VIALIS		*nunakun*	*nunagnegun*	*nunatgun*
	1SG	*nunamkun*	*nunagemkun*	*nunamkun*
	2SG	*nunavkun*	*nunagpegun*	*nunavkun*
	3SG	*nunaakun*	*nunagkenkun*	*nunainek*
	3RSG	*nunamikun*	*nunagmikun*	*nunamikun*
	1DU	*nunamegnegun*	*nunagmegnegun*	*nunamegnegun*
	2DU	*nunavtegnegun*	*nunagpetegnegun*	*nunavtegnegun*
	3DU	*nunaagnegun*	*nunagkegnegun*	*nunakegnegun*
	3RDU	*nunamegnegun*	*nunagmegnegun*	*nunamegnegun*
	1PL	*nunamteggun*	*nunagemteggun*	*nunamteggun*
	2PL	*nunavcetgun*	*nunagpecetgun*	*nunavcetgun*
	3PL	*nunaatgun*	*nunagketgun*	*nunaitgun*
	3RPL	*nunamegteggun*	*nunamegteggun*	*nunagmegteggun*
AEQUALIS		*nunatun*	*nunagtun*	*nunacetun*
	1SG	*nunamtun*	*nunagemtun*	*nunamtun*
	2SG	*nunavtun*	*nunagpetun*	*nunavtun*
	3SG	*nunaatun*	*nunagketun*	*nunaitun*
	3RSG	*nunamitun*	*nunagmitun*	*nunamitun*
	1DU	*nunamegtun*	*nunagmegtun*	*nunamegtun*
	2DU	*nunavtegtun*	*nunagpetegtun*	*nunavtegtun*
	3DU	*nunaagtun*	*nunagkegtun*	*nunakegtun*

Table 1. *Cont.*

POSSESSED→	SG	DU	PL
3RDU	nunamegtun	nunagmegtun	nunamegtun
1PL	nunamcetun	nunagkecetun	nunamcetun
2PL	nunavcetun	nunagpecetun	nunavcetun
3PL	nunaacetun	nunagkecetun	nunaicetun
3RPL	nunamegtun	nunagmegtun	nunamegtun

Providing paradigms can be a gruelling experience for speakers, even (or especially) for those with the best control of the language. (A majority of Yup'ik speakers are now bilingual in English, but the language is still spoken skilfully by thousands.) Because the recitation of paradigms is an inherently unnatural task, it may not provide a completely accurate reflection of the processes involved in the production of spontaneous speech. On occasion, however, the exercise can be revealing.

1.1. Yup'ik possessive inflection

One excellent Yup'ik speaker was asked to provide inflected forms of the noun *kaliqaq* 'paper'. The forms were requested one by one. This speaker had no trouble with the unpossessed absolutive forms, easily coming up with singular, dual, and plural.

(2)   Yup'ik absolutive *kaliqaq* 'paper'

kalikaq	'paper'	OK
kalikak	'two sheets of paper'	OK
kalikat	'three or more sheets of paper'	OK

The possessed forms for singular and plural papers also provided no difficulties. Asked for 'my two papers', however, he was stumped. He finally offered a form for plural papers plus the numeral two.

(3)   Yup'ik first person singular possessors

kalikaqa	'my paper'	OK
———	**'my two papers'**	?
kalikanka	'my (PL) papers'	OK

Speaker: 'My two. That's hard. It just jumps to plural. There is no dual.'

kalika**nka**   malruk
kalika-**nka**   malruk
paper-**1SG/PL**   two
'my two papers'

Forms with second person possessors came easily, for one, two, and more papers.

(4) Yup'ik second person singular possessors

kalikan	'your (SG) paper'	OK
kalikagken	'your (SG) two papers'	OK
kalikaten	'your (SG) papers (PL)'	OK

For third person singular possessors, however, again this speaker could not come up with a form for two papers.

(5) Yup'ik third person singular possessors

kalikaa	'his/her paper'	OK
————	**'his/her two papers'**	?
kalikai	'his/her papers (PL)'	OK

Speaker: 'I can't think of the dual if there is one. I'm sure there must be. It'll come to me later.'

For dual possessors, there were no problems, even with two papers.

(6) Yup'ik dual possessors

kalikapuk	'we two, our paper'	OK
kalikagput	'we two, our two papers'	OK
kalikaput	'we two, our papers (PL)'	OK
kalikakagtek	'you two, your paper'	OK
kalikagtek	'you two, your two papers'	OK
kalikatek	'you two, your bunch of papers'	OK
ingkuk kalikak	'those two, their paper'	OK
ingkuk kalikagket	'those two, their two papers'	OK
ingkuk kalikagket	'those two, their papers (PL)'	OK

With plural possessors, there were again hesitations and gaps for two papers.

(7) Yup'ik plural possessors

kalipaput	'we all, our paper'	OK
kalikagput	**'we all, our two papers'** 'Maybe this is wrong.'	OK
kalikaput	'we all, our papers (PL)'	OK
kalikaci	'you all, your paper'	OK
————	**'you all, your two papers'**	?
kalikaci	'you all, your papers (PL)'	OK
kalikat	'their paper'	OK
————	**'their two papers'**	?
kalikait	'their (PL) papers (PL)'	OK

Speaker: 'Can't remember the one for "their two papers", if there is a term.'

This speaker later suggested the plural *kalikait* 'their (PL) papers (PL)' for 'their two papers'. Interestingly, he had no trouble remembering possessed forms of other dual nouns, such as 'wife'.

(8) Yup'ik dual possession: 'wife'
    nuliagka   'my two wives'
    nuliagken   'your two wives'
    nuliarak   'his two wives'

It is significant that during elicitation tasks like this, speakers often comment on specific uses of particular forms and even the occasions on which they were heard. The possessed plural above brought forth such a comment.

(9) Yup'ik plural possession
    nulianka   'my wives (PL)'
    Speaker: 'My grandfather said this because he had three different wives, at three different times.'

As noted, the elicitation task is an inherently unnatural one, not something that most Yup'ik speakers normally do in the course of their daily lives. The results do, however, indicate that inflection is not simply the result of routinely applying regular rules to create regular forms. At the same time, there is evidence that not all inflected forms are memorized. Speakers produce some regular forms instantaneously, such as *kalikat* 'three or more papers', retrieving whole forms rather than assembling them. They apparently produce other forms by analogy or rule, then check them against their mental lexicon. Sometimes the products are confirmed, but sometimes they are rejected, like *kalikagput* 'we all, our two papers'. Finally, they find it impossible to create some forms, recognize that they have no memory of them, and substitute different ones, such as *kalikanka* 'my papers (PLURAL)' in place of 'my two papers'. Such substitution is of course a source of syncretism.

This Yup'ik elicitation task and others indicate that there is lexically-specific memory of inflected forms, even regular ones. The terms for 'my two papers' and 'my two wives' follow exactly the same regular inflectional pattern, but while this speaker was at a loss for the first, he immediately produced the second.

1.2. Yup'ik number inflection

As noted earlier, Yup'ik nouns are inflected for singular, dual, and plural number. The paradigms are somewhat complex but regular. There are several phonologically-conditioned patterns, as can be seen in Table 2. The majority of nouns end in -*q* in the absolutive singular, but singular nouns can also end in a vowel, *n*, or *k*.

Number inflection is robust: many mass nouns can be recategorized as count, with a unit or container meaning. Such recategorization is noticeably more prevalent in Yup'ik than in English.

Table 2. Yup'ik number inflection

SINGULAR	DUAL	PLURAL	
qayaq	qayqk	qayat	'kayak'
angyaq	angyak	angyat	'boat'
uluaq	uluak	uluat	'semi-lunar knife'
arnaq	arnak	arnat	'woman'
kass'aq	kass'ak	kass'at	'white person'
kaviaq	kaviak	kaviat	'fox'
qaltaq	qaltak	qaltat	'bucket'
irniaq	irniak	irniat	'baby, offspring'
amiq	amiik	amiit	'skin, pelt'
mikelnguq	mikelnguuk	mikelnguut	'child'
tan'gurraq	tan'gurraak	tan'gurraat	'boy'
nuna	nunak	nunat	'land, village'
qalu	qaluk	qalut	'dipnet'
agun	angutek	angutet	'open canoe'
cavun	cavutek	cavutet	'oar'
minek	minek	minet	'wake of fish or boat'

(10) Yup'ik count nouns

    uquq   'seal oil, now also fuel oil, lubricating oil, gasoline'
    uquk   'two seal pokes of oil, etc.'
    uqut   'three or more seal pokes of oil, etc.'

    meq   'fresh water'
    mer'ek   'two buckets/bottles of water'
    mer'et   'three or more buckets/bottles of water'

Pronominal suffixes on verbs agree in number with coreferential nouns. In (11) the dual number of the rabbits is indicated by both the dual number suffix -k on the noun and the dual pronominal suffix -k on the verb.

(11) Yup'ik pronominal number on verbs: Elizabeth Ali, speaker p.c.

    Amiira**k**   maqarua**k**
    amiir-a-**k**   maqarua-**k**
    skin-TR.IND-**3SG/3DU** snowshoe.hare-**DU**
    'She's skinning the (two) rabbits.'

As in many other languages, some nouns are defective in their number marking. There are nouns with apparently singular meaning but dual inflection, visible in the suffix -k. Their grammatical status is echoed in the possessive suffixes, as in (12)a, and on pronominal suffixes on associated verbs, as in (12)b and (12)c.

(12) Yup'ik dualia tantum

    a. aqsa**gka**
       aqsa-**gka**
       belly-**1SG/DU**
       'my abdomen, my belly'

    b. Qerrulliik   ang'uk
       qerrullii-**k**   ange-u-**k**
       trouser=DU   bc.big-INTR.IND-**3DU**
       'The pants are big.'   (one pair)

    c. ackii**gka**   tukniuk
       ackii-**gka**   tukni-u-**k**
       glasses-**1SG/DU** be.strong-INTR.IND-**3DU**
       'My glasses are strong'   (from Russian *očki*)

Often such terms show variation from speaker to speaker and dialect to dialect. The noun for 'abdomen, belly' is grammatically singular for some speakers, with the form *aqsaq*. Other inherently dual nouns are unsurprising, such as various terms for trousers (*atasuak* 'summer pants', *nalkiik* 'panties', *pelumessaak* from English *bloomers*) and tools with paired parts (*keggsuutek* 'pliers', *mangautek* 'scissors', *nunuutek* 'scissors', *pupsuuk* 'scissors').

There are also nouns with only plural forms. Some of these are plural for some speakers but singular for others.

(13) Yup'ik pluralia tantum

    a. atkuu**nka**   (with grammatically singular alternant *atkuq*)
       atkuk-**unka**
       parka-**1SG/PL**
       'my parka'

    b. ingler**enka**   (with grammatically singular alternant *ingleq*)
       ingler-**nka**   cf. *ingun* 'crosspiece on which one sits in
       bed-**1SG/PL**   a boat, slat of bed'
       'my bed'

    c. niicugnissuut**et**
       niite-yug-neq-i-cuun-**et**
       hear-DESID-result-make-device-**PL**
       'radio'

The term for 'radio' was apparently coined for the first instruments encountered by the Yup'ik, which consisted of numerous visible parts. (The derived stem *niite-yug-* hear-DESIDERATIVE means 'listen'.) Additional *pluralia tantum* are nouns identifiable from their plural suffix -*t*. One is *akret* 'ladder, stairs' (from *akeq* 'barb, stair, rung'). Jacobson (1984: 50) notes that notches on ladders made from a log resemble barbs of hooks or spears. Some others listed by Jacobson are *akut* 'trim at bottom of parka' (from *akuq* 'lower part of garment'), *ingqit* 'fancy, contrasting collared skin patchwork trim at hem of garment' (from *angqi-* 'to dice, cut up'), *evvaat* 'harmonica', dual or plural, and *it'gagka* or *it'ganka* 'my feet'. These plural nouns are represented by plural pronominal suffixes in verbs.

(14) Yup'ik concord

> Niicugnissuut**et** kumares**ki**!
> niite-yug-neq-i-cuun-**et** kumarte-**ki**
> hear-DESID-result-make-device-PL ignite-OPT.2SG/3PL
> 'Turn on the radio!'

The variability among speakers in their assignment of grammatical number to lexical items such as *aqsak* (DU)/*aqsaq* (SG) 'belly' and *atkut* (PL)/*atkuq* (SG) 'parka' suggests that both memory and computation must be involved in the production of inflected forms.

It is also significant that speakers do not necessarily share the same paradigmatic gaps. One excellent, fluent speaker was asked for the word for 'eye'. After much hesitation, he tentatively offered an uncertain guess, with apologies: *iik*. He asked other family members, and they responded with similar uncertainty. The dictionary form listed in Jacobson 1984: 159 is *ii*, without the final -*k*. The difficulties presented by this noun are not surprising. The unpossessed forms of body-part nouns are relatively rare as independent words. The same speaker easily produced the possessed forms *iika* 'my eye' and *iigka* 'my two eyes'. Furthermore, independent nouns for body parts even with possessors are not as common in speech as their English counterparts. Ideas expressed in English with separate body part nouns are more often expressed in verbs derived from the body part noun roots, as in (15).

(15) Yup'ik derived verbs: Jacobson 1984

> a. <u>ii</u>-lliqua   'I am eye-sore' = 'I have sore/infected eyes'
>   -lliqe-   suffix 'have poor quality N'
> b. <u>ii</u>-ngi'rtua   'I am eye-injured' = 'I have something in my eye, got injured in the eye'
>   -ngir-   suffix 'be injured in the N'
> c. <u>ii</u>-ngirtua   'He is eye-deprived' = 'He is snowblind'
>   -ngir-   suffix 'be deprived of N'
> d. <u>ii</u>-tuuq   'she is eye-large' = 'she has big eyes'
>   -tu-   suffix 'have large N'

Paradigm gaps like the singular form for *eye* again suggest that speakers do not simply inflect by rule; they search their memories for echoes of existing forms. This gap also reflects the role of frequency of use. Jacobson (1984: 159) notes that in another Yup'ik dialect, spoken on Nunivak Island, the singular form of 'eye' is now *iik*. The originally dual form, undoubtedly more frequent in speech than the singular, has been reinterpreted as the basic form of the noun.

1.3. Further lexicalization of inflected forms

As noted, the most common absolutive singular ending is -*q*. The majority of nouns show this singular suffix, which has the same form as the third person singular absolutive pronominal suffix on verbs. The same suffix is also added to loanwords (often with a linking vowel *a*) when they are integrated into the language.

(16) Yup'ik singular -*q* on loanwords
  kuskaq   'domestic cat'   Russian *koška*
  cukunaq   'cast iron pot'   Russian *čugunok*
  kalikaq   'paper'   Chukchi *kelikel*

But there are many nouns that end in -*k*. Some are loanwords that simply retain the final velar of their source. Many speakers use the form *cukunak* for 'cast iron pot', retaining the original *k* of the Russian *čugunok*. Others have language-internal sources. Yup'ik shows extensive zero derivation or conversion of noun stems to verb stems and vice-versa. Some of the nouns that end in *k* are directly related to verb stems ending in *k*/*g*. (Orthographic <g> represents a voiced velar fricative. Fricatives regularly appear as plain stops word-finally.)

(17) Yup'ik zero derivation
  kevek   'load'
  keveg-   'to lift'

Some nouns contain derivational suffixes that end in -*k*, such as -*vak* 'large'.

(18) Yup'ik suffix
  tuntu-vak   'caribou-large' = 'moose'

Some nouns ending in -*k* have histories much like that of 'eye'. They have been heard so much more often in the dual than in the singular that the dual form has been taken as basic, resulting in incipient syncretism.

(19) Yup'ik syncretism
  evsaik/esvaik 'female breast'
  iguuk   'testicle'

Though such nouns include some semantic element of 'two-ness' accessible to speakers, they are grammatically singular, as can be seen in the pronominal suffixes on associated verbs.

(20) Yup'ik grammatical singular: Elizabeth Ali, speaker p.c.

    nakacuk   kevkartu**q**
    nakacuk   kevkarte-u-**q**
    bladder   burst-INTR.IND-**3SG**
    bladder   **it** burst
    'The bladder burst.'

Mrs Ali spontaneously volunteered an explanation for the -*k* ending on 'bladder': 'It's because of the two tube-like things coming up out of the top on each side.' Some other nouns whose basic singular forms end in -*k* and which contain a semantic element of two-ness include *akiuk* 'echo' (from *aki*- 'reciprocate, answer back'), *amlek* 'crotch, area between legs', *pupsuk* 'pincer, pincher', *keluk* 'stitch', *iqsuq/iqsuk* 'left hand, left foot', *iquk* 'end (of object, time period, story), other end, tip'. Their referents are represented by singular pronominal suffixes on associated verbs and possessed nouns. In example (21), the noun 'crotch' which ends in -*k* presumably because of a semantic element of duality, is grammatically singular, as can be seen in the possessive ending and the pronominal suffix on 'it is torn'. The *dualia tantum* noun 'trousers' is grammatically dual, as can also be seen in the possessive suffix on 'crotch'.

(21) Yup'ik grammatical singular: Jacobson 1984: 63

    Qerrulliik   amel**gak**   allgumau**q**.
    qerrulli-ik   amlek-**gak**   alleg-uma-u-**q**
    trousers-DU   crotch-**3DU/SG**   tear-in.state.of.having.been-INTR.IND-**3SG**
    trousers   their crotch   it is torn
    'The crotch of the pants is torn.'

Developments of this type, where an originally dual form comes to be taken as the basic form of a noun, provide additional evidence that inflected forms can be remembered by speakers, even when they are fully regular.

2. Mohawk Kinship Paradigms

In Mohawk, all verbs are inflected with pronominal prefixes referring to their core arguments, one for intransitives and two for transitives. The prefixes distinguish first, second, and third persons, and singular, dual, and plural number. Within first person, inclusive and exclusive are distinguished. Within third person, neuter (N), zoic (Z), masculine (M), and indefinite (I) genders are distinguished. Neuters are used for inanimate objects, zoics for most animals, masculines for male persons and some male animals, and indefinites for generic 'one' or 'people'. Some female persons are referred to by zoic forms, so this category is also called feminine-zoic (FZ). Other female persons are referred to by indefinite forms, so this category is also called feminine-indefinite (FI). Groups containing both male and female persons are categorized as masculine dual or masculine plural.

The pronominal system shows an agent/patient pattern. The first person singular agent prefix is basically *k-*; the patient prefix is basically *wak-*. Participants who instigate and control situations are typically coded as grammatical agents, while those who are not in control but are significantly affected are typically coded as grammatical patients. Neuter arguments are not overtly represented in the prefixes unless no other argument is present.

(22) Mohawk grammatical agents and patients
 a. Agent pronominals
  k-atá:wens 'I swim'
  k-erihsiónkwahs 'I take it apart'
  k-enákere' 'I reside (somewhere)'
 b. Patient pronominals
  wak-í:ta's 'I am sleeping'
  wake-nonhwáktani 'I am sick'
  wak-káriahs '(It) bites **me**'
 c. Transitive pronominals
  kón-hsere' 'I am following **you**'
  rí-hsere' 'I am following **him**'
  rák-hsere' '**he** is following **me**'

The semantic basis underlying the system can still be discerned, but the distribution of the agent and patient pronominal paradigms is lexicalized, learned with each verb stem.

The basic forms of the pronominal prefixes that appear at the beginnings of verbs are in Table 3. Most of the prefixes show alternations in shape according to the preceding and following phonological context. Eight conjugation classes can be distinguished on the basis of the initial sound of the following stem. There is often fusion within the prefixes between the agent and patient components, as well as some syncretism. There are 221 possible cells in the paradigm and over sixty basic prefixes.

The verbal pronominal prefix paradigms are fully productive. Mohawk thus offers an example of a language with a rich and complex set of inflectional paradigms, of the type that might be assumed to be too extensive for speakers to memorize. Yet here, too, there are pockets of defectiveness.

Mohawk nouns contain prefixes related to the pronominal prefixes on verbs. On unpossessed nouns, the prefixes simply indicate gender. On possessed nouns, they indicate the person, number, and gender of the possessor and distinguish alienable and inalienable possession. Where the pronominal

Table 3. Mohawk pronominal prefixes basic verb-initial forms

	1SG	1DU	1PL	2SG	2DU	2PL	Ø	N	FZ.SG	M.SG	FI	FZ.DP	M.DP
1SG				kon-	keni-	kwa-	k-			ri-		khe-	
1.EXCL.DU							iakeni-			shakeni-		iakhi-	
1.EXCL.PL							iakwa-			shakwa-			
1.INCL.DU							teni-			tshiteni-		iethi-	
1.INCL.PL							tewa-			tshitewa-			
2SG	sk-/tak-						s-			tsh-		she-	
2DU	skeni-/takeni-						seni-			tshiseni-		ietshi-	
2PL	skwa-/takwa-						sewa-			tshisewa-			
Ø							ka-/w-		io-		iako-	ioti-	roti-
N	wak-	ionkeni-	ionkwa-	sa-	seni-	sewa-	ra-			ro-			
FZ.SG													
M.SG	rak-	shonkeni-	shonkwa-	ia-	tshiseni-	tshisewa-						shako-	
FI							ie-				iontat-	komwati-/	romwati-/
FZ.DU	ionk-	ionkeni-	ionkhi-	iesa-	ietshi-	ietshi-	keni-	konwa-		ronwa-		iakoti-	iakoti-
FZ.PL							konti-				iakoti-	komwati-/	romwati-/
M.DU							ni-					iakoti-	
M.PL							rati-				shakoti-	shakoti-	shakoti-

AGENTS (left axis) / PATIENTS (top axis)

Abbreviations

1	FIRST PERSON	SG	SINGULAR	N	NEUTER (*it*: inanimate objects)	INCL	INCLUSIVE
2	SECOND PERSON	DU	DUAL	FZ	FEMININE-ZOIC (*she, they*: women, animals)	EXCL	EXCLUSIVE
3	THIRD PERSON	PL	PLURAL	M	MASCULINE (*he, they*: males, mixed)		
		DP	DUO-PLURAL	FI	FEMININE-INDEFINITE (*one, they, she*)		

138 Marianne Mithun

prefixes on verbs begin with a palatal or velar glide (spelt <i> and <w> respectively), their counterparts on nouns lack the glide: *io-'taríhen* 'It is cold', *o-ra'wísta'* 'pancake'; *wake-nonhwáktani* 'I am sick', *ake-ra'wísta'* 'my pancake'.

(23) Mohawk nouns

    ora'wísta'
    o-ra'wist-a'
    N-pancake-NOUN.SUFFIX
    'pancake'

    akera'wísta'
    ake-ra'wist-a'
    1SG.ALIENABLE.POSS-pancake-NOUN.SUFFIX
    '**my** pancake'

The vast majority of Mohawk words are morphological verbs. Many are used as referring expressions, lexicalized as nominals.

(24) Mohawk lexical nominal with verbal morphology

    tehahonhtané:ken
    te-ha-ahonht-a-nek-en
    DUPLICATIVE-M.SG.AGENT-ear-LINKER-be.side.by.side-STATIVE
    'he is doubly ear-adjacent' = 'rabbit'

Some morphological verbs used as syntactic nominals still contain initial glides, and others lack them.

Most Mohawk kinship terms have the internal morphological structure of verbs, complete with pronominal prefixes. They can incorporate nouns, and can appear with tense suffixes, though these are rare. If they are incorporated into other verbs, they are first overtly nominalized. They can function as syntactic predicates, but they are normally used as referring expressions.

The kinship terms differ from possessive constructions in that they denote a bilateral relationship. For asymmetrical relationships, the senior kinsman is generally represented in the pronominal prefix like a grammatical agent, and the junior kinsman like a grammatical patient.

(25) Mohawk senior kinsmen

    rakhsótha
    rak-hsot=ha
    M.SG/1SG-be.grandparent.to=DIM
    '**he** is grandparent to **me**' = 'my grandfather'

    rake-'níha   '**he** is father to **me**'   =   'my father'
    rak-htsì:'a   '**he** is older sibling to **me**'   =   'my older brother']

(As noted earlier, the prefixes show some phonologically-conditioned allomorphy, like that between *rak-* and *rake-* in (25).)

140 *Marianne Mithun*

The pronominal prefixes follow the same pattern whether the whole word refers to the senior member of the relationship or the junior member. Which party the term refers to is usually indicated by the stem. One set of stems is used in terms referring to senior relatives, and another in those referring to junior relatives. Terms for grandparents are built on the stem *-hsot* 'be grandparent to', for example, while those for grandchildren are based on the stem *-atere'* 'have as grandchild'. Most kinship terms end in a diminutive =*ha* or =*a*.

(26) Mohawk junior kinsmen

riiaterè:'a
rii-atere'=a
1SG/M.SG-have.as grandchild=DIM
'I have him as grandchild' = 'my grandchild'

| **ri**-ièn:'a | 'I have **him** as offspring' | = | 'my son' |
| **ri**-'kèn:'a | 'I have **him** as younger sibling' | = | 'my younger brother' |

A few stems are used to refer to either member of a relationship, such as *-enhonsa'* 'be related as parent-in-law and son-in-law', and *-sa'wh* 'be related as parent-in-law and daughter-in-law'. There is potential ambiguity when both relatives are of the same gender, but it is seldom problematic. The term *rawenhónsa'* 'he is in-law to him' can mean either 'his father-in-law' or 'his son-in-law'.

Reciprocal relationships are based on intransitive reciprocal verb stems, such as *-ara'se'* 'be cousins to each other'.

(27) Mohawk reciprocal relationships

ionki-ara'sè:'a	'**we two** are cousins'	=	'my cousin'
ionkw-ara'sè:'a	'**we all** are cousins'	=	'my cousins'
tsi-ara'sè:'a	'**you two** are cousins'	=	'your cousin'
sew-ara'sè:'a	'**you all** are cousins'	=	'your cousins'
on-ara'sè:'a	'**they two** (F) are cousins'	=	'her (female) cousin'
ron-ara'sè:'a	'**they two** (MM, MF) are cousins'	=	'her (male) cousin, his cousin'

Terms referring to both members of an asymmetrical relation can be formed by adding a reflexive prefix to the stem usually used for the junior member: *iatatièn:'a* 'father and son' (*i-atat-ien'=a* M.DU.AGENT-REFLEXIVE-have.as. offspring=DIMINUTIVE).

Kinship terms used for junior kinsmen and reciprocal relationships show few if any paradigm gaps. Most of the terms referring to senior kinsmen are also as expected. Similarities between pronominal prefixes on regular verbs and on kinship terms can be seen in (28) and (29). Basic verbal prefixes involving masculine singular agents are in (28)a, and kinship terms with masculine singular senior kinsmen are in (28)b, (28)c, and (28)d.

(28) Some masculine pronominal prefixes
    a. Transitive verbs

rák-hsere'	'he is following **me**'	M.SG/1SG
iá-hsere'	'he is following **you**'	M.SG/2SG
ró-hsere'	'he is following **him**'	M.SG/M.SG
shonkení-hsere'	'he is following **us two**'	M.SG/1DU
tshisení-hsere'	'he is following **you two**'	M.SG/2DU
shonkwá-hsere'	'he is following **us all**'	M.SG/1PL
tshisewá-hsere'	'he is following **you all**'	M.SG/2PL

    b. Grandfathers

rak-hsótha	'my grandfather'	M.SG/1SG
ia-hsótha	'your grandfather'	M.SG/2SG
ro-hsótha	'his grandfather'	M.SG/M.SG
shonkeni-hsótha	'our grandfather'	M.SG/1DU
tshiseni-hsótha	'your grandfather'	M.SG/2DU
shonkwa-hsótha	'our grandfather'	M.SG/1PL
tshisewa-hsótha	'your grandfather'	M.SG/2PL

    c. Fathers

rake-'níha	'my father'	M.SG/1SG
ia-'níha	'your father'	M.SG/2SG
ro-'níha	'his father'	M.SG/M.SG
shonkeni-'níha	'our father'	M.SG/1DU
tshiseni-'níha	'your father'	M.SG/2DU
shonkwa-'níha	'our father'	M.SG/1PL
tshisewa-'níha	'your father'	M.SG/2PL

    d. Older brothers

rak-htsì:'a	'my older brother'	M.SG/1SG
ia-htsì:'a	'your older brother'	M.SG/2SG
ro-htsì:'a	'his older brother'	M.SG/M.SG
shonkeni-htsì:'a	'our older brother'	M.SG/1DU
tshiseni-htsì:'a	'your older brother'	M.SG/2DU
shonkwa-htsì:'a	'our older brother'	M.SG/1PL
tshisewa-htsì:'a	'your older brother'	M.SG/2PL

Similarities between prefixes involving Feminine-Zoic singular agents on basic verbs and those on kinship terms denoting relationships with Feminine-Zoic singular senior kinsmen can be seen in (29). As noted earlier, pronominal prefixes on verbs serving as predicates and those serving as referring expressions generally differ in a specific phonological way. Pronominal prefixes on referring expressions, whether they be morphological nouns or verbs, generally lack the initial glide *i* or *w* of their counterparts on predicates: ***iak**-hsere's* '**she** is following me', ***ak**-hsótha* '**she** is grandparent to me' = 'my grandmother'. (The initial glide of the kinterms in (28)b, (28)c, and (28)d above, such as *ia-hsótha* 'your grandfather', was protected by an initial *h* which subsequently disappeared word-initially before the consonant: **hia-hsótha > iahsótha*.)

(29) Some feminine pronominal prefixes

a. Transitive verbs

iák-hsere's	'she is following **me**'	FZ.SG/1SG
sá-hsere's	'she is following **you**'	FZ.SG/2SG
ió-hsere's	'she is following **her**'	FZ.SG/NZ.SG
ró-hsere's	'she is following **him**'	FZ.SG/M.SG
iakó-hsere's	'she is following **her**'	FZ.SG/FI
ionkení-hsere's	'she is following **us two**'	FZ.SG/1DU
ionkwá-hsere's	'she is following **us all**'	FZ.SG/1PL

b. Grandmothers

ak-hsótha	'my grandmother'	FZ.SG/1SG
sa-hsótha	'your grandmother'	FZ.SG/2SG
o-hsótha	'her grandmother'	FZ.SG/FZ.SG
ro-hsótha	'his grandmother'	FZ.SG/M.SG
onkeni-hsótha	'our grandmother'	FZ.SG/1DU
onkwa-hsótha	'our grandmother'	FZ.SG/1PL

c. Mothers and aunts

ake-'nisténha	'my mother/aunt'	FZ.SG/1SG
sa-'nisténha	'your mother/aunt'	FZ.SG/2SG
o-'nisténha	'her mother/aunt'	FZ.SG/FZ.SG
ro-'nisténha	'his mother/aunt'	FZ.SG/M.SG
onkeni-'nisténha	'our mother/aunt'	FZ.SG/1DU
onkwa-'nisténha	'our mother/aunt'	FZ.SG/1PL

d. Older sisters

ak-htsì:'a	'my older sister'	FZ.SG/1SG
sa-htsì:'a	'your older sister'	FZ.SG/2SG
o-htsì:'a	'her older sister'	FZ.SG/FZ.SG
ro-htsì:'a	'his older sister'	FZ.SG/M.SG
onkeni-htsì:'a	'we two, our older sister'	FZ.SG/1DU
onkwa-htsì:'a	'we all, our older sister'	FZ.SG/1PL

There are many more potential cells in each of these paradigms, as can be seen from Table 3. Most of the forms show allomorphy conditioned by preceding and following phonological contexts. The number of forms is so large that it might be thought that they could not possibly be memorized. If in fact they are assembled online by rule as needed, speakers should not be able to recognize paradigm gaps. But such gaps exist. They can be traced to several different causes.

2.1. Courtesy

Example (30), part of a conversation, is illuminating. The speaker was discussing an old man who had lived near the school when she was a child. She would greet him cheerily, saying 'Hi Gramps!', only to get a gruff response.

(30) Mohawk grandfather: Watshenní:ne Sawyer, speaker p.c.

Iah   newen'
iah   nowèn:ton
not   ever
'I've never

thé   tekoniatkon'seraterè:'a!
thé: te-koni-atkon-'ser-**atere'**=a
at.all   NEG-1SG/2SG-devil-NMLZ-**have.as.grandchild**=DIM
at all   do I have you as a darned grandchild
been your darned grandfather!'

The translation 'I've never been your darned grandfather' was later provided by the speaker herself, but the Mohawk term was not 'I am not grandparent to you'. It was built on the stem usually used to refer to junior kinsmen: 'I do not have you as grandchild' = 'You are not my grandchild'. One simply cannot say *konhsótha* 'I am grandparent to you' (*kon-hsot=ha* 1SG/2SG-be.grandparent.to=DIMINUTIVE) or *iah i: tekonhsótha* 'I am not your grandfather' (*iah i: te-kon-hsot=ha* not I NEG-1SG/2SG-be.grandparent.to=DIMINUTIVE). This is a paradigm gap.

Similarly, a mother talking to her daughter said what she later translated as 'Listen to me! I'm your mother.' She did not use the Mohawk equivalent of 'I am mother to you'. Instead, she shifted to the stem usually used to refer to children: 'I have you as child' = 'You are my child'. The emphatic pronoun *ì:'i* 'myself' reinforced the reference.

(31) Mohawk child: Watshenní:ne Sawyer, speaker p.c.

ì:'   konièn:'a
ì:'i   kon-**ien'**=a
I.EMPHATIC   1SG/2SG-**have.as.offspring**=DIM
I   I have you as a child
'I am your mother.'

Both of these gaps are part of a more general pattern involving relationships between speaker and hearer. In 1SG/2SG combinations, the stem appropriate for the hearer is used.

2.2. An evolving category

Some other gaps can be explained in terms of their pathways of development. The paradigms for *-hsot* 'grandfather' and *-'ni* 'father' lack forms for 'their grandfather' and 'their father'. To express these concepts, different lexical items are substituted.

(32) Mohawk grandfather and father gaps
  shakó-hsere' '**he** is following **them**' M./SG/3DP
  shako-htsì:'a '**he** is older sibling to **them**' = 'their older brother'

  Gaps
  *****shako**-hsótha '**he** is grandparent to **them**' = 'their grandfather'
  *****shako**-'níha '**he** is father to **them**' = 'their father'

  Replacements
  shako-**terè:'a** 'he has them as **grandchildren**' = 'their grandfather'
  shako-**ièn:'a** 'he has them as **children**' = 'their father'

These gaps are the result of a somewhat intricate history that has left traces throughout the inflectional system. To understand this history, we first turn our attention to another set of paradigmatic gaps.

The third person transitive pronominal prefixes on verbs are repeated in Table 4. As noted earlier, two gender categories are used for reference to female persons: the feminine-zoic (FZ) and the feminine-indefinite (FI). Patterns of usage are subtle and complex. In essence, feminine-zoic (FZ) forms are used for most animals and often for louder, more assertive women. Feminine-indefinite (FI) forms are used for generic persons ('one', 'people') and for highly respected and more refined women. Speakers are invariably quick to note that the prototypical referents of feminine-indefinite forms are one's grandmother and one's mother: no one would ever use feminine-zoic forms for these persons, at least in verbs. Yet the inflectional paradigms for kinship terms denoting grandmothers, mothers, and older sisters lack precisely these forms. Though these relatives are referred to by feminine-indefinite pronominals in verbs, they are designated by feminine-zoic pronominals in kinship terms.

Table 4. Third person transitive pronominal prefixes basic verb-initial forms

			PATIENTS			
		FZ.SG	M.SG	FI	FZ.DP	M.DP
AGENTS	Ø	*io-*	*ro-*	*iako-*	*ioti-*	*roti-*
	FZ.SG					
	M.SG	*ra-*	*ro-*	*shako-*		
	FI	*konwa-*	*ronwa-*	*iontat-*	*konwati-*	*ronwati-*
	FZ.DP			*iakoti-*	*iakoti-/konwati-*	*iakoti-/ronwati-*
	M.DP			*shakoti-*	*shakoti-/konwati-*	*shakoti-/ronwati*

(33) Mohawk disagreement
  Á:ke! *Akhsótha* *thó:* *nontiè:teron.*
  á:ke **ak**-hsot=ha thó: n-ont-**ie**-'teron
  gee FZ.SG/1SG-be.gp.to=DIM there PARTITIVE-CISLOCATIVE-FI-reside
  gee **she** is grandparent to me there **she** lives there
  'Oh no! That's where Grandma lives!'

The absence of feminine-indefinite forms for these kinship terms has a diachronic explanation. In Proto-Iroquoian, there was no gender distinction. The Proto-Iroquoian ancestors of the modern Mohawk feminine-zoic (FZ) forms were general third person forms. Sometime after the split of Proto-Iroquoian into Proto-Northern Iroquoian and Proto-Southern Iroquoian, a masculine category was added in the Northern branch. This left the original basic third person category as the non-masculine residue, that is, neuter-zoic-feminine, used for objects, animals, and female persons. Proto-Iroquoian also contained a third person indefinite category, used for generic persons ('one', 'people'). This category did not distinguish number. In some of the Northern Iroquoian languages, including Mohawk, the indefinite category is now used to refer to specific female persons as a sign of respect. This use is an innovation, though an ancient one. What is significant here is that though the feminine-indefinite (FI) category has assumed a place within the modern pronominal paradigms on verbs, and also in the paradigms on kinship terms referring to junior relatives, it has not penetrated the paradigms for senior female relatives. If the kinship terms were inflected purely by rule, the terms for grandmothers, mothers, and older sisters should have reflected the innovation immediately. In fact they have been the most resistant to change of all the kinship terms. These terms must be stored.

The earlier system has left traces in other parts of the inflectional paradigms of kinship terms as well. In the paradigms for certain terms referring to senior kinsmen, there is no feminine-indefinite form for the other member of the relationship: '***her** grandfather', '***her** father' (M.SG/FI). This is not a general property of the inflectional paradigms for all kinship terms, or even for all of those referring to senior kinsmen. It is lexically specific. The cells of the paradigms for older siblings contain forms for these combinations which are generally accepted. Speakers note that the corresponding forms for 'her grandmother' and 'her mother' have been heard, but they sound odd and are usually rejected.

(34)   Mohawk kinship gaps

        shakó-hsere'   'he is following **her**'   M.SG/FI
        shako-htsì:'a   'he is older sibling to **her**' = '**her (FI)** older brother'

        *shako-hsótha   'he is grandparent to **her**' = '**her (FI)** grandfather'
        *shako-'níha   'he is father to **her**' = '**her (FI)** father'

        akó-hsere'   'she is following **her**'   FZ.SG/<u>FI</u>
        ako-htsì:'a   'she is older sibling to **her**' = '**her (FI)** older sister'

        ?**ako**-hsótha   'she is grandparent to **her**' = '**her (FI)** grandmother'
        ?**ako**-'nisténha   'she is mother to **her**' = '**her (FI)** mother'

The extended feminine-indefinite category is now making its way through the inflectional paradigms of other kinship terms, as forms are created on the basis of a variety of perceived patterns.

We now return to the earlier mystery, the gaps for 'their grandfather' and 'their father'. The original indefinite category 'one/people' is being extended in a second direction. Groups of female persons are normally referred to by feminine-indefinite dual or feminine-indefinite plural pronominals in intransitive verbs. Groups of male persons, or mixed groups, are normally referred to by masculine dual of masculine plural forms. But transitive combinations containing indefinite grammatical patients ('it/**people**', 'she/**people**', 'he/**people**', etc.) have been extended to use for specific plural patients ('it/**them**', 'she/**them**', 'he/**them**').

(35) Mohawk extension of indefinite patient forms to plurals

shako-   M.SG/I   'he/people'   >   M.SG/3DP   'he/them'
iako-   FZ.SG/I 'she/people'   >   FZ.SG/3DP 'she/them'

These forms have completely replaced the original transitive pronominal prefixes containing plural patients in all verbal paradigms. The verb *shakó-hsere'* is now the only way to say '**he** is following **them**'. The innovation has not fully penetrated the inflectional paradigms for kinsmen, however. As seen earlier in (32), *shako-hsótha cannot be used for 'their grandfather'. The form is unacceptable, resulting in a gap. Similarly, **shako-'níha* is not accepted as a word and cannot be used for 'their father'. The innovation has made its way into the paradigms of some other kinship terms, however. It is fully accepted in terms referring to younger kinsmen, such as grandchildren and children. In fact these terms are used to replace the missing grandfather and father terms: *shako-terè:'a* 'he has them as **grandchildren**' = 'his grandchildren' or 'their grandfather', and *shako-ièn:'a* 'he has them as **children**' = 'his children' or 'their father'. The extension of indefinite patient forms to plural patients has also penetrated the paradigm for older siblings: *shako-htsì:'a* 'he is older sibling to them' = 'their older brother' is completely acceptable.

A hallmark of grammatical change in progress is variation and often uncertainty on the part of speakers. Speakers know, on some level, that they have heard a variety of forms. The complex Mohawk kinship inflection shows just these characteristics. In elicitation tasks, some Mohawk kinship terms are produced instantly and confidently, such as 'my grandmother', 'my grandfather', 'my mother', and 'my father'. The speed suggests that these forms are easily retrieved from memory as units. Other terms may require slightly more time for retrieval. Some are sought but never found. On occasion, gaps are filled by neologisms, formed according to patterns perceived in the inflection of other lexical items. Speakers vary considerably in their propensity to create new forms and in their acceptance of neologisms. There is also variation from one community to the next. The term *ontate-'nisténha* 'her mother' (FI/FI) was used spontaneously in conversation by an elder in one community but instantly rejected as completely impossible in another, though the formation is perfectly regular. To the extent that full inflected forms are stored in memory, such variation is to be expected. The variation also suggests that it is important not to draw conclusions prematurely about defectiveness on the basis of responses from a single speaker of a language.

3. Conclusion

Patterns of defectiveness in Yup'ik and Mohawk indicate that both rote and rule processing must be at work in the production of inflectional forms. If no regular inflected forms were stored, speakers could not know that a particular form does not exist. Yet speakers hesitate and stumble at certain cells in paradigms that could be filled by the application of quite regular morphological processes, such as the Yup'ik 'my two papers' and the Mohawk 'their grandfather'. If all inflected forms were formed by rule, speakers should always be able to access the base forms from which inflected forms are assembled. Yet at least some Yup'ik speakers cannot identify the base forms of some common nouns such as that for 'eye', forms which should occur as absolutive singular words. If inflected forms were not stored, it would be difficult to account for the reanalysis of certain regular inflected forms as basic, such as Yup'ik 'eye', 'breast', and 'testicle'. If inflected forms were not stored, there should be few differences among speakers and dialects concerning gaps.

At the same time, if all inflected forms were learnt and retrieved as units, there should be little innovation or restructuring of paradigms. Yet Yup'ik speakers have reanalysed certain *dualia tantum* and *pluralia tantum* forms as singulars, and extensive restructuring can be detected in the Mohawk inflectional pronominal prefix paradigms. It is significant that the Mohawk restructuring did not affect the paradigms throughout the language simultaneously. Changes observable in the Mohawk prefix paradigms on regular verbs have only begun to appear in the prefix paradigms on kinship terms. Furthermore, they have penetrated the paradigms of different kinship terms to varying degrees. The innovated patterns are now fully acceptable in most terms referring to junior kinsmen and older siblings. On occasion they are heard in terms for some senior kinsmen but not generally accepted. They are universally rejected in terms for other senior kinsmen.

The points in paradigms where gaps occur are significant. Elicited Yup'ik possessive paradigms showed gaps for dual objects with singular possessors ('my two papers') and plural possessors ('all of us, our papers') but not dual possessors ('we two, our two papers'). The distribution of the gaps is apparently related to frequency of occurrence. Further evidence of the effect of frequency comes from the differing retrieval rates for the same cells in paradigms of different lexical items: though one speaker failed to produce a form for 'my two papers', he instantly retrieved a form for 'my two wives'. The distribution of inflectional gaps in Mohawk kinship terms provides evidence of frequency effects of a different type. Gaps occurred for some of the most frequent forms: grandparents and parents. When the robust pronominal prefix paradigms used with other verbs were restructured, these core kinship terms were the most resistant to change. Their stability indicates that they are stored as fully formed words rather than constructed online by rule.

Overall, the distribution of gaps indicates that inflection must involve both rote and rule processing, with the division of labor related at least in part to frequency of use. These findings are in line with the ideas of lexical strength proposed by Bybee (1985, 2001) and the role of frequency in shaping grammar outlined by Bybee and Hopper (2001). Rote and rule processing may in fact enhance each other. The rich inflectional systems of Yup'ik and Mohawk are highly structured. We know that human beings are skilled at recognizing and learning patterns. Such learning need not replace memory; in fact it can even facilitate it. Learning a new, regularly patterned form is less taxing than learning a brand new word. At the same time, strong, frequently-occurring, easily identifiable patterns can facilitate the creation of new forms according to those patterns.

Defectiveness is by definition irregularity: unexpected gaps in what should be regular patterns. There can of course be generalizations within the irregularity. The elicited Yup'ik paradigm showed gaps in forms for two objects possessed by singular and plural possessors in all persons. In the Mohawk kinship terms, there were gaps for all senior feminine-indefinite referents. Work on defectiveness can advance our understanding on a different level when we pursue the reasons behind the irregularities and their persistence.

References

Baerman, Matthew. 2009. Diachrony of defectiveness. *Proceedings of the Chicago Linguistic Society* 43/2. 251–65.

Baerman, Matthew and Greville G. Corbett. This volume. Defectiveness: typology and diachrony, 1–18.

Butterworth, Brian. 1983. Lexical representation, *Language production 2: Development, writing, and other language processes*, ed. by Brian Butterworth, 257–94. London: Academic.

Bybee, Joan. 1985. *Morphology*. Amsterdam: John Benjamins.

Bybee, Joan. 1988. Morphology as lexical organization. *Theoretical morphology*, ed. by Michael Hammond and Michael Noonan, 119–42. San Diego: Academic.

Bybee, Joan and Paul Hopper. 2001. Introduction. *Frequency and the emergence of linguistic structure*, ed. by Joan Bybee and Paul Hopper, 1–26. Amsterdam: John Benjamins.

Hare, Mary, Michael Ford, and William Marslen-Wilson. 2001. Ambiguity and frequency effects in regular verb inflection. *Frequency and the emergence of linguistic structure*, ed. by Joan Bybee and Paul Hopper, 181–200. Amsterdam: John Benjamins.

Jacobson, Steven. 1984. *Yup'ik Eskimo dictionary*. Fairbanks, AK: Alaska Native Language Center, University of Alaska.

Kim, John. J., Steven Pinker, Alan Prince, and Sandeep Prasada. 1991. Why no mere mortal has ever flown out to center field. *Cognitive Science* 15. 173–218.

Pinker, Steven and Alan Prince. 1988. On language and connectionism: Analysis of a Parallel Distributed Processing model of language acquisition. *Cognition* 28. 73–193.

Prasada, Sandeep and Steven Pinker. 1993. Generalization of regular and irregular morphological patterns. *Language and Cognitive Processes* 8. 1–56.

Stemberger, Joseph Paul and Brian MacWhinney. 1988. Are inflected forms stored in the lexicon? *Theoretical morphology: Approaches in modern linguistics*, ed. by Michael Hammond and Michael Noonan, 101–16. San Diego: Academic.

9

Ineffability through Modularity: Gaps in the French Clitic Cluster*

MILAN REZAC

1. Modularity and Gaps

THE SET OF POSSIBLE COMBINATIONS OF PREVERBAL CLITICS in French has apparently 'arbitrary' gaps, whose absence does not obviously follow from independent syntactic or interpretive principles like the Theta-Criterion that restrict combinations of non-clitics as well. These gaps provide a powerful tool for investigating a foundational hypothesis about the architecture of language:[1]

(1) MORPHOPHONOLOGY-FREE SYNTAX (MFS): Syntax is autonomous of morphophonology.

Morphophonology is here a cover-term for the systems responsible for the form and arrangement of morphemes not due to syntax and interpretation. Its purview varies with the theory, but the allomorphy of the English past in *distribut-ed, let, ran, though-t, went* clearly belongs here, and even in

---

* I am grateful to the participants and organizers of the Defective Paradigms workshop, and to those of other venues of which this work formed a part: MIT LingLunch, seminar talks at the University of Ottawa, the University of Tromsø/CASTL, UMR 7023, conference presentations at LAGB 2007, Queen Mary PCC Fest, GLOW 2008, and a spring 2008 research course at the Leiden University Center for Linguistics. Particular thanks go to Matthew Baerman, Gilles Boyé, Anna Cardinaletti, Mélanie Jouitteau, Richard Kayne, Eric Mathieu, Andrew Nevins, David Pesetsky, Gillian Ramchand, Johan Rooryck, Michal Starke, Tarald Taraldsen, Anne Zribi-Hertz, and anonymous reviewers. To Mélanie Jouitteau I owe a further debt for much help with the empirical aspects of the work. Its flaws and errors are mine. The work was partly supported by NWO visiting researcher grant #B 30–669.

[1] See Baerman and Corbett (this volume), Zwicky (1992, 1996), Pullum and Zwicky (1988), Miller, Pullum, and Zwicky (1998), Halle and Marantz (1993), Embick (2000), Trommer (2002), Tseng (2005), Embick and Marantz (2008). MFS typically follows on realizationalist models of morphology, but also on early-insertion lexicalist ones to the extent there are principles to prevent syntax from accessing the morphophonology of the word node. It is explicitly absent in models where syntax and morphophonology are a single system, e.g. Bresnan (1998, 2001).

an exuberant syntax, so does the morpheme-internal prosody-sensitive infixation in *Du(-fuckin-)br(*-fuckin-)óvnik* (McCarthy 1982: 575). Under SYNTAX are included both syntax and aspects of interpretation dependent on it, such as theta and binding theory. MFS is a hypothesis about the MODULAR ARCHITECTURE of the cognitive system containing these domains: syntax is encapsulated from morphophonological information and the mechanisms that manipulate it. MFS seem to be as pervasively and systematically right as befits a fundamental architectural principle, whether or not it has exceptions that call for limited morphophonology-to-syntax communication. Syncretisms are a token: in French (2), non-strong, non-nominative plural pronouns neutralize gender across paradigms, as for *les*, yet this fails to influence their gender for participle and pronoun agreement in the syntax, *mises* and *elles*.

(2) Les cuillères$_i$, je les$_j$ ai mis-es là où elles$_i$/*ils$_i$ étaient.
 the spoon(F).PL, I them.M/F have put-FPL where they.F/*M were
 The spoons/glasses, I put them where they were.

(Rezac 2009)

In the domain of gaps, MFS individuates two classes of gaps and two classes of mechanisms, syntactic and morphophonological ones, and predicts that syntactic mechanisms do not respond to morphophonological gaps even if they may do so to syntactic ones. The syntactic invisibility of arbitrary gaps has been emphasized by Trommer (2002) and Embick and Marantz (2008) in arguing against Bresnan's (2001) model of violable constraints unhampered by MFS, designed to allow the arbitrary **amn't* gap of English license a unique syntactic structure as its 'REPAIR'.[2] The missing past participle of *stride* in English (Albright 2006) is a convenient illustration of their point: its absence licenses neither syntactic phenomena (*do*-support, **She has done stridden*) nor interpretations (the past for the perfect **By now, she strode across the desert for many years*) that are not available independently of the gap. Only independently available paraphrases can be resorted to. Syntax does not seem to react to the INEFFABILITY of a syntactic structure due to an arbitrary gap in its realization.

The French clitic cluster is a rich source for the study of MFS. Some of its gaps share their underlying principles with morphophonological mechanisms affecting the cluster, viewable as repairs of gaps that would emerge otherwise. Others condition a syntactic repair, and so should prove to be syntactic if MFS is right, furnishing a base-line against which to compare morphophonological gaps, one not available for *amn't* and *stride*. In the comparison, MFS

---

[2] Throughout, talk of 'repairing' of a gap is meant as neutral between two construals: responding to a gap as such, as by a constraint violation, and restating the conditions of a gap, which entails being able to state them.

seems to emerge as the over-arching principle governing gap-syntax interactions, differentiating gaps similar on the surface yet profoundly different in kind and behaviour.

Standard descriptions of French clitics propose the strictly ordered cluster in (3), filled by the clitics in (4), one per position, although we shall meet exceptions.[3] The cluster needs a left-adjacent finite or infinitival verb as host. The cluster-verb units have been treated as forming an inflectional 'paradigm' (Lambrecht 1981; Miller 1992; Miller and Sag 1997; Bonami and Boyé 2006), parallel to the object-agreement inflection of languages like Basque (Heger 1966).[4]

(3) Standard order: 1/2–3.DAT-3.ACC-GEN-LOC

(4) a. 1st/2nd person and *se* clitics: 1SG *me*, 2SG *te*, 1PL *nous*, 2PL *vous*, SE *se*
     b. 3rd person accusative clitics: 3MSG *le*, 3FSG *la*, 3PL *les*
     c. 3rd person dative clitics: 3SG *lui*, 3PL *leur*
     d. Adverbial clitics: locative LOC *y*, genitive GEN *en*

An example of the cluster is *lui en y* in (5). The example also shows one set of clitics set aside here: the *te me nous* group of 'ethical' clitics, glossed ETH, invoking a non-argumental discourse participant as witness or affected entity (Leclère 1976). They mostly precede other clitics and do not interact with them for co-occurrence restrictions (Jouitteau and Rezac 2008).

(5) Je   (*te*   (*me*   (*nous*)))   lui   en   y   ai   mis deux.
     I   2SG.ETH   1SG.ETH   1PL.ETH   him.DAT   GEN   LOC   have   put two
     I have put two of them (keys) there (in the bowl) for her.
                    (Jouitteau and Rezac 2008: 98; all the ethical datives are possible)

In the paradigm space defined by (3), many gaps exist, and some anomalous combinations that can be viewed as the repairs of other gaps. Two tools for investigating them are introduced first. Section 2 sorts out a set of gaps due to a syntactic principle, the Person Case Constraint, whose properties form a baseline against which other gaps are studied. Section 3 looks at the anomalous combinations, which betray the workings of an extra-syntactic

---

[3] Clitics are italicized. 1st/2nd/*se* person clitics make no case distinctions, but their case is recoverable by diagnostics like quantifier float, and is glossed (except for ethical clitics). The *se* clitic is glossed SE: it plays the role of a dative and accusative reflexive, an inchoative and a mediopassive formant, and an idiomatic part of some verbs.

[4] The separation of adverbial clitics and the verb by certain adverbs is unavailable in the grammars studied here (Kayne 1975: 79 note 7, 430). Space allows only proclisis to be discussed. Enclisis is distinct in form and ordering, with intriguing gaps often attributed to a mysterious 'euphony' (de Kok 1985: 379–383, Morin 1979b: 309–11; Miller 1992: 175ff.). Excluded are also gaps involving a single clitic only, such as *s'a* (Morin 1984, Abeillé and Godard 2002: 443ff.). For more on the morphophonology of the cluster, see Morin (1979a), Miller (1992), Auger (1994).

system manipulating morphological features and imposing constraints on their combinations. It reappears in the irreparable morphophonological gaps studied thereafter, and the remaining sections turn to these, resumed in Table 1. All appear to occur in the morphophonology and share invisibility to syntax, as MFS holds, heterogeneous though they are in their causes: repetition problems, morphological garden paths, unorderable clusters, and those that are presently mysteries.[5]

Table 1. French clitic cluster gaps

Cluster gap	Example	Gap type	Repair	Section
1/2/SE.ACC+3.DAT	*me lui*	syntax	syntactic	2
3.ACC+3.DAT	*la lui*	partial repetition	allomorphy	3
*LOC+LOC, *GEN+GEN	*en en*	clitic repetition	allomorphy/–	3
3.DAT+3.DAT	*leur lui*	partial repetition	–	4
3SG.DAT+LOC	*lui y*	garden path	–	5
3SG.ACC+LOC	*l'y*	garden path	–	5
GEN+LOC	*y en*	clitic ordering	–	6
pro-predicate *le*+X	*l'y*	?	–	7
se+DAT	*se lui*	?	–	7

2. The Person Case Constraint: A Syntactic Gap

Many of the logically possible combinations of clitics are missing for non-arbitrary syntactic reasons. Violations of the Theta Criterion, the Binding Theory, or the Case Filter belong here: there are no clusters of multiple accusative clitics, to the extent a cliticization domain does not include multiple accusative arguments (cf. (40)c). More intricate is (6). The genitive clitic originates as the complement of the object *le prix*, which cannot itself cliticize as the 3SGM.ACC clitic *le*. A plausible explanation is that *le* cannot stand for *le prix* to the exclusion of its complement, nor for *[le prix t$_{en}$]* by the Lexical Integrity Principle (cf. Blanche-Benveniste 1975: 106ff.; Rooryck 1988: 383).

---

[5] All gaps discussed here have been mentioned in the literature and discussed with various speakers, but detailed investigation focuses on the grammar of one consultant, M. Jouitteau (MJ), a middle-class speaker from Nantes with a register influenced by Cholet. For MJ we may distinguish a school-taught literary level set aside here (no subject clitic doubling; weak subject *nous* 'we'; *elle* [ɛ] 'she'), and spoken grammars ranging from ones at mid-distance from the literary level in familial and general informal settings (optional subject doubling, *on* 'we', *elle* [ɛ] 'she') to more remote ones restricted to certain contexts among peers (obligatory subject doubling, *on* 'we', *elle* [a], *y*-datives in section 5). Phenomena restricted to the last level are notated (MJ'), others (MJ). Cf generally Lambrecht (1981).

(6) a. J' en$_i$ connais [$_{DP}$ le prix   t$_i$]   b. Je l'(*en$_i$) connais
     I   GEN   know   the price
     I know the price of it.

Not all syntactic gaps are obvious, however. The *ME-LUI* or PERSON CASE CONSTRAINT (PCC) in (7) defines a set of impossible combinations superficially similar to others like **lui y* 3SG.DAT LOC which will turn out to belong outside syntax. Indeed, the seminal studies of Perlmutter (1971) and Bonet (1991) view the PCC as a set of gaps in the morphophonology. Yet the PCC belongs to syntax, and it makes for a minimal contrast with morphophonological gaps.

(7) PERSON CASE CONSTRAINT (PCC): *1st/2nd/*se* accusative clitic + non-ethical dative clitic.

Bonet's and subsequent work finds the PCC to recur across both Romance and otherwise typologically diverse clitic and agreement systems. This finding, the constraint's feature-based character, and its occasional independence of the morphological expression of these features, have led much research to place the constraint into the syntax (Postal 1990; Ormazabal and Romero 1998, 2002; Anagnostopoulou 2003; Béjar and Rezac 2003; Bianchi 2006; Adger and Harbour 2007; Rezac 2009; cf. Albizu 1997). A remarkable property of the PCC confirms this move by the MFS: it licenses otherwise impossible syntactic structures. In French, unfocussed dative and accusative pronouns must be clitics rather than strong pronouns, (8)a, except when a clitic would incur the PCC, (8)b (Kayne 1975; Couquaux 1975; Postal 1990; Rezac 2009).

(8) a. Philippe *la*   ⟨*leur*⟩   a présenté   ⟨*à eux/ √à EUX*⟩ hier.
       P   her.ACC them.DAT has introduced to them/to THEM yesterday
    b. Philippe *te*   ⟨**leur*⟩   a présenté   ⟨à eux/à EUX⟩   hier.
       P   you.ACC them.DAT has introduced to them/to me yesterday
    [Of course they$_i$ know her/you$_k$.] P has introduce her/you$_k$ to them/THEM$_i$ yesterday.

This clitic-strong pronoun alternation could in principle belong to the morphophonology. It resembles analytic-synthetic alternations that arguably occur there, such as *quick-er—more rapid*, save that the distance between the clitic and the strong pronoun seems too great for a morphophonological mechanism to span (Ackema and Neeleman 2003). Bonet (1991) finds an elegant way to relate the clitic and strong pronouns of (8) outside syntax as different spell-outs of the same movement chain. The dative moves out from a vP-internal position, the clitic spells out the top copy if possible, and the strong pronoun spells out the bottom copy if the clitic is banned by the PCC as a morphophonological constraint (see also Bošković 2002).

However, it turns out that the clitic and the strong pronoun in (8) involve different syntactic structures, not different spell-outs of the same one (Rezac 2009). Dative clitics and strong pronouns differ syntactically in ways other than focus in French, and for all such purposes, the unfocussed strong pronoun of the PCC repair behaves as a strong pronoun rather than as a clitic. Bare floating quantifiers like *tous* 'all' are a case in point. Only the syntax underlying a dative clitic can license one, and the PCC repair with its unfocussed strong pronoun behaves as if there were no clitic: *tous* can be added to (8)a to give *Philippe la leur a tous présenté hier* 'Philippe introduced her to all of them yesterday', but not to (8)b. Binding theory and constraints on right dislocation can make the same point. Thus the PCC licenses an otherwise unavailable syntactic structure of the repair and is visible to syntax. This proves a key contrast with non-syntactic gaps.

Visibility for syntax matches a different property of the PCC that furnishes another contrast: the PCC and its repair pay attention to syntactic primitives never differentiated by the morphophonology. For example, the repair only affects dative clitics that realize indirect objects, not those that correspond to possessors or benefactives (Kayne 1975; Couquaux 1975; Postal 1990; Rezac 2009). The realization of datives as clitics, and the morphophonological processes affecting clitic cluster in the next section, are blind to such distinctions. Morphophonological gaps are expected to be too. The actual situation is more nuanced, but not, it seems, so as to imperil this divide between syntax and morphophonology.

Such is the character of a gap that belongs to the syntactic component. MFS predicts that a morphophonological gap should avail itself of the mechanisms of the morphophonology solely, to be overcome or to remain as a gap. These gaps are introduced in the next section through a system that underlies and can repair some of them, leading into those that it cannot fix.

3. Morphophonological Repairs: Opaque Cliticization

Clitic cluster gaps due to the morphophonology should not have syntactic repairs, but they may have morphophonological ones. OPAQUE CLITICIZATION might be conceived of in these terms, where a clitic or Ø appears in a way unexpected from their typical distribution. The phenomenon is of interest because it makes use of the same features and constraints that underlie some irreparable gaps, and because both it and these gaps are invisible to syntax, as MFS predicts.

A particularly common context for opaque combinations in Romance are 3.DAT + 3.ACC clitic clusters, in contrast to ones involving 1st/2nd person (Bonet 1991). Partial morphological feature repetition has been suggested as the source of their troubles, falling under the OBLIGATORY CONTOUR PRINCIPLE (Grimshaw 1997; Pescarini 2007; Nevins 2007). This problem extends beyond these clusters to irreparable combinations, such as 3.DAT + 3.DAT in the next section. For 3.DAT + 3.ACC combinations, there is presumably strong functional pressure against gaps, and we find instead a variety of adjustments by clitic substitution or deletion:

(9) 3.ACC+3.DAT clitic clusters in Romance (French *le/la/les* + *lui/leur*)
 a. retained (standard French, Valencian)
 b. 3.ACC → Ø (French varieties)
 c. 3.DAT → *se* reflexive (Spanish: 'spurious *se*')
 d. 3SG/%3PL.DAT → *hi* locative (Catalan, various Italian dialects)
 e. 3SG.DAT → *ni* genitive (Castrovalvi, South Italy)
 f. features redistributed across 3rd person and LOC positions (Barceloní Catalan)
  (Bonet 1991, 1995; Pescarini 2005, 2007; Manzini and Savoia 2002)

These cluster transformations are not a matter of plain phonology because of Bonet's generalization in (10): they traffic in clitics and Ø, not in phonological features. Other work shows that the underlying ban on feature and clitic repetition is not phonological, for example Miller (1992), Pescarini (2007), Nevins (2007). Bonet's interpretation is that opaque cliticization occurs in a realizational component between syntax and phonology which operates over morphosyntactic features. The change of a 3SG.DAT to a locative for example consists of the impoverishment of [3SG OBL] to [OBL], where [3SG] are the phi-features 3SG.DAT shares with 3SG.ACC, and [OBL] is the feature that it shares with and that defines a locative.

(10) Opaque output forms in clitic combinations always result in another clitic form, indicating a closed system. (Bonet 1995: 612)

Placing opaque cliticization outside syntax with Bonet matches its apparent properties, without necessarily prejudging how syntax-like the mechanisms of this component might be, as in Distributed Morphology (cf. note 14). The relationship between the transformed features and their context seems arbitrary from a syntactic standpoint, as underscored by the variation in (9). The transformations only seem to pay attention to the local word-like context, the clitic cluster, and not to the larger syntactic structure around. One reflex of this is that a dative clitic behaves the same whether it is an indirect object or a possessor, syntactic distinctions that do matter for the PCC. Finally, a morphophonological approach to Romance clitic cluster transformations makes the following key prediction by MFS:

(11) Syntax (including its interpretation) is not affected by opaque cliticization.

The prediction is significant, for opaque clitics do exist independently, engendering proposals where opaque cliticization is really the contextual use of the usual syntax of the opaque clitic: a locative replacing a dative really is a locative (Manzini and Savoia 2002). Yet Romance opaque cliticization appears to be inert for syntax, like the syncretism in (2). The Spanish SPURIOUS *SE* rule (9)c, shown in (12), is a good example. In the context of a 3.ACC clitic, the 3SG/PL.DAT *le, les* clitics surface as *se*, which is elsewhere a reflexive and impersonal subject clitic. Additionally, in some varieties the features of the dative clitic are realized by the form of the accusative. Neither phenomenon affects the syntax. This follows by MFS if they occur outside syntax, such as the morphological feature deletion and re-linking of Bonet (1995).

(12) El libro$_i$, a ellos$_j$, ¿quién *se$_j$* *lo/los$_i$* prestó?
the book to them who SE.DAT [< *les* 3PL.DAT] 3SG/PL.ACC lent
Who lent the book to them?
(Iberian (*lo*)/American (*los*) Spanish, Bonet 1995: 634)

The same syntactic inertness obtains of the other 3.DAT+3.ACC cluster transformations (Bonet 1991: 211 for (9)d). It holds also of clitic deletion, instantiated in French (13), and the addition of a spurious *le* in the same example.[6] There is no theta-role deleted or added, and the phi-features of the deleted accusative clitic remain interpreted while those of the added one are not. More subtly, the deletion fails to affect binding possibilities and quantifier float, which we have seen PCC repair do. The deleted accusative clitic in (14) must remain disjointed from its local subject, and it continues to license a bare floating quantifier (Rezac 2009; cf. Zink 1997: 247).

(13) Elle la lui → *lui/le la lui/la le lui* a envoyé.
she her.ACC him.DAT has sent
She sent it (e.g. the table) to him. (MJ)

---

[6] For deletion, see Miller (1992: 172ff.), Auger (1994: 82ff.) who notes it to be obligatory, Bonami and Boyé (2006: 296); Grevisse and Goosse (1993: §1070.2); for dialects, e.g. Remacle (1952: 229), Svenson (1959: 56). Auger (1994: 83) and Bonami and Boyé (2006: 296) point out that the deletion cannot be object drop (of which it lacks at any rate the characteristic non-specific reading), since it is available with *apporter* 'bring' that cannot drop its object. Bonami and Boyé along with Miller (1992: 172) argue that it is not a plausible phonological process in French.

Spurious *le* does not seem to be mentioned in the literature, though it recalls Catalan reflexive splitting of Bonet (1991: 119–22) or the doubling in *donne-le-me-le* 'give-it-me-it' of Bürgi (1998: 44), (MJ' *refais-le/la-me/?nous-le* 'redo-him/her-(for) me/us'), and the *l*-gemination in *(œ)ll'avez-vous vu* 'him. A have-you' of Morin (1979a: 26) *for MJ. It affects all 3.DAT+3.ACC clusters, e.g. *Elle la/les le lui a envoyé/fait envoyer* 'She sent her/them to him, She had her/them sent to him'. It is not always limited to 3.DAT+3.ACC clusters, optionally affecting *Elle me l'/les a envoyé* 'She sent it/them to me' to give *Elle me le l'/*les a envoyé*. Cf. note 13. It is not perceived as informal, seems common for Nantes speakers of MJ's generation but not that of their parents, and I have not found it elsewhere.

(14) Elle$_{i \notin X}$ les→Ø$_X$ lui$_{k \notin X}$ a   tous$_X$ déjà   présenté.
     she   them.ACC   her.DAT   has all   already introduced
     She has already introduced all of them to her.   (MJ)

An extreme instance of repetition is the repetition of whole clitics, incurring the REPEATED MORPH CONSTRAINT (Menn and McWhinney 1984). Miller's (1992: 143–5) study of its repair by HAPLOLOGY in the case of French *en en* clitic clusters illustrates its syntactic inertness. In (15), the quantifier *deux* 'two' requires the genitive clitic *en* to represent its restrictor, and the left-dislocated *ce vin* must link to another *en* realizing the genitive argument of the verb. Independently, neither *en* is omissible. However, combining the two requirements results in a sole *en* clitic only, (15). It is possible to imagine what a genuinely syntactic reduction of two *en*s to a single one might yield, as in the parasitic gap in (16) where a single *en* links to two positions, (16). This is not the interpretation of (15). Syntax does not see the haplology.

(15) Ce vin$_j$,   il   *en* [< *en*$_i$ *en*$_j$]   remplit   [deux   *e*$_i$].
      this wine   he   GEN   fills   two
      This wine, he fills two of them$_i$ with it$_j$.

(16) Marie *en*$_i$ a   présenté   [le frère   *e*$_i$]   à   [la sœur   *e*$_i$]
      Marie GEN   has introduced the brother   to the sister
      Marie introduced his$_i$ brother to his$_i$ sister.
                                   (Sportiche 1996: 255; cf. Blanche-Benveniste 1975: 113)

Haplology as a repair of the repeated morph constraint is common.[7] Opaque cliticization can occur elsewhere, as in GEN GEN *n n* > GEN LOC *n i* in Barceloní versus haplology in other Catalan varieties (Bonet 1991: 86–97, 112).[8] Neither need be available. In that case, a repeated sequence sometimes survives: GEN GEN *n n* in Catalan varieties, REFL IMPERS *si si* in Conegliano Italian, 3PL.DAT 3PL.ACC *els els* in Valencian (Bonet 1995: 627ff.; for *en en* retained in literary French, Rowlett 2007: 128 note 46). However, sometimes it does not, and then an irreparable gap in the clitic cluster emerges: combinations of impersonal and spurious *se* in Spanish (Perlmutter 1971: 33; Bonet 1991: 169) or multiple dative clitics in French (Miller 1992: 264f.; cf. the next section). These gaps arise in the domain where the Repeated Morph Constraint lives. Neeleman and van de Koot (2005) conclude it to lie outside syntax, given its language, construction, and morpheme specificity, and

---

[7] See Miller (op. cit.) for locative clitics; for an apparent instance with reflexive *se*, see Kayne (1975: 372), Postal (1989: 132 note 15, 1990: 195 note 62). Elsewhere, cf. for Italian 1PL LOC *ci* + *ci* haplology Pescarini (2005: 245, 2007 ex. 24), for Rocca Imperiale 1PL GEN *nə* + *nə*, Pescarini (2007 ex. 42).

[8] So also GEN GEN > SE GEN *se ne* in Italian (Cardinaletti and Giusti 2005: ex. 197), or > LOC GEN *ce ne* (Pescarini 2005); reflexive + impersonal SE *si si* in Italian > LOC/1PL SE *ci si* (Bonet 1995; Grimshaw 1997).

sensitivity to factors like adjacency. By MFS it follows that any repair should be syntactically invisible, as it is.

It is time now to turn to the irreparable gaps, first those due to the same causes as the ones in this section: partial repetition. Lacking morphophonological repairs, they permit a different test of their invisibility to syntax, because they would yet cannot be fixed by the PCC repair.

4. Double Dative Clusters

It is possible in French to create clusters with multiple dative clitics, typically by combining the arguments of distinct predicates through CLITIC CLIMBING. A variety of such clusters are unacceptable.[9] Contexts that require clitic climbing yet run into a ban on multiple datives are simply ineffable. Not only are the clitics impossible, but the PCC repair that realizes one of the datives as an unfocussed pronoun is not available either (Kayne 1975: 172ff., 290f., 296f.; Couquaux 1975: 53, 71 note 11; Postal 1981: 308–14, 1983: 412, 1984: 122; Rezac 2009).

The simplest scenario is raising. French mostly permits raising only out of adjectival small clauses, and some adjectives take a dative complement, such as *reconnaissant (à)* 'grateful to'. If the dative is an unfocussed pronoun, it must be a clitic, and the raising verb is its only host. The raising verb may itself have a dative experiencer clitic. The resulting double dative combination is tolerated by many but not all if 1/2.DAT+3.DAT (*me lui*), homophonous with the 1/2.ACC+3.DAT clusters banned by the PCC; by none if it gives 3.DAT+3.DAT; and with a great deal of variation for 1/2.DAT+2/1.DAT. Unacceptable clusters are not amenable to the PCC repair, substituting an unfocussed strong pronoun for one of the datives:

(17) Paul *me*   ⟨*leur⟩   semble   reconnaissant   ⟨?*à eux⟩
      Paul me.DAT   them.DAT   seems   grateful   to them
      Paul seems to me to be grateful to them.
                                        (Couquaux 1975: 53; cf. Kayne 1975: 175)

Causatives of ditransitives (and unergatives + dative) are more complex. In the relevant causative construction, the verb is an infinitive embedded under *faire* 'do', the subject/causee of the (di)transitive is dative, and clitic

---

[9] There is no comprehensive investigation, to my knowledge. See especially Morin (1978: 358ff.), Postal (1983, 1984, 1990), Tasmowski (1985: 297 note 36, 360ff.), de Kok (1985: 383, 386, 479), as well as briefer mentions in Bissel (1944: 333), Blanche-Benveniste (1975: 224), Couquaux (1975: 53), Kayne (1975: 175, 2000: 118), Roetgiest (1987: 152ff.), Miller (1992: 265), Miller and Sag (1997: 598), Nicol (2005: 159ff.). Cf. Rivas (1977) on Spanish, where dative clusters of 3+3 are excluded but those of 1/2+3 are permitted.

climbing is obligatory. If the dative causee-subject and the dative indirect object of the ditransitive are both unfocussed pronouns, both must cliticize, and they find themselves in the same cluster. The details of permissible clusters are mostly as with raising, except that some speakers who permit 1/2.DAT+3.DAT for raising permit them in causatives only if an accusative clitic intervenes, 1/2.DAT+3.ACC+3.DAT, while others permit them as such. Impossible clusters cannot be ameliorated by the PCC repair, as in (19). To express such sentences, alternative causative structures with no clitic climbing are used.[10]

(18) a. Elle *me* *les* *lui* a fait envoyer(, les chocolats, à maman.)
b. *Elle *leur* *les* *lui* a fait envoyer(, les chocolats, à maman.)
c. Elle **leur/??me* *lui* a fait envoyer les chocolats(, à maman.)
   she me/them.DAT them.ACC her.DAT has made send the chocolates to mom
She has made me send them (the chocolates) to her (mom).
(MJ) (cf. Kayne 1975: 291; Tasmowski 1985: 361)

(19) Paul va *lui* faire porter les livres aux étudiants TOUT DE SUITE.
Paul va *lui* ⟨?*leur⟩ faire porter les livres ⟨*à eux⟩ TOUT DE SUITE.
Paul will him.DAT them.DAT make carry the books to them/the students immediately
[Eric forgot to bring the books to Paul's students! What will they do now?]
Paul will make him carry the books to them/to the students immediately.
(MJ) (cf. Kayne 1975: 296f.; Postal 1981: 308–14)

In these structures, datives come together from distinct predicates. Double datives can also occur with a single predicate to some extent, by adding a benefactive clitic to a verb that takes an indirect object (Rouveret and Vergnaud 1980: 169–71). For some speakers, the indirect object can then also cliticize, and curiously, 3.DAT+3.DAT clusters may then become available, in direct contrast to multipredicate structures. Even in these double dative clusters however, repetition of the same dative morpheme is strictly impossible, a gap again invisible to the PCC repair.[11]

---

[10] For one with distinctive binding properties, see Morin (1978: 358ff.), Kayne (1975: 295 note 23, 2000: 23), Postal (1981: 315), de Kok (1985: 598 note 2). For another, see Tasmowski (1985), Miller (1992), Abeillé et al. (1997).
[11] The possibility to cumulate datives is far from general: contrast Kayne (1975: 172 note 122) for a possessor and Postal (1990: 131 ex. 61) for a benefactive. In sentences like (20), one of the clitics must bind *se*, it seems.

(20) (Barbara$_j$,)

   a. On   te   lui   a chanté sa$_j$ chanson à Pauline$_i$.
       One you.ETH   him.DAT has sung her song   to Pauline
       We sang her$_j$ song to Pauline for him, you see

   b. On   te   leur/*lui   lui$_i$ a chanté sa$_j$ chanson.
       One you.ETH them/him.DAT her.DAT
       We sang her$_j$ song to her$_i$ for them/*him, you see.

   c. On   te   lui   a chanté sa$_j$ chanson à elle$_i$.
       One you.ETH him.DAT   has sung her song   to her
       *We sang her$_j$ song to her$_i$ for him, you see.

(MJ)

For all these double dative clusters, the unacceptable dative combinations cannot undergo the PCC repair, and the underlying syntactic structure is ineffable. That matches the mechanical character of these gaps. From the perspective of syntax, the distinctions between good and bad dative clusters appear arbitrary and hard to refer to without ad hoc devices: other selection and movement, for example, do not do so. On the other hand, the Obligatory Contour Principle over features from the preceding section seems to capture well the scale 1/2.DAT+3.ACC+3.DAT > 1/2.DAT+3.DAT > 3.DAT+3.DAT. If the gaps belong outside syntax, then the syntactic PCC repair is correctly unavailable by MFS.

An intriguing caveat comes from differences among raising, causatives, and benefactives in the types of double dative clusters tolerated. For many speakers like MJ, raising (17) but not causatives (18) tolerate *me lui*; moreover, monopredicate and not multipredicate structures tolerate *leur lui*. To differentiate these, dative types might have to be featurally differentiated in the morphophonology, but this is unappealing insofar as dative realization and opaque cliticization treat all homogeneously. More satisfying would be to rely on independent principles, thinking notably of the pragmatic account of Tasmowski (1985) for various causative restrictions, including *me la lui*—**me lui*. For the raising-causative difference, we might depart from the observation that clitics signal a highly accessible discourse antecedent for a following gap (Ariel 1990; Delfitto 2002). This facilitates linking discourse referents to gaps, but also incurs processing complexity with an increase in the number of clitics (Lepschy and Lepschy 1988: 212). Causatives of ditransitives have three gaps at the point where the clitic cluster is met, raising structures have two, and speaker intuitions about their judgements suggest a correlated difficulty with their resolution. Causativizing an unergative, which yields only two gaps as in (21), seems to eliminate the ban on 1/2.DAT+3.DAT clusters of (18).[12] Another

---

[12] The example, which seems robust, violates the generalization that dative clitics come in the order of gaps, perhaps a factor: Kayne (1975: 290), Rouveret and Vergnaud (1980: 177), Postal

story along these lines would have to be told for 3+3 clusters, starting perhaps from the optionality of one of the datives in monopredicate in contrast to multipredicate structures.

(21) Ca   *nous*   *lui*   a   fait   apparaître   fatiguée,   *(à) nous
     That us.DAT   her.DAT   has made   appear/seem   tired   to us
     That made her seem tired to us. (= *Nous on a cru qu'elle était fatiguée.*)

(MJ)

The alternative is to state these restrictions on clusters and their invisibility to PCC repairs in the syntax and to restrict the PCC repair to the PCC by syntactic means in a model with corresponding means, as in Postal (1990) deploying the power of Arc Pair Grammar.

5. Dative-Locative Interactions

The gaps in this and the following sections are perhaps the most widely-noted ones in French: clusters containing the adverbial clitics. Incompatibilities between the locative clitic and datives are discussed in this section, and locative-genitive interactions in the next. Unlike the foregoing gaps where a high degree of consensus exists among French varieties close to the standard, these ones are subject to a great deal of variation along multiple parameters. They are little understood, and the following discussion has two unequal components: good evidence that the gaps are outside syntax and not visible for syntactic repair, and tentative suggestions about their causes. For the gaps of this section, the problem seems to come from interference in the morphological parse between features shared by datives and locatives.

Let us begin with a highly specific gap affecting only 3SG.DAT LOC *lui y*, as in *m/leur/*lui y parler* 'speak to me/*him there' (Miller and Monachesi 2003: 3.4; Couquaux 1975: 50; Blanche-Benveniste 1975: 77f., 85; Morin 1981: 99 note 6, Herslund 1988: 60f., 320f., de Kok 1985: 368, Grevisse and Goosse 2008: 682. 3°). The gap does not license the PCC repair. In (22)a, a strong pronoun for an unfocussed dative is bad whether or not cliticizing the dative runs into the *lui y* gap. Modifying the example to create a PCC context makes the strong pronoun fine in (22)b. Simply omitting *y* distorts the meaning in the same way as omitting 'there' in English.

(1981: 319 note 30, 1984: 135, 152), Tasmowski (1985). One should like to relate the fact that the lower dative clitic may be coreferential with the matrix subject in a causative but not raising or monoclausal structures, presumably due to the intervening causee, but here unergatives pattern with (di)transitives (Morin 1978: 359; cf. Postal 1983: 401; Kayne 2000: 23 118).

(22) a. C'est parce que le nid protège ses petits$_i$/son petit$_i$ que
l'oiseau ⟨leur$_i$/?*lui$_i$⟩ y donne à manger ⟨*à eux$_i$/*à lui$_i$⟩.
the bird them/him.DAT LOC gives to eat to them/to him
It's because the nest protects its young (one) that the bird feeds them/*him there.

b. C'est parce que son petit$_i$ a faim que
l'oiseau nous ⟨*lui$_i$⟩ donne à manger ⟨à lui$_i$⟩.
the bird us.ACC him.DAT gives to eat to him
It's because his youngling is hungry that the bird gives us (worms) to him to eat.

(MJ)

The gap might be attributed to the phonological hiatus in the *lui y* sequence, [(l)ɥii] (Grevisse and Goosse op. cit., Littré 1872–7 s.v. *lui*[1]). Probably, phonology does play a role. For MJ, the gap disappears when the subject is clitic-doubled at the colloquial level as in (23), which results in the pronunciation [iji] and resolves the hiatus (thus also *on* 'one/we' *lui y* [ɔ̃ji], *je* 'I' *lui y* [ʒiji], etc.). The gap is also absent when the genitive clitic disrupts the *lui y* sequence, *lui en y* in (5), and when the order of the two clitics is reversed as some speakers permit, (24) cf. Zink 1997: 232 note 79.[13] A phonological gap irreparable by the syntactic PCC repair fits well with MFS.

(23) l'oiseau *(i) lui y a donné à manger. (Ø *lui y* [(l)ɥii] ~ *i lui y* [iji])
the bird *(he) him.DAT LOC has given to eat

(=(22)a) (MJ)

(24) Marie l' y lui soumettra demain.
Marie him.ACC LOC him.DAT submit tomorrow
Marie will submit it to him there tomorrow.

(Posner 1997: 405)

Still, a hiatus is not all there is to the story. Such hiatus is either tolerated or repaired by deletion in situations involving a clitic and a non-clitic, as Miller (1992: 176f., 145), Auger (1994: 55f.) demonstrate. Locative *y* is fine when it follows the strong pronoun *lui* 'he', or when followed by *i*-initial verbs like *illustrer* 'illustrate', save for *ir*- 'will go' when *y* is simply deleted. The *lui y* problem is also attenuated or disappears despite the hiatus when both clitics are subcategorized, as in (25).

---

[13] For MJ however, the *l'* here is the spurious *le* of (13), also in (i) (there is no accusative DP clitic doubling).

(i) Marie *(l') y lui/leur soumettra le dossier demain.
Marie him.ACC LOC him/them.DAT will.submit the dossier tomorrow

(MJ)

(25) Je *(l)ui   y   *parle / √ferai   penser.   (*je lui y* [ʒɥii])
     I   him.DAT LOC   speak   will.make think
     I will talk to him (*there), √I will make him think of that.

(MJ)

In looking for what renders hiatus problematic for *lui y*, the close Romance relationship between locative and 3.DAT clitics comes to mind. Morphologically, dative clitics often seem to contain the locative clitic as a component, indicated in Table 2 and example (26). The dative may be realized as a locative alone, or in conjunction with various expressions of its phi-features: some identical to accusative clitics or to their subcomponents like the plural *z*, some to dative clitics in related dialects, with these modes transitioning smoothly one to another (as in Rohlfs 1935: 124). Particularly striking is Barceloní, where the 3rd person and locative components of a dative can be separated by the genitive clitic *n*: 3PL.DAT *lz-i*, 3PL.DAT + GEN is *lz-n-i* [ɔlzɔni] (Bonet 1995: 641f.; cf. Ahlborn 1946: 59–61 for Occitan).

(26) a. Je *leur(-zy)* [ʒə lœʁzi] *y-eur* [ʒjœʁ] / *lui(*-z)(-y)* [ʒɥiji]   casserai   la figure.
        I them.DAT   him.DAT   will.break   the face
        I'll break their/his face.

(MJ')

     b. On   *leur z'y/lui (*z'y)*   raconte   des histoires.
        one them/him.DAT   tells   stories
        We tell them/him stories.

(Bürgi 1998: 52, Vaudois)

Table 2. Dative-locative relationships

DAT =	3SG	3PL	Variety
LOC	y ^liaison^[i] ≠ lui > '(u)i *^liaison^[(ɥ)i]	(leur)	F: Morin 1981: 99, Lambrecht 1981: 31
	y		Québec: Auger 1994
LOC (+ PL)	i	i-z / z-i,	F; FP; Béarn: Rohlfs 1935: 124
		y-eu-(z-y), etc.	
ACC +LOC	l-i	lous-i	FP; Catalan variety: Bonet 1993
	l-i	lèz-i	Walloon: Remacle 1952: 196
DAT + LOC	lui(-z)-y	leu(r)-z-y	FP; F
	l-i	(leus)	FP; Marais Vendéen: Svenson 1959: 56
	l-i	(lor)	FP; Old French

Legend: F means wide-spread in colloquial French (cf. Giraud 1969: 42); FP refers to the Occitan varieties surveyed in Ronjat (1937: §505–6).

This recurrent relationship suggests that the locative clitic is somehow a component of the dative clitic (Ahlborn 1946: 59–61). Partly on this basis and partly from the opaque cliticization of datives as locatives, Bonet (1991, 1995) decomposes dative clitics into phi-features, which is the content of accusative clitics, plus the feature [OBL], which defines locatives: 3SG.DAT = [3SG OBL].

Among the realizations of this feature combination are both forms like *lui*, and others like *lui-z-y* that appear to have multiple exponence of [OBL]. Both differ from the sequence *lui y* [3SG OBL]$_{lui}$ [OBL]$_y$ only in the number and grouping of features. The *lui y* gap may then be thought to arise partly from a difficulty in differentiating [3SG OBL] [OBL] from [3SG OBL] in the morphology or its parsing, as an instantiation of the mechanisms underlying the Obligatory Contour Principle effects (Walter 2007: 168–72). Recurrence of the same problem in the phonology as [(l)ɥii] exacerbates it. It is ameliorated or eliminated by realizing *lui* as [j] distinct from [i], fixing the phonology; by subcategorization for a dative and a locative argument, priming the expectation of two distinct elements; and if *lui* and *y* are separated by another clitic in *lui en y* or if they come in reverse order *y lui* (especially if the $lu_{3SG} > i_{LOC}$ order means that [3SG OBL]$_{lui}$ has trouble being followed but not preceded by [OBL]$_y$).[14]

The same logic should apply to *leur y*, save that the phonological factor is absent. Consonant with this is Morin's (1981: 99 note 6) observation that it is also dispreferred (Herslund 1988: 60ff.), although better than *lui y* 'everything else being equal'. Its acceptability varies with context, from best to worst in (27). The first example involves a subcategorized *y*, the second unlike the others is at a distinctly literary level, the last has no redeeming qualities.

(27) a. Il   leur   y   fera   penser.
        he   them.DAT   LOC   will.make   think
        He will have them think of it.

    b. Il   leur   y   succèdera.
        he   them.DAT   LOC   will.follow
        He will replace them in the position.

---

[14] The dative-locative relationship can be articulated in ways other than Bonet's feature composition of terminals without affecting the proposal to be made, notably through distinct LOC and DAT syntactic terminals as in Manzini and Savoia (2002), Kayne (2008). In this light Vaudois French is interesting. As (26)b indicates, *y* cannot be attached to *lui*; it does however surface attached to the sole auxiliary that permits clitic climbing if present, *veux* in (i). A syntactic approach lends itself to this. So must a morphophonological approach: in some Romance varieties where clitic climbing is clitic copying as in (ii), what gets spelt out at which copy can depend on prosodic properties of the infinitive, as Morin (1979b: 304ff. note 5) points out, and that ought to belong to morphophonology by modularity. Bonet's copy spell-out proposal in section 2 has the means to make it so. The scope of morphology is unclear when it comes to features shared across copies or extended projections like auxiliary plus participle, letting opaque cliticization affect these.

(i) J'   y   veux   le   lui/*leur   prêter.   (ii) La   podes   pourta-*lo* au   lieit
     I   LOC   want   it.ACC him/*them.DAT   lend   her you.can   carry-her   to.the   bed
     I want to lend it to them.   You can put her to bed.
                    (Bürgi 1998: 53, cf. 99ff.)   (Piat 1911: §44)

c. Max   *leur*   *y*   parlera.
   Max   them.DAT LOC   will.speak
   Max will speak to them there.

(Morin 1981: 99 note 6)

There occur other problematic interactions between datives and locatives that fit this picture. McA'nulty (1971), discussed in de Kok (1985: 196), observes that in a sentence containing a dative argument gap, (28)a, a locative clitic is excluded, while the reverse is not true, (28)b. A similar effect obtains in (29), with further nuances: an adjunct locative clitic is impossible with a verb subcategorizing for a dative, *donner* 'give', better if the dative is optional, *amener* 'bring', and fine if there is a dative clitic. These patterns suggest that a verb looking for a dative argument seeks to interpret an [OBL] feature as belonging to the dative and pre-empts a locative parse for it, causing a morphological garden-path, unless already satisfied by a dative clitic.

(28) a. *C'est à lui/à toi   que j' *y*   parle / j' *y*   ai   remis   le livre.
        it's   to him/to you that I LOC speak / I LOC have returned the book
        He is/you are the one that I spoke to there/that I returned the book to there.

     b. C'est là   que je *lui*   parle / je *t'*   ai   remis   le livre.
        it's there that I him.DAT speak / I you.DAT have returned the book
        There's where I spoke to him/where I returned the book to you.

(McA'nulty 1971: 63) (MJ)

(29) a. Des articles$_i$, dans le bar$_j$, elle *en*$_i$ *y*$_j$ a   ?amené/*donné trois à Pierre.
        articles   into the bar   she GEN   LOC   has   brought/given three to
                                                                              Pierre
        Of articles, in the bar, she ?brought/*gave there three of them to Pierre.

(MJ)

     b. Je vais   *leur*   *y*   ⟨*en*⟩   envoyer   un   ⟨de nos projets⟩.
        I am.going them.DAT   LOC   GEN   send   one   of our projects
        I'm going to send them one of them/of our projects there.

(MJ)

The same dative-over-locative garden-path may account for a gap observed by Heggie and Ordóñez (2005: 12ff.): 3SG.ACC LOC *l'y*. *L'y* is fine in (30), where it is subcategorized and the verb does not take a dative argument, but quite strongly out in (31)b where *y* is an adjunct and the verb subcategorizes for a dative. The problem disappears when the dative argument is a clitic, giving *le lui y*, realized either as [lə lɥi i] in a slow distinctive tempo or as [(l)ɥiji] in a rapid one, not [(l)ɥii], to avoid the *lui y* gap. The gap does not occur with another choice of accusative: 3PL.ACC LOC *les y* is fine in (31)b. Repair by a strong pronoun is impossible, (32).[15]

---

[15] The gap is stronger than the *lui y* gap, and holds at different levels of language. It is considerably attenuated for the verb *présenter*, perhaps because the location is more of an argument. A

(30) a. Il a mis le   livre sur la table.   b. Il l'   y   a   mis.
        he has put the book on the table.   he it.ACC LOC has put
        He put the book on the table.   He put it there.
                                                  (MJ) (Heggie and Ordóñez 2005: 12ff.)

(31) a. Il ⟨y⟩   a donné le livre   à Marie   ⟨au congrès⟩.
        he LOC   has given the book   to Marie   at.the meeting
     b. Il l'   ⟨*y⟩   a donné   à Marie   ⟨au congrès⟩.
           it.ACC   LOC
     c. Il le   lui   y   a donné.   (le lui y = [lə lɥi i], [(l)ɥiji],
           it.ACC her.DAT LOC   *[(l)ɥii])
        He gave the book/it to Marie/to her at the meeting/there.
                                                  (MJ) (cf. Heggie and Ordóñez 2005: 12ff.)

(32) Maï voulait de nos hérissons/notre hérisson, mais c'était embêtant de (les/le) lui
     donner à la boutique. C'est parce que c'était calme au bar qu'
     Maï wanted our hedgehog(s), but it was difficult to give him/them to her at the
     shop. It's because it was calm at the bar that

     on   ⟨les/??l'⟩   y   a   donnés   ⟨*eux/*lui⟩ à Fañch.
     one   them/??him.ACC   LOC   has   given   them/him   to Fañch
     we gave them/??him to Fañch (Maï's friend) there.
                                                                              (MJ)

This gap too suggests a morphological garden-path. Adopting the dative-locative relationship of Bonet, 3SG.DAT [3SG OBL] and 3SG.ACC LOC [3SG] [OBL] are featurally identical, as they are morphologically in many Romance varieties. The hypothesis that would account for the foregoing paradigms is that the sequence 3SG, OBL tends to be parsed as [3SG OBL] rather than [3SG] [OBL] if there is a dative expected. The presence of a dative clitic impedes this garden-path, since it discharges the expectation of the dative argument. The effect seems abetted by the phonological similarity of *l'y* [li] and 3SG.DAT *lui* [(l)ɥi], and disappears for 3PL LOC *les y*. The reasons for the contrast are not

---

gap recalling this one is the exclusion of 3SG/PL.ACC GEN *l'/les en* in the presence of a dative argument, as in (i) (cf. Morin 1981: 101 note 10). However, the pattern is not the same: it is weaker than *l'y*, both *l'en* and *les en* are excluded about equally, and cliticizing the dative does not seem to help. If one wanted to pursue a parallel explanation nontheless, there comes to mind the opaque cliticization of some Catalan varieties, 3SG.ACC GEN > LOC *l'i* (Bonet 1991: 86–97). (Some varieties of Spoken French, but not MJ's, generally exclude *l'y/en* and less so *les y/en*, besides good *m'y/en*: see Morin 1979a: 7ff., 1981: 100 note 8, and Lepschy and Lepschy 1988: 212 for variability of *ne lo* in Italian.)

(i)   Je   *l'/les*   en   ramènerai (??à Maï), de Paris.
      I   it/them.ACC   GEN   will.bring   to Maï, from Paris.
                                                          (MJ) (cf. Morin 1981: 101 note 10)
(ii) *Je   *le   lui*   en   ramènerai
            him.DAT
                                                          (Morin 1981: 101 note 10)

fully clear, relating perhaps to the unmarkedness of SG vs. PL and the absence of number specification for LOC, perhaps to the greater prevalence of 3.DAT— 3S.ACC + LOC parallelisms for 3SG than for 3PL in Romance, including Old French.

The garden-path character of dative-locative gaps is suggested by their pattern of degradation and amelioration in function of factors such as hiatus. The hypothesis needs much further exploration. In the literature, morphological garden-paths of this sort have already been occasionally invoked to explain arbitrary gaps. Noyer (1992: 164-6) proposes one for a state of affairs in Mam illustrated in (33), under his analysis. There is a unique suffixal position of exponence, underlined, expressing the features of the agent preferentially and of the patient otherwise. In (33), the agent *he* controls the suffix Ø expressing its [-I, -you] features. Because the position is unique, Ø also pre-empts an expression of the patient's features for the two translations: a suffix *a* for [+I, -you] of *us (excl.)*, and Ø for [+I, +you] of *us (incl.)*. The morphology should therefore be ambiguous between the two. However, the reading with the patient as *us (incl.)* is strongly preferred. Noyer posits that the reading with *us (excl.)* is excluded as a garden path in parsing the morphology, which assumes that a form ending in Ø does not 'hide' the *a* that would express the features of the patient if not pre-empted by the agent. On the preferred reading, the suffix Ø is surface-true to the features of the agent and patient alike.

(33) ... qo   ... t-   tzeeq'an-   Ø
       [+I -sg]   [elsewhere]   hit   [(αI) αyou]
    he hit us (incl.), */?he it us (excl.)

In Noyer's proposal, the surface form is compatible with a featural make-up that leads the parser down one type of analysis, the more surface-true one, and blocks another. The Tamashek gap discussed by Baerman and Corbett (this volume) might lend itself to such an approach as well. French locative/dative interactions differ slightly. A garden path is created by a parse that attaches an [OBL] feature to an expected dative gap in the McA'nulty paradigm, combining further with an adjacent [3SG] to give [3SG OBL] (3SG.DAT) in the *l'y* gap, while in the *lui y* gap the local repetition of [OBL] in [3SG OBL]$_{lui}$ [OBL]$_y$ either also results in [3SG OBL] or plain confusion. However, these dative parses are not themselves legitimate in any of the above gap examples. It is important therefore to note that ungrammaticality generally does not prevent garden-paths. German (34) closely resembles Noyer's proposal. A genitive can be expressed by the preposition *von* or the suffix *-s*, but for nouns like *Paris* whose genitive is homophonous with the unsuffixed nominative for phonological reasons, the nominative parse beats out the genitive one despite its ungrammaticality (Bayer et al. 2001; cf. Di Sciullo 2000: 8). Similarly in

English (35), there arises an irrecoverable parsing garden-path analysing *DP₁ of DP₂'s DP₃* as [1 of [2's 3]] rather than [[1 of 2]'s 3], despite any local disambiguation clues and ungrammaticality or nonsense of the outcome (Fodor and Inoue 1994: 441f.; Green 1971).[16]

(34) a. Bewohner von London/Paris   b. Bewohner Londons/*Paris
      inhabitants of London/Paris   inhabitant London's/*Paris'
                                                                   (Bayer et al. 2001: 467)

(35) a. a picture of *me's/*my/*mine recipient/frame
      the recipient/frame of a picture of me
cf. b. the person talking to me's purpose
                                                                        (q.v. Zwicky 1995)

Morphological parsing problems thus seem to furnish one source of gaps in the clitic cluster. They are incurred by principles operating over the features manipulated by the opaque cliticizations of section 3 and partly identical to those seen there, the Obligatory Contour Principle. The next section turns to gaps also arising in the extra-syntactic systems that put morphological features to use, but this time in realization: to ordering problems.

6. Locative-Genitive Combinations

LOC + GEN combinations are widely noted to be rare, save for two *y en* sequences that might have an idiomatic status: in the existential *il y en a* 'there is' lit. '(it) LOC GEN has', and *s'y en* SE LOC GEN (Blanche-Benveniste 1975: 77f., 137, 220ff; Morin 1981: 101; de Kok 1985: 385).[17] Morin (1981) observes that the acceptability of other LOC + GEN combinations varies with subtle factors: its literary character induced by *naît* helps (36)a, whereas (36)b shows more arbitrary variation. He also points out that nothing is wrong with the phonology. In varieties that replace 3(SG).DAT by *y*, the resulting DAT GEN *y en* sequences are no more restricted than *lui en* (cf. Auger 1994: 105, 107).

(36) a. Il   naît   à Paris plus de femmes   qu'il n' *y*   *en*   meurt. (92%)
      it   is.born at Paris more women   than it   LOC   GEN   dies
      There are born in Paris more women than die there.

---

[16] Brought to my attention by D. Pesetsky, p.c.
[17] With reflexive *se*, we should get the 1st/2nd person clitics as in *Je m'y en vais* or *Je m'en y vais* 'I am going away there'. The former is literary (Littré 1872–7, s.v. *y*¹; de Kok 1985: 385), the latter condemned as a frequent vice by Molard (1803, s.v. *aller*, noted by M. Jouitteau p.c.), though neither now in use in varieties familiar to me.

b. J'   y   en   ai   ajouté/planté deux.   (54%/15%)
   I   LOC   GEN   have   added/planted two
   I added two of those to it/planted two of those there.

> (Morin 1981: 99 note 6, rate of acceptation out of thirteen speakers of diverse localities)

Probing the GEN+LOC sequences a little further, we find a great variability of and uncertainty about ordering. Prescriptive works propose *y en*, but in the linguistic literature there are both cases of *y en/*en y* and attested *en y*, in otherwise apparently parallel examples (Morin 1979b: 300 note 3 vs. Lambrecht 1981: 32; cf. Rowlett 2007: 128 note 46). Consider the initial judgements on such sequences for one speaker, in (37), (38), and in (29) above. Grammaticality judgements are available and can be crisp, and completion scenarios lead to the spontaneous production of the two clitics, but the order varies greatly. Indeed, the judgements may reverse within a short time: (37)a is not good on both orders, but on one at a time, engendering an experience reported similar to the reversal of a bistable percept. At the same time, there are islands of stability where independent factors force a certain order: the cluster in (5), where the *lui y* gap forces *lui en y*, is a spontaneous production of unmitigated enduring goodness.

(37) a. T'étais saoule, t'as rien vu!—Je te jure, j' *en   y / y en* ai   vu   trois.
                                                   I GEN LOC   have seen three
   You were drunk, you didn't see anything!—I swear, I SAW THREE OF THEM THERE.

b. Je ?*t'*   *y*   *en* / **t'*   *en*   *y*   verse (, de l'eau, dans le verre)
   I   you.DAT LOC GEN   you.DAT GEN LOC pour of water, into the glass
   Shall I pour you some in it?

(38) a. Il nous faudra faire quelque chose de la fenêtre$_i$ dans la cuisine$_j$—il y a deux rideaux de couleurs différentes. Je crois qu'

   il faut *y$_j$*   *en$_i$* / ?*en$_i$*   *y$_j$*   ôter   le jaune et garder le rouge.
   it must LOC   GEN   GEN   LOC   remove the yellow and keep the red

   We'll have to do something about the windows of the kitchen—there are two curtains of different colours. I think that we should remove the yellow one from it (the window) there (in the kitchen), and keep the red.

b. Les rideaux ne sont pas mal, sauf pour celui$_i$ de la fenêtre$_j$ dans la cuisine$_k$.

   Il faut *l'$_i$*   *en$_j$*   *y$_k$* / **l'*   *y*   *en*   ôter   au plus vite.
   it must it.ACC   GEN   LOC   it.ACC LOC GEN   remove as fast as possible

   The curtains are not bad, except for the one of the window of the kitchen. We should remove it (the curtain) from it (the window) there (in the kitchen) as fast as possible.

(MJ)

Usually, these clusters are simply avoided. A common strategy is to omit one clitic. *Là* 'there' may complete (39), but a contextually salient bowl or a pointing gesture will do as well.

(39) A: Ou est-ce que je mets la nourriture pour le lapin/les lapins? B: Tu vois ce bol-là?
A: Where do I put the food for the rabbit(s)? B: Do you see that bowl?
Tu peux   *lui/leur*   (*y)   *en*   mettre (là).
you can   him/them.DAT LOC GEN   put   there
You can put some (GEN) in it (LOC) for them (DAT).

(MJ, *y* only literary)

GEN+LOC combinations thus run into some problem that has speakers avoid them if possible and linearize them variably otherwise. The latter suggests that the grammar might be uncertain about the relative order of the two clitics. This proposal is related to the classical view that GEN and LOC share the same clitic cluster slot, but it permits the exceptions seen above. The Obligatory Contour Principle might be responsible, since many Romance varieties spell en out as *en* + *y* generally or contextually (e.g. Benincà and Poletto 2005: 233, cf. Zink 1997: 309f.); cf. Bonet's (1995) analysis of *y* as [OBL], *en* [OBL [GEN]]. Diachrony helped. The order of the clitics changed from *en y* to *y en* in the history of French (de Kok 1985: 366ff.). Subsequently, the combinations of the two clitics have been rare, save for the fixed *il y en a* and *s'y en*, and do not seem to have established a sufficiently robust ordering (compare Albright 2006 for the causes of *stridden). When independent principles like the *lui y gap establish the order, the problem disappears, and the GEN+LOC combination is fine.

7. Mystery Gaps

The foregoing gaps in French clitic combinations seem amenable to explanations built on reasonable assumptions and with the potential to explain their properties in some detail. The last two gaps considered here are more elusive (cf. note 15 for another gap). They are not amenable to the PCC repair and lack an obvious syntactic reason, but a non-syntactic one is also not evident.

The first gap is the failure of the NEUTER clitic to combine with others. French has a pro-predicate clitic *le*, homophonous with 3SGM.ACC, where some other Romance varieties like Barceloní use a dedicated neuter clitic. The French pro-predicate *le* cannot combine at all with the adverbial clitics, (40)a (more impossible than (30)b), though it is better with datives, (40)b (Kayne 1975: 299 note 27; Heggie and Ordóñez 2005: 12ff.). In Barceloní, combinations of the neuter clitic with others also give rise to gaps or to opaque cliticizations (Bonet 1991: 19, 95, 151ff., 122–4, 86ff.). This recalls the difficulties of note 15 that *l'y*, *l'en* occasionally experience independently, but is not reducible to them. The neuter clitic might interact with adverbial ones because like them it is not pro-nominal, and indeed in other Romance varieties the pro-predicate clitic may rather be locative or genitive (Ronjat 1937: §511 for Occitan *en*, Zink 1997: 302 for Middle French *y*; cf. Walloon below).

(40) a. Jean   l'   ⟨*y⟩   est   ⟨à Paris⟩.   (*l'* = *connu, président*)
     Jean   it.ACC   LOC   is   at Paris   known, president
     Jean is one (president) at Paris/*there, Jean is such (known) at Paris/*there.

   b. ?Dévouée, elle   *me*   *l'*   est depuis longtemps
      devoted, she   me.DAT   it.ACC is   since   a.long.time.ago
      Devoted, she has been to me for a long time.
                                    (Kayne 1975: 299 note 27) (MJ)

   c. je ne veux pas qu'elle soit malade, encore moins qu'
                                    elle *se*   *la*   fasse
                                    that se.ACC her.ACC makes
      I do not wish her to be ill, still less that she makes herself such (ill).
                                    (de Kok 1985: 384) (*MJ, with *la* or *le*)

Instead of an invariant pro-predicate *le*, older and dialectal French deploy the full array of 3.ACC clitics to reflect the phi-features of the replaced predicate, such as *la* in (40)c (Posner 1997: 397, Grevisse-Goosse 2008, §673b). The accusative-neuter similarity thus goes farther, though not, as far as I know, to give 1st/2nd person pro-predicates. De Kok (1985: 384ff.) observes that in literary usage, pro-predicate clitics rarely combine with accusative clitics to give sequences like (40)c. He notes that attested clusters are all homophonous with ones existing independently, so while (40)c stands beside *se* SE.DAT + *le/la* 3SG.ACC, there is no *le le/la* because there is no double-accusative *le le/la*. That too might suggest that the difficulties of combining neuter clitics with others relate to realizing the result. In (40)c the pro-predicate clitic is of the agreeing type; in other examples gathered by De Kok it is not. However, none are remotely acceptable in the French discussed here (MJ; Blanche-Benveniste 1975: 140f., Jones 1996: 303; in Gleize Walloon of Remacle 1952: 256, the 3 ACC pro-predicate clitic changes to LOC if combined with a true 3 ACC).[18]

The second gap consists of the mediopassive *se* + dative clitic. As a reflexive internal argument, *se* participates in the PCC and its repair. It also serves to form MEDIOPASSIVES, where the external argument is interpreted as an impersonal agent and the direct object if any is promoted to nominative case and agreement (Fellbaum and Zribi-Hertz 1989; Dobrovie-Sorin 2005).

---

[18] Accusative clitic climbing is impossible across an accusative when fine otherwise, suggesting a Case problem (Solà 2002: 241f., cf. Rivas 1977; see Tasmowski 1985: 314, 362 note 7, Postal 1990: 196 note 69 for exceptional French varieties immune to this, perhaps relatable to (13)). For MJ, the neuter clitic might run into this ban.

Mediopassive *se* cannot combine with a dative clitic, although it can combine both with dative arguments and with the locative and genitive clitics. For the resulting gaps, the PCC repair is not available, as observed by Blanche-Benveniste (1975: 214–9), Kayne (1975: 398), Postal (1990: 167ff.).

(41) Bien sûr qu'Azenor$_i$ aime danser,
mais ça ne se ⟨*lui$_i$⟩ dit pas ⟨à ses parents/*à elle$_i$⟩, c'est tout.
but that NEG SE her.DAT says not to her parents/to her that's all
Of course Azenor likes to dance, but one does not say that to her parents/*to her.

(MJ)

Although superficially identical to a subset of the PCC in French, there is reason to think the mediopassive *se* clusters are unrelated to it. Some older French varieties seem to permit it without permitting other PCC combinations (de Kok 1985: 384), and so do Occitan varieties (Ronjat 1937: §792, §798). In Spanish, the reflexive accusative *se* is not subject to the PCC as it is in French, but mediopassive *se* + dative clitic is still excluded, (42) (with *n*).[19] By contrast, NOMINATIVE *se* is fine, (42) (without *n*); absent in French, this *se* differs in keeping direct object as an accusative and not promoting it to an agreeing nominative.

(42) Se les vende(*-n) libros a los chicos.
SE them.DAT sell.3SG(-3PL) books to the boys
One sells books to the boys.

(Mendikoetxea 1992: 319)

It is unclear what underlies this gap. Mendikoetxea (1992: 319ff.) proposes that mediopassive but not nominative *se* forms an inseparable morphological unit with the verb, within a theory where the mediopassive *se* is lower in the structure than the nominative *se* and attaches to the verb as a passive-like suffix. That is untenable for French, where locative and genitive clitic may freely separate the mediopassive *se* from the verb: modifying (41), we get *Ça ne s'y est pas dit* 'One has not said that there' (*y* LOC 'there'). Spanish in turn renders difficult another sort of explanation. Since the PCC bleeds all other *se* + dative clitic clusters in French, this remaining set might encounter difficulties in realization as in the last section, or even be learnt as a gap (Boyé and Hofherr this volume). But in Spanish *se* + dative surface clusters are fine, as in the nominative *se* version of (42) or with its reflexive *se* unaffected by the PCC, yet the mediopassive *se* + dative clitic combinations are still out.

---

[19] Mendikoetxea (1992: 319 note 8) notes some speaker variation, and indeed the ungrammatical (42) type seems not infrequent elsewhere, e.g. Fernández-Ordóñez (1999, ex. 157).

8. Conclusion: Gaps in Morphology and Gaps in Syntax

The gaps in the French clitic cluster fall into two groups. Syntactic gaps make up one, and the Person Case Constraint belongs among them, invoking syntactic information and licensing a syntactic repair superficially similar to non-syntactic gaps though it is. The other group is constituted by gaps invisible to syntax and dependent on morphophonological information and mechanisms, properties which reappear in opaque cliticization. MFS expects non-syntactic mechanisms and syntactic invisibility to correlate, and to a considerable extent that seems true, indicating some version of the modular architecture from which MSF derives.

The syntactic status of the PCC and the blindness of its repairs to other gaps may be valid cross-linguistically (Rezac 2008, 2009). For this, the least suitable architectures are ones where morphophonological gaps are visible to a syntax modelled through violable constraints, predicting their automatic repair by the emergence of otherwise ungrammatical syntactic structures (Bresnan 2001; see Poser 1992: 123–5 for related discussion). In more modular conceptions of the syntax-morphology relationship, there are a variety of ways to draw the necessary distinctions. One is to put the PCC squarely into the syntax, or at the syntax-morphology interface where syntax could see it but not the internals of external module(s), as much of the work cited in section 2 proposes. The notion of interface could be broadened to include parts of an extra-syntactic morphological component defined precisely by being visible to syntax, lending itself to the proposals of Albizu (1997) or Bonami and Boyé (2006: 304ff.). Similarly, a gamut of approaches to morphophonological gaps is compatible with MFS, from ones wholly autonomous of syntax to the syntactic but post-spell-out realizational component of Distributed Morphology. In weighing these options, the key will prove a theory of the limitations of the PCC repair, and the existence and nature of other systematic differences between the two groups of gaps, some seen above: the (in)visibility of syntactic distinctions neutralized in the morphophonology (types of datives), and vice versa, the syntactic (non-)arbitrariness of feature couplings in gaps (*les/*l'y*), and the role played by phonology (**lui/?leur y*).

References

Abeillé, Anne and Danièle Godard. 2002. The syntactic structure of French auxiliaries. *Language* 78. 404–52.

Abeillé, Anne Danièle Godard, and Philippe Miller. 1997. Les causatives en français: un cas de compétition syntaxique. *Langue française* 115. 62–74.

Ackema, Peter and Ad Neeleman. 2003. Context-sensitive spell-out. *Natural Language and Linguistic Theory* 21.681–735.

Ackema, Peter and Ad Neeleman. 2005. *Beyond morphology: Interface conditions on word formation*. Oxford: Oxford University Press.

Adger, David and Daniel Harbour. 2007. Syntax and syncretisms of the Person Case Constraint. *Syntax* 10. 2–37.

Ahlborn, Gunnar. 1946. *Le patois de Ruffieu-en-Valromey (Ain)*. Göteborg: Elanders Boktryckeri Aktiebolag.

Albizu, Pablo. 1997. Generalized Person-Case Constraint: A case for a syntax-driven inflectional morphology. *Theoretical issues on the morphology-syntax interface*, ed. by Myriam Uribe-Etxebarria and Amaya Mendikoetxea, 1–33. Donostia: Gipuzkoako Foru Aldundia/EHU.

Albright, Adam. 2006. Lexical and morphological conditioning of paradigm gaps. Ms., MIT.

Anagnostopoulou, Elena. 2003. *The syntax of ditransitives: Evidence from clitics*. The Hague: Mouton de Gruyter.

Aricl, Mira. 1990. *Accessing NP Antecedents*. London: Routledge.

Auger, Julie. 1994. Pronominal clitics in Québec colloquial French: A morphological analysis. Doctoral dissertation, University of Pennsylvania.

Baerman, Matthew and Greville G. Corbett. This volume. Defectiveness: typology and diachrony, 1–18.

Bayer, Josef, Markus Bader and Michael Meng. 2001. Morphological underspecification meets oblique case: Syntactic and processing effects in German. *Lingua* 111. 465–514.

Béjar, Susana, and Milan Rezac. 2003. Person licensing and the derivation of PCC effects. *Romance Linguistics: Theory and acquisition*, ed. by Ana Teresa Pérez-Leroux and Yves Roberge, 49–62. Amsterdam: John Benjamins.

Benincà, Paola and Cecilia Poletto. 2005. On some descriptive generalizations in Romance. In *The Oxford handbook of comparative syntax*, ed. by Guglielmo Cinque and Richard Kayne, 221–58. Oxford: Oxford University Press.

Bianchi, Valentina. 2006. On the syntax of person arguments. *Lingua* 116. 2023–67.

Bissel, Clifford H. 1944. *Faire, laisser, voir* and *entendre* with a dependent infinitive. *The Modern Language Journal* 28. 325–37.

Blanche-Benveniste, Claire. 1975. *Recherches en vue d'une théorie de la grammaire française: Essai d'application à la syntaxe des pronoms*. Paris: Champion.

Bonami, Olivier and Gilles Boyé. 2006. French pronominal clitics and the design of Paradigm Function Morphology. *On-line Proceedings of the Fifth Mediterranean Morphology Meeting*. University of Bologna. Available at <http://mmm.lingue.unibo.it/>

Bošković, Željko. 2002. On multiple *wh*-fronting. *Linguistic Inquiry* 33. 351–83.

Bonet, Eulàlia. 1991. Morphology after syntax: Pronominal clitics in Romance. Doctoral dissertation, MIT.

Bonet, Eulàlia. 1993. Third person pronominal clitics in dialects of Catalan. *Catalan Working Papers in Linguistics* 3. 85–111.

Bonet, Eulàlia. 1995. Feature structure of Romance clitics. *Natural Language and Linguistic Theory* 13.607–47.

Bouvier, Yves-Fernard. 2001. Some audible effects of a silent operator. *Snippets* 4.

Bresnan, Joan. 1998. Morphology competes with syntax: Explaining typological variation in weak cross-over effects. *Is the best good enough? Optimality and competition in syntax*, ed. by Pilar Barbosa, Danny Fox, Paul Hagstrom, Martha McGinnis and David Pesetsky, 59–92. Cambridge, Mass.: MIT Press.

Bresnan, Joan. 2001. Explaining morphosyntactic competition. *Handbook of contemporary syntactic theory*, ed. by Mark Baltin and Chris Collins, 1–44. Oxford: Blackwell.

Bürgi, Anne. 1998. Le pronom *ça* en français vaudois: description et analyse. MA thesis, Université de Sherbrooke.

Cardinaletti, Anna and Giuliana Giusti. 2005. The syntax of quantified phrases and quantitative clitics. *The Blackwell companion to syntax*, ed. by Martin Everaert and Henk van Riemsdijk, vol. V, case 71. Oxford: Blackwell.

Couquaux, Daniel. 1975. Une règle de réanalyse en français. *Recherches linguistiques de Vincennes* 4. 32–72.

de Kok, Ans. 1985. *La place du pronom personnel régime conjoint en français: une étude diachronique*. Amsterdam: Rodopi.

Delfitto, Denis. 2002. On the semantics of pronominal clitics and some of its consequences. *Catalan Journal of Linguistics* 1. 29–57.

Di Sciullo, Anna-Maria. 2000. Parsing asymmetries. *Natural Language Processing— NLP 2000, Lecture Notes in Artificial Intelligence 1835*, ed. by Dimitris N. Christodoulakis, 1–15. Springer.

Dobrovie-Sorin, Carmen. 2005. The *se*-anaphor and its role in argument realization. *The Blackwell companion to syntax*, ed. by Martin Everaert and Henk van Riemsdijk, vol. IV, case 56. Oxford: Blackwell.

Embick, David. 2000. Features, syntax, and categories in the Latin perfect. *Linguistic Inquiry* 31. 185–230.

Embick, David and Alec Marantz. 2008. Architecture and blocking. *Linguistic Inquiry* 39. 1–53.

Fellbaum, Christiane and Anne Zribi-Hertz. 1989. *The middle construction in French and English: A comparative study of its syntax and semantics*. Bloomington, Ind.: Indiana University Linguistics Club.

Fernández-Ordóñez, Inés. 1999. Leísmo, laísmo y loísmo. *Gramática descriptiva de la lengua española*, ed. Ignacio Bosque and Violeta Demonte, 1317–97. Madrid: Espasa Calpe.

Fodor, Janet Dean and Atsu Inoue. 1994. The diagnosis and cure of garden paths. *Journal of Psycholinguistic Research* 23. 407–34.

Green, Georgia M. 1971. Unspeakable sentences: Book 2. *Linguistic Inquiry* 2. 601–2.

Grevisse, Maurice and André Goosse. 1993. *Le bon usage*: 14th edition, Grammaire française. Bruxelles: De Boeck & Larcier.

Grimshaw, Jane. 1997. The best clitic: Constraint conflict in morphosyntax. *Elements of Grammar*, ed. by Liliane Haegeman, 169–96. Dordrecht: Kluwer.

Guiraud, Pierre. 1969. *Le français populaire*. Paris: Presses Universitaires de France.

Halle, Morris and Alec Marantz. 1993. Distributed morphology and the pieces of inflection. *The view from building 20*, ed. by Kenneth Hale and Jay Keyser, 111–76. Cambridge, Mass.: MIT Press.

Heger, M. Klaus. 1966. La conjugaison objective en français et en espagnol. *Persée* 1. 19–38.

Heggie, Lorie and Francisco Ordóñez. 2005. Clitic ordering phenomena: The path to generalizations. In *Clitic and Affix Combinations: Theoretical perspectives,* ed. by L. Heggie and F. Ordóñez, 1–29. Amsterdam: John Benjamins.

Herslund, Michael. 1988. *Le datif en français*. Louvain-Paris: Peeters.
Jones, Michael. *Foundations of French syntax*. Cambridge, Cambridge University Press.
Jouitteau, Mélanie and Milan Rezac. 2008. The French ethical dative: Thirteen syntactic tests. *Bucharest Working Papers in Linguistics* 9. 97–108.
Kayne, Richard. 1975. *French syntax*. Cambridge, Mass.: MIT Press.
Kayne, Richard. 2000. *Parameters and universals*. Oxford University Press.
Kayne, Richard. 2008. Expletives, datives, and the tension between morphology and syntax. *The limits of syntactic variation*, ed. Theresa Biberauer, 175–217. Amsterdam: John Benjamins.
Lambrecht, Knud. 1981. *Topic, antitopic, and verb agreement in non-standard French*. Amsterdam: John Benjamins.
Leclère, Christian. 1976. Datifs syntaxiques et datifs éthiques. *Méthodes en grammaire française*, ed. by Jean-Claude Chevalier and Maurice Gross, 73–96. Paris: Klincksieck.
Lepschy, Anna Laura and Giulio C. Lepschy. 1988. *The Italian language today*. New York: Hutchinson.
Littré, Émile. 1872–7. *Dictionnaire de la langue française* (2nd ed). Hachette. Available at <http://francois.gannaz.free.fr/Littre>
Manzini, Rita and Leonardo M. Savoia. 2002. Clitics: Lexicalization patterns of so-called 3rd person datives. *Catalan Journal of Linguistics* 1. 117–55.
McA'nulty, Judith. 1971. La co-occurrence des clitiques en français. *Cahiers de linguistique de l'université du Québec* 1. 43–69.
McCarthy, John J. 1982. Prosodic structure and expletive infixation. *Language* 58. 574–90.
Mendikoetxea, Amaya. 1992. On the syntax of constructions with ARB SE in Spanish. *Anuario del Seminario de Filología Vasca "Julio de Urquijo"* 24(1). 307–26.
Menn, Lise and Brian MacWhinney. 1984. The repeated morph constraint: Toward an explanation. *Language* 60. 519–41.
Miller, Philip H. 1992. *Clitics and constituents in phrase structure grammar*. New York: Garland.
Miller, Philip H. and Paola Monachesi. 2003. Les pronoms clitiques dans les langues romanes. In *Les langues romanes: Problèmes de la phrase simple*, ed. Danièle Godard, 67–123. Paris: CNRS Editions.
Miller, Philip H. and Ivan A. Sag. 1997. French clitic movement without clitics or movement. *Natural Language and Linguistic Theory* 15. 573–639.
Miller, Philip H., Geoffrey K. Pullum and Arnold M. Zwicky. 1998. The principle of phonology-free syntax: Four apparent counter-examples in French. *Journal of Linguistics* 33. 67–90.
Molard, Etienne. 1803. *Dictionnaire grammatical du mauvais langage, où recueil des expressions et des phrases vicieuses usitées en France, et notamment à Lyon*. Lyon: C. F. Barret.
Morin, Yves-Charles. 1978. Interprétation des pronoms et des réfléchis en français. In *Cahiers de linguistique* 8. 337–76.
Morin, Yves-Charles. 1979a. La morphophonologie des pronoms clitiques en français populaire. *Cahiers de linguistique* 9. 1–36.
Morin, Yves-Charles. 1979b. More remarks on French clitic order. *Linguistic Analysis* 5. 293–312.

Morin, Yves-Charles. 1981. Some myths about pronominal clitics in French. *Linguistic Analysis* 8(2). 95–109.
Morin, Yves-Charles. 1984. De quelques lacunes dans la distribution réfléchis/ réciproques. *Le français moderne* 52. 61–5.
Neeleman, Ad and Hans van de Koot. 2005. Syntactic haplology. *The Blackwell companion to syntax*, ed. by Martin Everaert and Henk van Riemsdijk, vol. 4, case 69. Oxford: Blackwell.
Nevins, Andrew. 2007. The representation of third person and its consequences for person-case effects. *Natural Language and Linguistic Theory* 25. 273–313.
Nicol, Fabrice. 2005. Strong and weak person restrictions: A feature checking analysis. In *Clitic and affix combinations*, ed. by Lorie Heggie and Francisco Ordóñez, 141–97. Amsterdam: John Benjamins.
Noyer, Rolf R. 1992. Features, positions, and affixes in autonomous morphological structure. Doctoral dissertation, MIT.
Ormazabal, Javier, and Juan Romero. 1998. On the syntactic nature of the *me-lui* and the Person-Case Constraint. *Anuario del Seminario Julio de Urquijo* 32. 415–34.
Ormazabal, Javier, and Juan Romero. 2002. Object agreement restrictions. Ms., University of the Basque Country/LEHIA and University of Alcalá/U. Autónoma de Madrid.
Perlmutter, David. 1971. *Deep and surface constraints in syntax*. New York: Rinehart & Winston Inc.
Pescarini, Diego. 2005. Clitic clusters and morphological repairs: Evidence from Italian, Spanish and Barceloní. *Studi linguistici e filologici on line* 2.2.
Pescarini, Diego. 2007. Elsewhere in Romance: Counter-levelling, syncretism, and clitic clusters. Ms.
Piat, Louis. 1911. *Grammaire générale populaire des dialectes occitaniens: Essai de syntaxe*. Montpellier: Imprimerie générale du Midi.
Poser, William J. 1992. Blocking of phrasal constructions by lexical items. *Lexical matters*, ed. by Ivan Sag and Anna Szabolcsi, 111–30. Stanford, CA: CSLI.
Posner, Rebecca. 1997. *Linguistic change in French*. Oxford: Clarendon Press.
Postal, Paul M. 1981. A failed analysis of the French cohesive infinitive construction. *Linguistic Analysis* 8. 281–323.
Postal, Paul M. 1983. On characterizing French grammatical structure. *Linguistic Analysis* 11. 361–417.
Postal, Paul M. 1984. French indirect object cliticisation and SSC/BT. *Linguistic Analysis* 14. 111–72.
Postal, Paul M. 1989. *Masked inversion in French*. Chicago: University of Chicago Press.
Postal, Paul M. 1990. French indirect object demotion. *Studies in Relational Grammar 3*, ed. by Paul M. Postal and Brian D. Joseph, 104–200. Chicago: University of Chicago Press.
Pullum, Geoffrey K. and Arnold M. Zwicky. 1988. The syntax-phonology interface. *Linguistics: The Cambridge survey*, ed. by Frederick J. Newmeyer, I: 255–80. Cambridge: Cambridge University Press.
Remacle, Louis. 1952. *Syntaxe du parler wallon de La Gleize*, vol. 1, *Noms et articles— Adjectifs et pronoms*. Paris: Les Belles Lettres.

Rezac, Milan. 2008. The syntax of eccentric agreement: The Person Case Constraint and Absolutive Displacement in Basque. *Natural Language and Linguistic Theory* 26. 61–106.

Rezac, Milan. 2009. Modular architecture and uninterpretable phi-features. Ms. Available at <lingbuzz/00845>

Rivas, Alberto. 1977. Clitics in Spanish. Doctoral dissertation, MIT.

Roetgiest, Eugeen. 1987. L'ordre des clitiques objets en français moderne. *Travaux de linguistique* 14/15. 145–58.

Rohlfs, Gerhard. 1935. *Le gascon: Études de philologie Pyrénéenne*. Halle: Max Niemeyer.

Ronjat, Jules. 1937. *Grammaire istorique des parlers provençaux modernes*, vol. 3. Montpellier. Société des Langues Romanes.

Rooryck, Johan. 1988. Formal aspects of French nonlexical datives. *Folia Linguistica* 22. 373–86.

Rouveret, Alain and Jean-Roger Vergnaud. 1980. Specifying reference to the subject: French causatives and conditions on representations. *Linguistic Inquiry* 11. 97–202.

Rowlett, Paul. 2007. *The syntax of French*. Cambridge: Cambridge University Press.

Solà, Jaume. 2002. Clitic climbing and null subject languages. *Catalan Journal of Linguistics* 1. 225–55.

Sportiche, Dominique. 1996. Clitic structures. In *Phrase Structure and the Lexicon*, ed. by Johan Rooryck and Lauri Zaring, 213–76. Dordrecht: Kluwer.

Svenson, Lars-Owe. 1959. *Les parlers du Marais Vendéen*, vol. I. Göteborg: Elanders Boktryckeri Aktiebolag.

Tasmowski, Liliane. 1985. Faire Infinitif. *Les constructions de la phrase française. Invitation à la réflexion sur le passif, le pronominal, l'impersonnel et le causatif*, ed. by Ludo Melis, Liliane Tasmowski, Paul Verluyten and Dominique Willems, 223–365. Gent: Communication and Cognition.

Trommer, Jochen. 2002. Modularity in OT-Morphosyntax. *Resolving conflicts in grammar: Optimality Theory in syntax, morphology and phonology*, ed. by Gilbert Fanselow and Carol Féry, *Linguistische Berichte Sonderheft* 11. 49–82.

Tseng, Jesse. 2005. Prepositions and complement selection. In *Proceedings of the 2nd ACL-SIGSEM Workshop on the linguistic dimensions of prepositions and their use in computational linguistics formalisms and applications*, ed. by A. Villavicencio and V. Kordoni. 11–19. Essex: University of Essex.

Walter, Mary Ann. 2007. Repetition avoidance in human language. Doctoral dissertation, MIT.

Zink, Gaston. 1997. *Morphosyntaxe du pronom personnel (non réfléchi) en moyen français (XIVe–XVe siècles)*. Paris: Librairie Droz.

Zwicky, Arnold M. 1992. Some choices in the theory of morphology. *Formal grammar: Theory and implementation*, ed. by Robert D. Levine, 327–71. Oxford: Oxford University Press.

Zwicky, Arnold M. 1995. Exceptional degree markers: A puzzle in internal and external syntax. *Ohio State University Working Papers in Linguistics* 47. 111–23.

Zwicky, Arnold M. 1996. Syntax and phonology. *Concise Encyclopedia of Syntactic Theories*, ed. by Keith Brown and Jim Miller, 300–5. Oxford: Elsevier Science.

10

Interactions Between Defectiveness and Syncretism

GREGORY STUMP

1. Introduction

A THEORY OF INFLECTION DEFINES THE PRINCIPLES by which language users infer the form and meaning of the words realizing a language's lexemes. The phenomenon of defectiveness poses an important challenge for any such theory: that of accounting for the non-existence of certain words whose form and meaning would seem to be predicted by a language's inflectional morphology. One way to address this challenge would be to pursue the hypothesis that all instances of defectiveness actually involve words whose existence is excluded by independently motivated principles; this is, in effect, the hypothesis that there is no true defectiveness.

Certainly there are apparent instances of defectiveness that can be dismissed by reference to independent principles. For instance, the French verb *falloir* 'be necessary' lacks first and second person as well as plural forms because its sole argument is invariably a propositional complement and its subject is therefore invariably the third-person singular masculine expletive pronoun *il*; similarly, the fact that the verb *traire* 'milk' lacks simple past indicative and imperfect subjunctive forms might be explained by claiming that this verb lacks the special stem on which these two tense/mood combinations are built (compare the verb *faire* 'do', whose simple past indicative and imperfect subjunctive forms are built on the special stem *fi-*, which lacks any counterpart in the paradigm of *traire*; see Boyé and Hofherr (this volume) for relevant discussion).

But although some instances of defectiveness can be reduced to independent phenomena, it is clear that not all can: that is, at least some patterns of defectiveness must be directly specified by rules in a language's morphology, as Baerman and Corbett (2006) have observed. An important kind of evidence in favour of this conclusion is the fact that patterns of defectiveness may interact with a language's patterns of syncretism in more than one way;

my claim here is that these alternative interactions afford an important insight into the ways in which irreducible patterns of defectiveness may be specified.

In §2, I discuss the various possible interactions between defectiveness and syncretism. In §3, I show that each of these varied sorts of interaction is attested in early Indic declensional morphology. In §4, I propose a formal account of these various interactions in a realizational theory of morphology.[1]

2. Interactions of Defectiveness with Syncretism

In instances of syncretism, distinct cells in a lexeme's paradigm have the same inflectional realization. Consider, for instance, the hypothetical paradigm in Table 1; here, A, B, C, D and E represent distinct morphosyntactic properties, so that the six cells in this paradigm realize the six morphosyntactic property sets {A, D}, {B, D}, {C, D}, {A, E}, {B, E}, and {C, E}. This paradigm exhibits syncretism because the property sets {A, D} and {B, E} are identically realized as v. In such a paradigm, I shall refer to a set of cells that are identical in their realization as a DOMAIN OF SYNCRETISM.

In instances of defectiveness, certain morphosyntactic property sets are left unrealized in a paradigm in which they are nevertheless available for realization. For instance, the hypothetical paradigm in Table 2 is defective because three of the morphosyntactic property sets available for realization—those containing the property E—go unrealized. In such a paradigm, I shall refer to the set of cells that are unrealized as a DOMAIN OF DEFECTIVENESS.

Table 1. A hypothetical pattern of syncretism

	A	B	C
D	v	w	x
E	y	v	z

Domain of syncretism: {A, D}, {B, E}

Table 2. A hypothetical pattern of defectiveness

	A	B	C
D	v	w	x
E	—	—	—

Domain of defectiveness: {A, E}, {B, E}, {C, E}

In some paradigms, defectiveness and syncretism compete with one another, in the sense that the same cell is a candidate both for defectiveness and for syncretic realization. In such instances, there are various possible

---

[1] I thank the participants at the British Academy's defectiveness conference, and particularly the editors of this volume, for their helpful comments. In addition, I thank Steven Collins, Margaret Cone, James Gair and Ole Pind for helpful insights on the Pāli anaphoric enclitic pronoun NA, whose properties I investigated as part of this research but do not discuss in detail here.

interactions between defectiveness and syncretism. I regard three such interactions as canonical, in the sense that they obviously contrast with one another and can serve as a simple point of reference for the analysis of more complex interactions.[2] These three canonical interactions are described in (1) and are represented schematically in Table 3.

(1) Three canonical interactions between defectiveness and syncretism

   a. Where P_1, P_2 are paradigms belonging to the same inflection class: DEFECTIVENESS OVERRIDES SYNCRETISM in P_2 if two cells belonging to a domain of syncretism in P_1 correspond to two cells in P_2 one of which is defective (where cell C_1 in P_1 corresponds to cell C_2 in P_2 if and only if C_1 and C_2 realize the same morphosyntactic property set). Thus, suppose that P_1 and P_2 are the respective paradigms in Tables 1 and 3(a): in that case, cell {B, E} belongs to a domain of syncretism in P_1, but the corresponding cell in P_2 belongs to a domain of defectiveness; defectiveness therefore overrides syncretism in P_2.

   b. SYNCRETISM OVERRIDES DEFECTIVENESS in a paradigm P if P contains a morphosyntactically coherent set S of cells having two complementary subsets S_1, S_2 such that (i) the cells in S_1 are defective and (ii) there is a domain of syncretism to which all of the cells in S_2 belong. Thus, in Table 3(b), the set of cells associated with property E (i.e. the morphosyntactically coherent set {{A, E}, {B, E}, {C, E}} has the two complementary subsets {{A, E}, {C, E}} and {{B, E}}, the first of which contains defective cells and the second of which contains a cell belonging to a domain of syncretism. Syncretism therefore overrides defectiveness in the paradigm represented in Table 3(b).

   c. Where P_1, P_2 are paradigms belonging to the same inflection class: SYNCRETISM DETERMINES A DOMAIN OF DEFECTIVENSS in P_2 if the cells constituting a domain of defectiveness in P_2 correspond to the cells constituting a domain of syncretism in P_1. Thus, suppose that P_1 and P_2 are the respective paradigms in Tables 1 and 3(c): in that case, just as cells {A, D} and {B, E} constitute a domain of syncretism in P_1, the corresponding cells likewise constitute a domain of defectiveness in P_2. Syncretism therefore determines a domain of defectiveness in P_2.

Table 3. Three canonical interactions between defectiveness and syncretism

(a) Defectiveness overrides syncretism				(b) Syncretism overrides defectiveness				(c) Syncretism determines a domain of defectiveness			
	A	B	C		A	B	C		A	B	C
D	v ↖	w	x	D	v ↖	w	x	D	↖	w	x
E		↘		E		↘ v		E	y	↘	z

---

[2] See Corbett 2005 for discussion of the canonical approach in linguistic typology.

Complex combinations of these canonical interactions are of course possible; for instance, a pattern of syncretism might override a pattern of defectiveness which itself overrides another pattern of syncretism. There are also other, less canonical interactions—for instance, one in which a morphosyntactically coherent set of cells that is otherwise defective has two realized cells, only one of which is syncretic.

In §3, I show that early Indic declensional morphology presents examples of the three canonical interactions in Table 3 as well as more complex interactions. In §4, I argue that the way in which defectiveness interacts with syncretism depends straightforwardly upon the way in which it is defined; I develop this idea in the context of the formal theory of inflection discussed by Stump (2002, 2006) and Stewart and Stump (2007).

3. Interactions Between Defectiveness and Syncretism in Early Indic Declensional Paradigms

In this discussion, I draw upon evidence from several stages of early Indic: from Vedic, the earliest form of attested Sanskrit (§3.1); from post-Vedic Sanskrit (§3.2); from Classical Sanskrit (§3.3); and from the Prākrits (§3.4).

3.1. The pronoun ENA in Vedic: defectiveness overrides and is overridden by syncretism

Consider first the inflection of the third person anaphoric clitic pronoun ENA in Vedic, in which defectiveness overrides and is overridden by syncretism.

In Vedic, several pronouns participate in a pattern of inflection for case, number and gender which I shall here call the DEFAULT PRONOMINAL DECLENSION. The formal peculiarities of this declension are exemplified by the paradigm of the relative pronoun YA in Table 4.

As this table shows, YA inflects for seven cases, three numbers and three genders.[3] The resulting paradigm embodies nine patterns of syncretism. These patterns vary in their breadth in the Sanskrit declensional system. Some are patterns exhibited by all declensional paradigms:

  (i) each nominative dual form is identical to the accusative dual form for the same gender;

---

[3] Sanskrit has an eighth, vocative case, irrelevant here because members of the default pronominal declension never occur in the vocative case.

Table 4. Forms of the relative pronoun YA in Vedic (Whitney 1889: §509; Macdonell 1910: §398)

	Singular			Dual			Plural		
	Masc.	Neut.	Fem.	Masc.	Neut.	Fem.	Masc.	Neut.	Fem.
nominative	yás	yát	yā́	yáu[a]	yé		yé	yā́ni[a]	yā́s
accusative	yám		yā́m				yā́n		
instrumental	yénā[b]		yáyā	yā́bhyām			yébhis, yáis		yā́bhis
dative	yásmai		yásyai				yébhyas		yā́bhyas
ablative	yásmāt		yásyās	yós, yáyos					
genitive	yásya						yéṣām		yā́sām
locative	yásmin		yásyām				yéṣu		yā́su

a. sometimes yā́   b. sometimes yénā

(ii) the instrumental, dative, and ablative of all three genders are alike in the dual; and
(iii) the genitive and locative of all three genders are alike in the dual.

One is exhibited by all non-pronominal declensional paradigms, in addition to that of YA:

(iv) each dative plural form is identical to the ablative plural form for the same gender.

One is exhibited by all feminine declensional paradigms:

(v) the feminine ablative singular form is identical to the feminine genitive singular form.

One is exhibited by all neuter declensional paradigms:

(vi) in each number, the neuter nominative form is identical to the neuter accusative form.

The remainder are restricted to a subset of the declension classes exhibiting the relevant morphosyntactic contrasts:

(vii) in both the singular and the plural, each oblique masculine form is identical to the neuter form for the same case;
(viii) neuter and feminine direct-case forms are alike in the dual; and
(ix) the feminine nominative plural form is identical to the feminine accusative plural form.

Among the third person pronouns in Vedic is the highly defective pronoun ENA, whose forms are unaccented (hence clitic) and whose interpretation is invariably anaphoric, never deictic. Its inventory of forms is given in Table 5.

Table 5. Forms of the pronoun ENA 'he/she/it' in Vedic (Whitney 1889: §500; Macdonell 1910: §395)

	Singular			Dual			Plural		
	Masc.	Neut.	Fem.	Masc.	Neut.	Fem.	Masc.	Neut.	Fem.
nominative		Ⓢ		Ⓢ	Ⓢ			Ⓢ	Ⓢ
accusative	enam	enat	enām	enau	ene		enān	enāni	enās
instrumental	enena		enayā						
dative								
ablative								
genitive				enos, enayos					
locative								

Ⓢ: Syncretism with the cell immediately below is overridden

The defectiveness of this paradigm is not the effect of any independent principle. First, one cannot plausibly say that ENA lacks certain forms because it lacks the stem on which those forms are based. All of the forms in Table 5 conform to the default pronominal declension exemplified by the relative pronoun in Table 4, and paradigms conforming to this declension are in general built on a single stem in *a* (e.g. *ya-*); thus, the forms missing from Table 5 would all presumably arise from the same stem *ena-* as the forms present in Table 5. For this reason, the defectiveness of Vedic ENA cannot be likened to that of French TRAIRE 'milk' (§1).

Second, there is no independent syntactic or semantic reason why the shaded cells in Table 5 should go unrealized. Consider first the absence of nominative forms from Table 5. It has been suggested to me that this is a principled consequence of ENA's clitic status, perhaps in conjunction with the fact that Vedic is a pro-drop language. But one cannot in fact say that clitic pronouns always lack nominative forms in Vedic: for instance, the clitic pronoun TVA 'one, many a one' has nominative forms (Macdonell 1910: §396), as does ENA itself in post-Vedic Sanskrit (see §3.2 below).

Consider now the absence of oblique forms other than the instrumental singular and the genitive/locative dual in Table 5. It would be very difficult to contend that the incidence of these forms is excluded by some independent syntactic or semantic principle, particularly in view of the fact that synonymous forms are not excluded from the paradigm of the demonstrative pronoun IDAM 'this'. This latter pronoun can be used deictically or anaphorically, and as Table 6 shows, its paradigm is built upon two pronominal stems: *i-* (in direct-case forms other than the masculine nominative singular) and *a-* (in all remaining forms, some of which involve regular sandhi modifications of *a* to *e* or *ā*); the forms based on *a-* are enclosed within dark borders in Table 6. The oblique forms, all based on *a-*, have unaccented (clitic) counterparts whose interpretation (like that of ENA) is invariably anaphoric: in view of the fact that these clitics are prosodically, syntactically, and semantically like the forms of ENA, it is unclear how one could attribute the gaps in the oblique cells of ENA's paradigm to a syntactic or semantic principle without wrongly predicting gaps in the corresponding parts of IDAM's inventory of clitic forms.

Table 6. Paradigm of Vedic IDAM 'this' (Whitney 1889: §§501f; Macdonell 1910: §393)

	Singular			Dual			Plural		
	Masc.	Neut.	Fem.	Masc.	Neut.	Fem.	Masc.	Neut.	Fem.
nominative	ayám	idám	iyám	imā́, imáu	imé		iámé	imā́ni	imā́s
accusative	imám	idám	imā́m	:::	:::	:::	iámā́n	:::	:::
instrumental	enā́		ayā́	ābhyā́m			ebhís		ābhís
dative	asmái		asyái	:::	:::	:::	ebhyás		ābhyás
ablative	asmā́t		asyā́s	:::	:::	:::	:::	:::	:::
genitive	asyá		asyā́s	ayós			eṣā́m		āsā́m
locative	asmín		asyā́m	:::	:::	:::	eṣú		āsú

Given that the paradigm of ENA and the clitic inventory of IDAM each supply forms that the other lacks, one might try to argue that the forms of ENA are nothing other than suppletive members of IDAM's clitic inventory. But in Vedic, the paradigm of ENA and IDAM's clitic inventory are not merely complementary (Whitney 1889: §§501f; Macdonell 1910: §393). For example, *enā* (IDAM's masculine/neuter instrumental singular clitic) and *enena* (ENA's masculine/neuter instrumental singular form) clearly contrast, as the examples in (2) (both from the *Taittirīya Brāhmaṇa*) show.

(2) a. etáṃ   te   stómam   tuvijāta   vípraḥ
       this: thee: hymn: of.powerful.nature: singer:
       MASC.ACC.SG DAT.SG MASC.ACC.SG MASC.VOC.SG   MASC.NOM.SG

       rátham   ná   dhī́raḥ   svápā   atakṣam;
       chariot: not,   skilful: craftsman: fashion:
       MASC.ACC.SG   i.e. 'as it were' MASC.NOM.SG MASC.NOM.SG   1SG.IMPRF.ACT

   O you of powerful nature, I, a singer, have made for you this hymn, as a skilful craftsman (makes) a chariot;

   yádī́d   agne   práti   tvám   deva   háryāḥ
   if.indeed   Agni: thou: god: accept.gladly:
               MASC.VOC.SG PREVERB   NOM.SG   MASC.NOM.SG 2SG.PRS.SBJV.ACT

   súvarvatīr   apá   enā   jayema.
   celestial: waters: it [=the hymn]: win, obtain:
   FEM.ACC.PL   FEM.ACC.PL MASC.INS.SG   1PL.PRS.OPT.ACT

   if indeed, O god Agni, you accept (it) gladly, may we obtain by it the celestial waters.

   (Taittirīya Brāhmaṇa 2.4.7.66–7)

b. bháradvāja   yát   te   caturthám   āyur   dadyém
   Bharadvāja: if   thee: fourth: life: give:
   MASC.VOC.SG   DAT.SG   NEUT.ACC.SG   NEUT.ACC.SG   1SG.PRS.OPT.ACT

   kím   enena   kuryā́?
   what: it [= the life]   do:
   NEUT.ACC.SG   NEUT.INS.SG   2SG.PRS.OPT.ACT

O Bharadvāja, if I gave you a fourth life, what would you do with it?
(Taittirīya Brāhmaṇa 3.10.11.45)

Moreover, ENA is, in very rare cases, accented, in which case it contrasts with an accented form of IDAM; in the Vedic verse in (3), for instance, the feminine accusative singular form of ENA appears with accent (and in pada-initial position, from which clitics are excluded); here it contrasts with IDAM's feminine accusative singular form *imā́m*, which would have been metrically admissible in the same position. One therefore cannot maintain that the forms in Tables 5 and 6 all actually realize a single lexeme. (This situation changes, however, in post-Vedic Sanskrit, as I show in §3.2.)

(3) imā́s   ta   indra   pŕ́śnayo   ghr̥tám
    these: thee: Indra: spotted: ghee:
    FEM.NOM.PL   DAT.SG   MASC.VOC.SG   FEM.NOM.PL   NEUT.ACC.SG

    duhata   āśíram
    yield: milk.mixture:
    3PL.PRS.IND.MID   FEM.ACC.SG

    enā́m   r̥tásya   pipyúṣīḥ.
    this [= milk mixture]   sacred.custom: swollen:
    FEM.ACC.SG   NEUT.GEN.SG   PRF.ACT.PTCP, FEM.NOM.PL

To you, O Indra, these spotted cows, swollen, yield ghee (and) the milky mixture, this thing of sacred custom.
(R̥gveda 8.6.19)

In view of these facts, I conclude that in Vedic, ENA's paradigm is defective, and that its defectiveness is irreducible—that it cannot be plausibly attributed to any independent principle of morphology, syntax, or semantics. The Vedic paradigm of ENA therefore presents two canonical interactions between defectiveness and syncretism. The first of these is that of defectiveness overriding syncretism (as in (1a)): in the default pronominal declension, the nominative and the accusative are ordinarily syncretized in each of the five instances in (4) (as in Table 4); but in the paradigm of ENA, the domain of nominative defectiveness cuts across the domain of syncretism in all five of these instances.

(4) Nominative/accusative syncretism in the default pronominal declension in Vedic
    a. neut nom sg   =   neut acc sg
    b. masc nom du   =   masc acc du

c. neut/fem nom du = neut/fem acc du
d. neut nom pl = neut acc pl
e. fem nom pl = fem acc pl

The second of these canonical interactions is that of syncretism overriding defectiveness (as in (1b)): among all the genitive cells in Table 5, the only overt realizations are syncretic forms; similarly for the locative cells. I will consider the theoretical significance of these facts in §4.

3.2. A follow-up on the pronoun ENA in post-Vedic Sanskrit

Before considering an example of the third canonical interaction between defectiveness and syncretism, I must say a word or two about the subsequent development of the pronoun ENA in post-Vedic texts. In post-Vedic Sanskrit, the lexeme ENA exhibits a slightly wider range of syntactic uses: certain accusative forms in the paradigm of ENA begin exhibiting nominative uses as well, in accordance with the patterns of syncretism in (4) (Wackernagel and Debrunner 1930: 523f). In particular, the neuter accusative singular form *enat* also begins to be used in the nominative, as in (5) and (6).

(5) Brahmaṇe svāheti, tad enat prīṇāti.
 holy.power: = svāhā + iti thus it: please:
 NEUT.DAT.SG hail! DIRECT NEUT.ACC.SG 3SG.PRS.IND.ACT
  DISCOURSE MARKER

 'To the holy power hail' (he says); thus he delights it [= the holy power].

 tad enat prītam kṣatrād gopāyati.
 thus it: pleased: lordly.power: guard:
  NEUT.NOM.SG NEUT.NOM.SG NEUT.ABL.SG 3SG.PRS.IND.ACT

 Thus, delighted, it guards (him) from the lordly power.
  (Aitareya Brāhmaṇa 7.22.4; cf. Keith 1920: 74, 311)

(6) yā vai sā mūrtir ajāyata annam
 REL.PRON: indeed that: form: be.born: food:
 FEM.NOM.SG FEM.NOM.SG FEM.NOM.SG 3SG.IMPRF.MID NEUT.NOM.SG
 vai tat.
 indeed that:
  NEUT.NOM.SG

 The form that was born was indeed food.

 tad enat sṛṣṭam parāṅ-atyajigāṃsat.
 then it: created: directed.away-escape.DESID:
  NEUT.NOM.SG NEUT.NOM.SG 3SG.IMPRF.ACT

 It [= the food], when created, sought to go away
  (Aitareya Āraṇyaka 2.4.3; cf. Keith 1909: 229)

The masculine accusative dual form *enau* also takes on nominative uses, as in (7) and (8).

(7) athainau   dadhi-madhu samaśnuto
= atha + enau   sour.milk-honey: obtain:
 then they: MASC.NOM.DU NEUT.ACC.SG 3DU.PRS.IND.ACT

Then those two [bride and groom] obtain sour milk and honey

 yad   vā havis̩yam̐   syāt.
 REL.PRON: or fit.for.sacrifice: be:
 NEUT.NOM.SG   NEUT.NOM.SG 3SG.OPT.ACT

or whatever might be suitable for sacrifice.
            (Mānavagr̥hyasūtra 1.12.5; cf. Dresden 1941: 63)

(8) tasmād enau   prathamau śasyete   svargyau
  therefore they: first: recite: heavenly:
       MASC.NOM.DU MASC.NOM.DU 3DU.PRS.IND.PASS MASC.NOM.DU

Therefore these two are recited first as being heavenly.
            (Kauśītaki-Brāhman̩a 22.1.21; Keith 1920: 74, 467)

Thus, in post-Vedic Sanskrit, defectiveness no longer overrides nominative/accusative syncretism in the neuter singular and the masculine dual; that is, nominative defectiveness in the paradigm of ENA is overridden by two instances of nominative/accusative syncretism, as in Table 7.

Table 7. Forms of the pronoun ENA 'he/she/it' in post-Vedic Sanskrit

	Singular			Dual			Plural		
	Masc.	Neut.	Fem.	Masc.	Neut.	Fem.	Masc.	Neut.	Fem.
nominative	enam	enat	enām	enau	Ⓢ		Ⓢ	Ⓢ	Ⓢ
accusative					ene		enān	enāni	enās
instrumental	enena		enayā						
dative									
ablative									
genitive				enos, enayos					
locative									

Ⓢ: Syncretism with the cell immediately below is overridden

It is unclear, however, why this override of nominative defectiveness by nominative/accusative syncretism is limited to the two instances in (4a,b) (i.e. to the neuter singular and the masculine dual), and why it isn't extended to the remaining instances in (4c–e) (i.e. to the neuter/feminine dual, the neuter plural, and the feminine plural).

In addition to these post-Vedic changes in the paradigm of ENA, the demonstrative pronoun IDAM undergoes changes of its own (Burrow 1965:

276) which have the effect of integrating ENA's paradigm into its inventory of clitic forms. Recall that the forms in IDAM's paradigm are based on the pronominal stems *i-* and *a-*, and that it is the oblique forms based on *a-* that serve (unaccented) as IDAM's clitic forms. In post-Vedic Sanskrit, the paradigm of IDAM is slightly different; cf. Table 8. Three of the forms in this paradigm are based neither on *i-* nor on *a-*, but on the stem *ana-*: these are the instrumental singular forms *anéna* and *anáyā* and the genitive/locative dual form *anáyos*; these correspond to the Vedic forms *enā́*, *ayā́* and *ayós*. (Exceptionally, *anáyā* does show up twice in the *Ṛgveda*, but is the only form of *ana-* observable in the Saṃhitās; Macdonell 1916: 108.) Despite this difference in IDAM's post-Vedic paradigm, it is still the forms based on *a-* that determine the membership of IDAM's inventory of clitic forms; as a consequence, IDAM's post-Vedic clitic inventory has gaps in the instrumental singular and the genitive/locative dual. For this reason, every cell that is realized in the post-Vedic paradigm of ENA (Table 7) corresponds to a gap in IDAM's post-Vedic inventory of clitic forms, so that the paradigm of ENA can be integrated into this inventory as an instance of what Juge (1999) calls non-overlapping suppletion. This, indeed, is how Pāṇini portrays it (*Aṣṭādhyāyī* 2.4.34; cf. Katre 1987: 165).

Table 8. Paradigm of post-Vedic IDAM 'this' (Whitney 1889: §§501)

	Singular			Dual			Plural		
	Masc.	Neut.	Fem.	Masc.	Neut.	Fem.	Masc.	Neut.	Fem.
nominative	ayám	idám	iyám	imáu	imé		imé	imā́ni	imā́s
accusative	imám	idám	imā́m				imā́n		
instrumental	anéna		anáyā				ebhís		ābhís
dative	asmái		asyái	ābhyām			ebhyás		ābhyás
ablative	asmā́t		asyā́s						
genitive	asyá			anáyos			eṣā́m		āsā́m
locative	asmín		asyā́m				eṣú		āsú

3.3. Defective neuter an-stems in Classical Sanskrit: syncretism determines a domain of defectiveness

Consider now the inflection of the neuter noun YAKAN 'liver' in Classical Sanskrit. As the paradigm in Table 9 shows, this noun is defective, lacking nominative, vocative, and accusative forms in all three numbers. YAKAN is sometimes said to have a heteroclite paradigm, because traditionally, these gaps are filled by the corresponding forms of the synonymous noun YAKṚT; YAKṚT does, however, have a full paradigm of its own, as in Table 10. This sort of relationship, in which defectiveness is compensated for by borrowing from an independent paradigm, exists with a number of other neuter nouns belonging to the *an*-stem declension, including those in (9) (Whitney 1889: §432).

Table 9. The paradigm of the neuter noun YAKAN 'liver' in Classical Sanskrit

	singular	dual	plural
NOM			
VOC			
ACC			
INS	yaknā		yakabhis
DAT	yakne	yakabhyām	
ABL			yakabhyas
GEN	yaknas		yaknām
		yaknos	
LOC	yakni, yakani		yakasu

Table 10. The paradigm of the neuter noun YAKṚT 'liver' in Classical Sanskrit

	singular	dual	plural
NOM			
VOC	yakṛt	yakṛtī	yakṛnti
ACC			
INS	yakṛtā		yakṛdbhis
DAT	yakṛte	yakṛdbhyām	
ABL			yakṛdbhyas
GEN	yakṛtas		yakṛtām
		yakṛtos	
LOC	yakṛti		yakṛtsu

(9)   ASAN 'blood' (nominative, vocative, and accusative forms supplied by the full paradigm of ASṚJ)
     ŚAKAN 'ordure' (... by the full paradigm of ŚAKṚT)
     ĀSAN 'mouth' (... by the full paradigm of ĀSYA)
     UDAN 'water' (... by the full paradigm of UDAKA)
     DOṢAN 'forearm' (... by the full paradigm of DOS)
     YŪṢAN 'broth' (... by the full paradigm of YŪṢA)

There is no independent phonological, morphological, syntactic or semantic motivation for the absence of the direct-case forms from YAKAN's paradigm; that is, this is apparently an instance in which the morphology of the language must simply stipulate the absence of these forms.

The defectiveness in this example is sensitive to a regular pattern of syncretism in most neuter declensions: in this pattern, the nominative, the vocative, and the accusative are realized identically; this same pattern appears in the singular, the dual, and the plural. Thus, the domain of defectiveness in Table 9 subsumes nine cells that would ordinarily constitute the three domains of nominative/vocative/accusative syncretism exemplified in Table 11.[4] For this reason, the paradigm in Table 9 exemplifies the third canonical interaction of defectiveness with syncretism, in which syncretism determines a domain of defectiveness as in (1c).

---

[4] Note that the nominative, vocative, and accusative forms in the paradigm of NĀMAN are built on three different stems (the zero grade stem (prevocalically *nāmn*-, elsewhere *nāma*-), the normal grade stem *nāmān*-, and the lengthened grade stem *nāman*-), two of which appear in other cases as well. Thus, the defective cells in the paradigm of YAKAN cannot be attributed to the absence of a particular stem from its stem inventory.

Table 11. The paradigm of the neuter noun NĀMAN 'name' in Classical Sanskrit

	singular	dual	plural
NOM			
VOC	nāma[a]	nāmnī, nāmanī	nāmāni
ACC			
INS	nāmnā		nāmabhis
DAT	nāmne	nāmabhyām	
ABL			nāmabhyas
GEN	nāmnas		nāmnām
LOC	nāmni, nāmani	nāmnos	nāmasu

a. voc. sg. sometimes *nāman*

3.4. The pronoun ṆA in Prākrit: a complex interaction between defectiveness and syncretism

In Middle Indic, the pronoun ENA becomes more defective than ever: thus, in the Māhārāṣṭrī, Śaurasenī, and Māgadhī Prākrits, its use becomes restricted to a single accusative singular form *eṇaṃ* for all three genders (Pischel 1981: §431).

But alongside the pronoun EṆA, the Prākrits exhibit a distinct pronoun ṆA which, like EṆA, is enclitic in form and anaphoric in interpretation. Though defective, the paradigm of ṆA realizes a wider range of case/number/gender combinations than that of EṆA. In the twelfth century Prākrit grammar of Hemacandra, ṆA is assigned the paradigm of forms in Table 12. (Here and henceforth, cited Prākrit forms are from the Māhārāṣṭrī Prākrit.)

Table 12. Forms of the Prākrit pronoun ṆA 'he/she/it' according to Hemacandra III.70,77 (Pischel 1877–80, vol. 1: 87ff.; 1981: §431)

	singular			plural		
	Masculine	Neuter	Feminine	Masculine	Neuter	Feminine
NOM		Ⓢ		Ⓢ		
ACC	ṇaṃ			ṇe		
INS	ṇeṇa		ṇāe	ṇehiṃ		ṇāhiṃ
ABL						
DAT						
GEN						
LOC						

Ⓢ: Syncretism with the cell immediately below is overridden.

The nature of the relation between ENA and NA has been a matter of debate. On the one hand, Pischel (1900: §431) has suggested that NA derived from ENA by aphaeresis (i.e. loss of initial *e*-); similarly, Johansson (1907–8: 90ff.) argues that NA arose as a sandhi variant of ENA in postvocalic contexts in which the initial *e* of ENA's stem was either contracted or elided. By contrast, Torp (1881) and Smith (1953) have argued that NA is the reflex of an earlier pronominal stem **no-*, whose derivative **e-no-* persists as ENA in Sanskrit and as ENA in the Prākrits but whose basic form **no-* has no reflex in Sanskrit. (Compare the pronouns **to-/*e-to-* and their reflexes TA/ETA, attested in both Sanskrit and the Prākrits.) Finally, Scheller (1967: 22) proposes that NA is a Middle Indic innovation arising from the proportional analogy X: *eṇa-* = *ta-*: *eta-*.

I will not pursue this complex issue here; it is in any event clear that in the Prākrits, the pronouns NA and ENA are distinct lexemes, since their paradigms, though both defective, are defective to different degrees.

In the Prākrits, the default pronominal declension exhibits the patterns of nominative/accusative syncretism in (10). Like Vedic ENA, Prākrit NA lacks nominative forms; thus, in the paradigm in Table 12, defectiveness overrides the two patterns of syncretism in (10a,b). At the same time, Prākrit NA lacks accusative plural forms in the neuter and feminine genders. Thus, the two patterns of nominative/accusative syncretism in (10c,d) partially determine the domain of defectiveness within the paradigm of NA.[5]

(10) Nominative/accusative syncretism in the default pronominal declension in Prākrit

    a. neut nom sg   =   neut acc sg
    b. masc nom pl   =   masc acc pl
    c. neut nom pl   =   neut acc pl
    d. fem nom pl   =   fem acc pl

The early Indic facts presented here pose a challenge for morphological theory, namely that of representing the alternative ways in which defectiveness and syncretism may interact in a language. I now address this issue.

---

[5] The paradigm of NA in Table 12 also exhibits a pattern of masculine/neuter/feminine syncretism in the accusative singular. In Sanskrit, non-pronominal masculine and neuter *a*-stems inflect alike in the accusative singular, and the paradigm of NA reflects the spread of this pattern to some pronominal paradigms in Prākrit. The further identity of the feminine accusative singular form of NA with its masculine/neuter accusative singular form *ṇaṃ* is the effect of a moraic restriction on syllable structure that emerges in Middle Indic (Geiger 1994: 4). By virtue of this restriction, all nasal vowels become short; consequently, the Sanskrit distinction between *a*-stem masculines/neuters and *ā*-stem feminines is neutralized in the accusative singular (compare Sanskrit *dharmam* 'law', *kanyāṃ* 'girl' with Pāli *dhammaṃ, kaññaṃ*).

4. A Theoretical Conception of Interactions Between Defectiveness and Syncretism

In this section, I present an independently motivated theoretical framework in which interactions between defectiveness and syncretism can be insightfully represented. I present the details of this framework in §4.1–3. These include a systematic distinction between content paradigms and form paradigms (§4.1); formally defined notions of inflectional category instantiation, morphosyntactic property specification, and what I call the encompass relation (§4.2); and the crucial notions of paradigm function and paradigm linkage from Stump (2001, 2002, 2006) and Stewart and Stump (2007) (§4.3). In §4.4, I analyse the early Indic facts in the context of this framework.

4.1. Content paradigms and form paradigms

Following Stump (2002) and Stewart and Stump (2007), I assume that a language's inflectional morphology is defined by reference to two types of paradigm: content paradigms and form paradigms. A CONTENT PARADIGM is a set of pairs of the form ⟨L, σ⟩, where L is a lexeme and σ is a set of morphosyntactic properties with which L may be associated in syntactic structure. In particular, the content paradigm of a lexeme L is the set containing every pairing of L with a morphosyntactic property set with which it may be syntactically associated. Each such pairing is called a CONTENT CELL. A content paradigm expresses the range of syntactic uses to which a lexeme may be put.

A FORM PARADIGM is a set of pairs of the form ⟨R, σ⟩, where R is a lexeme's root form and σ is a set of morphosyntactic properties for which R may inflect. In particular, the form paradigm of a root R is the set containing every pairing of R with a morphosyntactic property set for which R may inflect. Each such pairing is called a FORM CELL. A form paradigm expresses the range of inflectional realizations to which a root may give rise.

One might expect that the content cells in the content paradigm of a lexeme L will stand in a one-to-one correspondence to the form cells in the form paradigm of L's root form. Very often, however, this is not the case. Consider, for instance, the relative pronoun lexeme YA in Vedic (Table 4). As a member of the default pronominal declension in Vedic, this lexeme can be syntactically associated with any combination of a gender (masculine, neuter, or feminine) with a non-vocative case (nominative, accusative, instrumental, dative, ablative, genitive, or locative) and a number (singular, dual, or plural). There are sixty-three such combinations; these are given in Table 13. Thus, the content paradigm of YA has sixty-three cells, each consisting of the pairing of YA with one of the morphosyntactic property sets in Table 13.

Table 13. The morphosyntactic property sets defining the content paradigm of a Vedic pronoun

{G:masc, C:nom, N:sg}	{G:neut, C:nom, N:sg}	{G:fem, C:nom, N:sg}
{G:masc, C:acc, N:sg}	{G:neut, C:acc, N:sg}	{G:fem, C:acc, N:sg}
{G:masc, C:ins, N:sg}	{G:neut, C:ins, N:sg}	{G:fem, C:ins, N:sg}
{G:masc, C:dat, N:sg}	{G:neut, C:dat, N:sg}	{G:fem, C:dat, N:sg}
{G:masc, C:abl, N:sg}	{G:neut, C:abl, N:sg}	{G:fem, C:abl, N:sg}
{G:masc, C:gen, N:sg}	{G:neut, C:gen, N:sg}	{G:fem, C:gen, N:sg}
{G:masc, C:loc, N:sg}	{G:neut, C:loc, N:sg}	{G:fem, C:loc, N:sg}
{G:masc, C:nom, N:du}	{G:neut, C:nom, N:du}	{G:fem, C:nom, N:du}
{G:masc, C:acc, N:du}	{G:neut, C:acc, N:du}	{G:fem, C:acc, N:du}
{G:masc, C:ins, N:du}	{G:neut, C:ins, N:du}	{G:fem, C:ins, N:du}
{G:masc, C:dat, N:du}	{G:neut, C:dat, N:du}	{G:fem, C:dat, N:du}
{G:masc, C:abl, N:du}	{G:neut, C:abl, N:du}	{G:fem, C:abl, N:du}
{G:masc, C:gen, N:du}	{G:neut, C:gen, N:du}	{G:fem, C:gen, N:du}
{G:masc, C:loc, N:du}	{G:neut, C:loc, N:du}	{G:fem, C:loc, N:du}
{G:masc, C:nom, N:pl}	{G:neut, C:nom, N:pl}	{G:fem, C:nom, N:pl}
{G:masc, C:acc, N:pl}	{G:neut, C:acc, N:pl}	{G:fem, C:acc, N:pl}
{G:masc, C:ins, N:pl}	{G:neut, C:ins, N:pl}	{G:fem, C:ins, N:pl}
{G:masc, C:dat, N:pl}	{G:neut, C:dat, N:pl}	{G:fem, C:dat, N:pl}
{G:masc, C:abl, N:pl}	{G:neut, C:abl, N:pl}	{G:fem, C:abl, N:pl}
{G:masc, C:gen, N:pl}	{G:neut, C:gen, N:pl}	{G:fem, C:gen, N:pl}
{G:masc, C:loc, N:pl}	{G:neut, C:loc, N:pl}	{G:fem, C:loc, N:pl}

While the content paradigm of YA has sixty-three content cells, its root *ya* has many fewer distinct realizations, as Table 4 shows. This suggests that the form paradigm of *ya* includes some form cells in which morphosyntactic property sets stand in a disjunctive relation. For instance, given that the form *yat* realizes both of the morphosyntactic property sets in (11), one might assume that *yat* realizes the form cell in (12), whose morphosyntactic property specification is a disjunction of the two property sets in (11). I shall henceforth refer to form cells containing disjunctive property specifications (such as (12)) as SYNCRETIC form cells. If each instance of syncretism in the inflection of *ya* is assumed to involve a syncretic form cell, then *ya*'s form paradigm has only thirty cells: each cell is the pairing of the root *ya* with one of the thirty morphosyntactic property specifications in Table 14 (where I abbreviate GENDER-CASE-NUMBER specifications like {G:masc, C:acc, N:sg} as {m-acc-s}, etc.).

(11) a. {G:neut, C:nom, N:sg}
     b. {G:neut, C:acc, N:sg}

(12) ⟨ya, [{G:neut, C:nom, N:sg} ∨ {G:neut, C:acc, N:sg}]⟩

Thus, the sixty-three content cells defined for YA by the morphosyntactic property sets in Table 13 do not stand in a one-to-one correspondence to the thirty form cells defined for *ya* by the morphosyntactic property specifications in Table 14. Here and in general, each domain of syncretism in a

Table 14. The morphosyntactic property specifications defining the form paradigm of a root belonging to the default pronominal declension in Vedic
(N.B.: {G:masc, c:acc, N:sg} is abbreviated as {m-acc-s}, etc.)

{m-nom-s}	[{n-nom-s} ∨ {n-acc-s}]	{f-nom-s}
{m-acc-s}		{f-acc-s}
[{m-ins-s} ∨ { n-ins-s}]		{f-ins-s}
[{m-dat-s} ∨ {n-dat-s}]		{f-dat-s}
[{m-abl-s} ∨ { n-abl-s}]		[{f-abl-s} ∨ {f-gen-s}]
[{m-gen-s} ∨ { n-gen-s}]		
[{m-loc-s} ∨ { n-loc-s}]		{f-loc-s}
[{m-nom-d} ∨ {m-acc-d}]	[{n-nom-d} ∨ {n-acc-d} ∨ {f-nom-d} ∨ {f-acc-d}]	
[{m-ins-d} ∨ {m-dat-d} ∨ {m-abl-d} ∨ {n-ins-d} ∨ {n-dat-d} ∨ {n-abl-d} ∨ {f-ins-d} ∨ {f-dat-d} ∨ {f-abl-d}]		
[{m-gen-d} ∨ {m-loc-d} ∨ {n-gen-d} ∨ {n-loc-d} ∨ {f-gen-d} ∨ {f-loc-d}]		
{m-nom-p}	[{n-nom-p} ∨ {n-acc-p}]	[{f-nom-p} ∨ {f-acc-p}]
{m-acc-p}		
[{m-ins-p} ∨ {n-ins-p}]		{f-ins-p}
[{m-dat-p} ∨ {m-abl-p} ∨ {n-dat-p} ∨ {n-abl-p}]		[{f-dat-p} ∨ {f-abl-p}]
[{m-gen-p} ∨ {n-gen-p}]		{f-gen-p}
[{m-loc-p} ∨ {n-loc-p}]		{f-loc-p}

content paradigm corresponds to a single, syncretic cell in the associated form paradigm.

4.2. Some definitions

In the morphosyntactic property specifications in Table 14, the notation [σ ∨ τ] represents the disjunction of property sets σ and τ; thus, the realization *yat* of the form cell ⟨ya, [{G:neut, c:nom, N:sg} ∨ {G:neut, c:acc, N:sg}]⟩ realizes neuter gender, singular number, and either nominative or accusative case. To clarify the nature of such disjunctive property sets, I assume the following definitions.

(13) Instantiation
Where F is an inflectional category to which property p belongs, F:p is a well-formed INSTANTIATION of F.
Example. c:dat, c:abl, and c:ins are some well-formed instantiations of the inflectional category c (= CASE).

(14) Well-formed morphosyntactic property specifications
a. Where σ is a set of compatible instantiations appropriate to some syntactic category C, σ is a well-formed SIMPLE MORPHOSYNTACTIC PROPERTY

SPECIFICATION for C. A simple morphosyntactic property specification for some C that is not a proper subset of any other simple morphosyntactic property specification for C is said to be COMPLETE.
b. Where $\sigma_1, \ldots \sigma_n$ are well-formed simple morphosyntactic property specifications for some C, $[\sigma_1 \vee \ldots \vee \sigma_n]$ is a well-formed DISJUNCTIVE MORPHOSYNTACTIC PROPERTY SPECIFICATION for C. In those instances in which $\sigma_1, \ldots \sigma_n$ are complete, $[\sigma_1 \vee \ldots \vee \sigma_n]$ is likewise said to be COMPLETE.

Example. (15a) is a simple morphosyntactic property specification for N and (15b) is a disjunctive morphosyntactic specification for N.

(15) a. {G:neut, C:nom, N:sg}
b. [{G:neut, C:nom, N:sg} ∨ {G:neut, C:acc, N:sg}]

(16) The ENCOMPASS relation
a. Where σ and τ are well-formed simple morphosyntactic property specifications and $\tau \subseteq \sigma$, σ encompasses τ. That is, a simple morphosyntactic property specification encompasses each of its subsets.
b. Where $\sigma_1, \ldots \sigma_n$ are well-formed simple morphosyntactic property specifications and σ_i encompasses τ (where $1 \leq i \leq n$), $[\sigma_1 \vee \ldots \vee \sigma_n]$ encompasses τ. That is, a disjunctive morphosyntactic property specification encompasses what each of its disjuncts encompasses.

Example. The morphosyntactic property specifications in the left column of Table 15 encompass the specifications in the right column.

Table 15. Examples of the encompass relation

Morphosyntactic property specification	Encompassed morphosyntactic property specifications
{G:masc, C:nom, N:sg}	{G:masc, C:nom, N:sg}, {G:masc, C:nom}, {G:masc, N:sg}, {C:nom, N:sg}, {G:masc}, {C:nom}, {N:sg}, {}
[{G:neut, C:nom, N:sg} ∨ {G:neut, C:acc, N:sg}]	{G:neut, C:nom, N:sg}, {G:neut, C:acc, N:sg}, {G:neut, C:nom}, {G:neut, C:acc}, {G:neut, N:sg}, {C:nom, N:sg}, {C:acc, N:sg}, {G:neut}, {C:nom}, {C:acc}, {N:sg}, {}

(17) Morphosyntactic property specifications in content cells and form cells

In a content cell ⟨L,σ⟩, the morphosyntactic property specification σ is simple and complete; in a form cell ⟨R,τ⟩, the morphosyntactic property specification τ is complete, and may be simple or disjunctive.

Example. The morphosyntactic property set τ in a form cell ⟨R,τ⟩ can be either a simple morphosyntactic property specification such as (15a) or a disjunctive specification such as (15b); but the morphosyntactic property set σ in a content cell ⟨L,σ⟩ can only be a simple specification (e.g. (15a) but not (15b)).

4.3. Paradigm functions and rules of paradigm linkage

Each of the cells in the content paradigm of YA and each of the cells in the form paradigm of *ya* has an inflected form of the root *ya* as its realization. The relation between a cell and its realization may be schematically represented by means of a PARADIGM FUNCTION (a function PF that applies to a given cell to yield its realization): that is, the realization of the content cell ⟨L, τ⟩ may be schematically represented as PF(⟨L, τ⟩), and that of the form cell ⟨R, σ⟩ may be schematically represented as PF(⟨R, σ⟩). Under this assumption, the way in which a cell's realization is defined depends upon whether the cell in question is a content cell or a form cell.

In general, the realization PF(⟨R, σ⟩) of a form cell ⟨R, σ⟩ is defined as the result of applying a particular sequence of realization rules. Consider, for instance, the inflection of the Sanskrit root *aśva* 'horse': the accusative singular cell in the form paradigm of this root is (18), and the realization of this cell is *aśvam*. PF(⟨aśva, {G:masc, C:acc, N:sg}⟩) is therefore defined as the result of applying a particular rule to *aśva*; this is a rule realizing the properties 'accusative' and 'singular' through the suffixation of *-m*. Of course, such realizations needn't be defined piecemeal (with specific reference to particular roots and particular morphosyntactic property sets), but can ordinarily be specified by definitions generalizing over whole classes of roots and whole classes of morphosyntactic property sets; see Stump 2001 for extensive discussion of such generalized definitions.

(18) ⟨aśva, {G:masc, C:acc, N:sg}⟩

The realization of a content cell may be equated with that of a particular form cell; a rule specifying this sort of equation is a RULE OF PARADIGM LINKAGE. For instance, the realization of the content cell ⟨AŚVA, {G:masc, C:acc, N:sg}⟩ is that of the form cell (18); that is, PF(⟨AŚVA, {G:masc, C:acc, N:sg}⟩) = PF(⟨aśva, {G:masc, C:acc, N:sg}⟩). Where the realization of a content cell ⟨L, τ⟩ is equated in this way with that of a form cell ⟨R, σ⟩, I will call this form cell the FORM CORRESPONDENT of ⟨L, τ⟩.

Often, a content cell and its form correspondent share the same morphosyntactic property specification. This fact is captured by the very general, default rule of paradigm linkage in (19).

(19) Universal default rule of paradigm linkage: Where R is L's root, PF(⟨L, σ⟩) = PF(⟨R, σ⟩).

While the generalization expressed by (19) might appear to be trivial, it is not, because it is sometimes overridden by more specific rules of paradigm linkage. As Stump (2002) and Stewart and Stump (2007) show, there is a variety of ways in which (19) might be overridden. In instances of deponency, a content cell's morphosyntactic property set contrasts with that of its form correspondent: schematically, PF(⟨L, σ⟩) = PF(⟨R, σ′⟩), where σ′ doesn't encompass σ. In instances of heteroclisis, different cells in a lexeme's content paradigm have form correspondents in different form paradigms: schematically, PF(⟨L, σ_1⟩) = PF(⟨R_1, σ_1⟩) but PF(⟨L, σ_2⟩) = PF(⟨R_2, σ_2⟩), where $R_1 \neq R_2$ and $σ_1 \neq σ_2$. Instances of suppletion involve this same sort of relation between the cells in a content paradigm and cells in two or more form paradigms.[6] These special patterns of paradigm linkage are schematically represented in Figures 1 and 2.

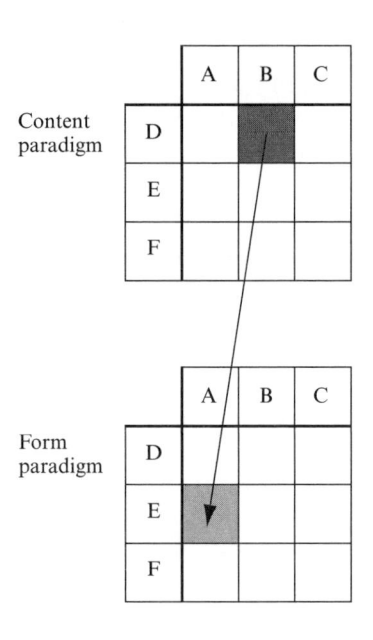

Figure 1. Deponency

Syncretism is a third phenomenon involving overrides of the default rule of paradigm linkage in (19). In instances of syncretism, distinct cells in a lexeme's content paradigm share the same form correspondent: schematically, PF(⟨L, σ_1⟩) = PF(⟨L, σ_2⟩) = PF(⟨R, σ_3⟩), where $σ_1 \neq σ_2$ and $σ_3$ encompasses both $σ_1$ and $σ_2$; this pattern of paradigm linkage is represented in Figure 3.

An example of a rule of paradigm linkage that induces syncretism in this way is the Sanskrit rule of paradigm linkage in (20):

---

[6] In instances of suppletion, the roots of the form paradigms differ in form, but may nevertheless belong to the same inflection class; in instances of heteroclisis, the roots of the form paradigms belong to different inflection classes, but may be identical in form. Nothing, of course, excludes the possibility of heteroclitic suppletion.

DEFECTIVENESS AND SYNCRETISM 201

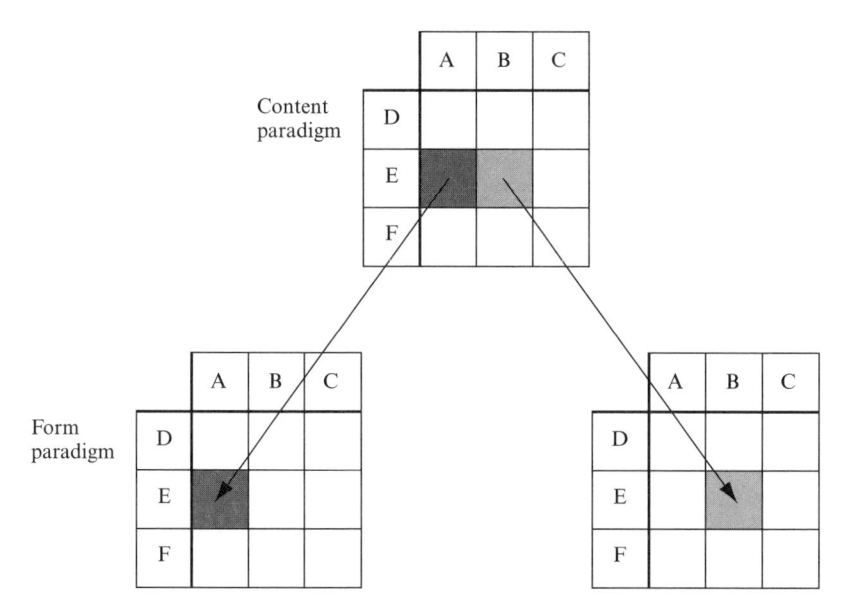

Figure 2. Heteroclisis and suppletion

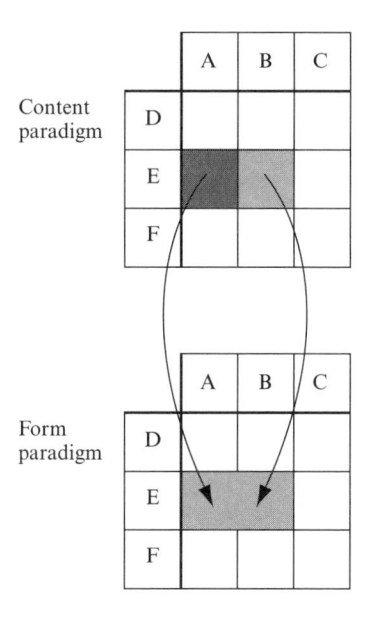

Figure 3. Syncretism

(20) Sanskrit rule of paradigm linkage:
Where (a) lexeme L belongs to category C,
(b) the root R of L belongs to inflection class I,
(c) the morphosyntactic property specification τ is appropriate to C,
(d) the morphosyntactic property specification σ is appropriate to I, and
(e) PF(⟨L, τ⟩) is definable[7] as PF(⟨R, σ⟩):
PF(⟨L, τ⟩) = PF(⟨R, σ⟩) if and only if σ encompasses τ.

(19) and (20) make the same predictions when σ = τ; but when σ ≠ τ, (20) overrides (19). Thus, consider the Sanskit lexeme YA, whose content paradigm is based on the morphosyntactic property specifications in Table 13 and whose root *ya* has a form paradigm based on the morphosyntactic property specifications in Table 14 and the realizations in Table 4: according to (20) (and contrary to (19)), the realization of the content cells in (21a) and (22a) (whose property specifications are simple) equals the realization of the form cells in (21b) and (22b) (whose property specifications are disjunctive). These two form cells have disjunctive property sets because each has a realization that syncretizes two simple property sets.

(21) a. ⟨YA, {G:neut, C:nom, N:sg}⟩
b. ⟨*ya*, [{G:neut, C:nom, N:sg} ∨ {G:neut, C:acc, N:sg}]⟩

(22) a. ⟨YA, {G:masc, C:abl, N:sg}⟩
b. ⟨*ya*, [{G:masc, C:abl, N:sg} ∨ {G:neut, C:abl, N:sg}]⟩

In this conception of inflectional morphology, syncretism is enforced by a rule of paradigm linkage that links a content cell to a form correspondent whose morphosyntactic property specification is disjunctive. Moreover, syncretism is directly represented both in the structure of form paradigms and in the property specifications of syncretic form cells. For instance, the form paradigm of *ya* in Table 4 has only four dual cells because of the extensive syncretism among its dual forms; in addition, the disjunctive property specifications in these dual form cells explicitly identify them as syncretic. Thus, in this theory, syncretism is a characteristic of form paradigms but not of content paradigms.

Logically, defectiveness could be stipulated either within a content paradigm or within a form paradigm. This is exactly what I shall argue: that the different ways in which defectiveness interacts with syncretism follow from the fact that defectiveness may be stipulated in a content paradigm (where there is never any syncretism) or in a form paradigm (where there may be syncretism). I develop this idea concretely in the following section, where I

---

[7] The significance of this requirement will become clear immediately below, in §4.4.

propose a formal account of the observed interactions of defectiveness and syncretism in early Indic.

4.4. A formal analysis of interactions between defectiveness and syncretism in Paradigm Function Morphology

Once a distinction is assumed between content paradigms and form paradigms, the question arises whether patterns of defectiveness are defined with respect to content paradigms or with respect to form paradigms. The answer, I argue, is that both sorts of definition are necessary.

Where a content cell $\langle L, \tau \rangle$ and its form correspondent $\langle R, \sigma \rangle$ have a realization, I will say that $PF(\langle L, \tau \rangle)$ IS DEFINABLE AS $PF(\langle R, \sigma \rangle)$. Given a lexeme L with root R, whether $PF(\langle L, \tau \rangle)$ is definable as $PF(\langle R, \sigma \rangle)$ may depend on the value of σ, that of τ, or those of both σ and τ. In other words, defectiveness may be associated with content cells, with form cells, or with both. Because domains of syncretism are represented in form cells, domains of defectiveness that are sensitive to domains of syncretism are most easily defined with reference to form cells. By contrast, domains of defectiveness that are insensitive to domains of syncretism are often most easily defined with reference to content cells.

I assume that in those instances in which it is irreducible, defectiveness is enforced by a stipulated restriction on the realization of a content cell and its form correspondent. My claim here is that there is more than one way in which a domain of defectiveness may be defined, and that the different types of interaction between defectiveness and syncretism stem from these different types of definition. In particular, I propose the following theoretical characterization of the three canonical interactions between defectiveness and syncretism:

(23) Canonical interactions between defectiveness and syncretism
    a. **Defectiveness overrides syncretism** when the domain of defectiveness is defined as including one or more content cells.
    b. **Syncretism overrides defectiveness** when the domain of defectiveness is defined as excluding one or more syncretic form cells.
    c. **Syncretism determines a domain of defectiveness** when the domain of defectiveness is defined as including one or more syncretic form cells.

Consider again the inflection of Vedic pronouns. A pronominal lexeme has a content paradigm whose cells should, by default, correspond to the property sets in Table 13; similarly, the form paradigm of a pronominal root should, in the default case, have cells corresponding to the morphosyntactic property specifications in Table 14. The Sanskrit rule of paradigm linkage in (20) entails that if L is a pronominal lexeme with root R, then for each morphosyntactic property specification τ in Table 13 and each morphosyntactic property specification σ in Table 14, PF(⟨L, τ⟩) = PF(⟨R, σ⟩) if and only if σ encompasses τ. But this equation is subject to the precondition (20e) that PF(⟨L, τ⟩) be definable as PF(⟨R, σ⟩).

Ordinarily, there will be no special restrictions on the definability of PF(⟨L, τ⟩) as PF(⟨R, σ⟩); but in the special case in which L = ENA (so that R = *ena*), stipulation (24) restricts the values of τ and σ for which PF(⟨L, τ⟩) is definable as PF(⟨R, σ⟩). According to (24), PF(⟨ENA, τ⟩) is undefinable as PF(⟨*ena*, σ⟩) unless: (a) ⟨ENA, τ⟩ is an accusative content cell; (b) ⟨ENA, τ⟩ is an instrumental singular content cell; or (c) ⟨*ena*, σ⟩ is the form cell encompassing the genitive dual.[8]

(24) Defectiveness of ENA in Vedic
Where σ encompasses τ, PF(⟨ENA, τ⟩) is definable as PF(⟨*ena*, σ⟩) only if
    (a) τ encompasses {C:acc},
    (b) τ encompasses {C:ins, N:sg}, or
    (c) σ encompasses {C:gen, N:du}.

Because τ doesn't encompass {C:nom} in instances (a) and (b) and σ doesn't encompass {C:nom} in instance (c), nominative content cells are inevitably relegated to the domain of defectiveness; that is, where ⟨ENA, τ⟩ is a nominative content cell, PF(⟨ENA, τ⟩) is not definable as PF(⟨*ena*, σ⟩), even if ⟨*ena*, σ⟩ happens to be a syncretic form cell. Thus, in accordance with (23a), nominative defectiveness canonically overrides nominative/accusative syncretism in the inflection of ENA because (24) determines the domain of defectiveness as including nominative content cells.

In addition, (24) stipulates that the domain of defectiveness excludes the genitive dual form cell; this is the form cell having the syncretic property set in (25a). For this reason, PF(⟨ENA, τ⟩) is definable as PF(⟨*ena*, σ⟩) if τ is any of the six property sets in (25b). Thus, in accordance with (23b), the syncretism of genitive with locative in the dual canonically overrides the defectiveness of locative cells in the inflection of ENA because (24) defines the domain of defectiveness as excluding the syncretic form cell encompassing the genitive dual.

(25) a. [{m-gen-d} ∨ {m-loc-d} ∨ {n-gen-d} ∨ {n-loc-d} ∨ {f-gen-d} ∨ {f-loc-d}]
    b. {G:masc, C:gen, N:du}
       {G:masc, C:loc, N:du}
       {G:neut, C:gen, N:du}
       {G:neut, C:loc, N:du}

---

[8] My reference to the genitive dual rather than to the locative dual in this definition is an arbitrary one. I make an analogously arbitrary choice of the nominative over the vocative and the accusative in definition (26).

{G:fem, C:gen, N:du}
{G:fem, C:loc, N:du}

Stipulation (24) defines the pattern of defectiveness represented in Tables 16 and 17, in which the domain of defectiveness is shaded and in which non-defective cells are labelled (a), (b), or (c) according to the clause of (24) that identifies them as non-defective. Non-defective cells that are unlabelled are non-defective by inference: if σ encompasses τ and (24) identifies τ as non-defective, then σ is non-defective; if σ encompasses τ and (24) identifies σ as non-defective, then τ is non-defective.

Table 16. Content paradigm of Vedic ENA

	Singular			Dual			Plural		
	m.	n.	f.	m.	n.	f.	m.	n.	f.
Nom									
Acc	(a)	(a)	(a)	(a)	(a)	(a)	(a)	(a)	(a)
Ins	(b)	(b)	(b)						
Dat									
Abl									
Gen									
Loc									

Table 17. Form paradigm of Vedic *ena*

	Singular			Dual			Plural		
	m.	n.	f.	m.	n.	f.	m.	n.	f.
Nom									
Acc									
Ins									
Dat									
Abl									
Gen					(c)				
Loc									

Now consider the case of Classical Sanskrit YAKAN 'liver'. Comparably to the situation with ENA, a special stipulation here restricts the values of τ and σ for which PF(⟨YAKAN, τ⟩) is definable as PF(⟨*yakan*, σ⟩). According to (26), PF(⟨YAKAN, τ⟩) is undefinable as PF(⟨*yakan*, σ⟩) if ⟨*yakan*, σ⟩ is a nominative form cell.

(26) Defectiveness of YAKAN in Classical Sanskrit
Where σ encompasses τ, PF(⟨YAKAN, τ⟩) is definable as PF(⟨*yakan*, σ⟩) unless σ encompasses {C:nom}.

According to (26), the domain of defectiveness in YAKAN's paradigms includes all nominative form cells: there are three such cells (one singular, one dual, and one plural), each of which exhibits a nominative/vocative/accusative syncretism. Thus, in accordance with (23c), syncretism determines the domain of YAKAN's defectiveness because the domain of defectiveness is defined as including three syncretic form cells.

Stipulation (26) defines the pattern of defectiveness represented in Tables 18 and 19, in which the labelled cells are those that (26) explicitly identifies as defective. Shaded cells that are unlabelled are defective by inference: if σ encompasses τ and (26) identifies σ as defective, then τ is defective.

Table 18. Content paradigm of Classical Sanskrit YAKAN

	Singular	Dual	Plural
Nom			
Voc			
Acc			
Ins			
Dat			
Abl			
Gen			
Loc			

Table 19. Form paradigm of Classical Sanskrit *yakan*

	Singular	Dual	Plural
	(26)	(26)	(26)

Consider finally the case of the Prākrit pronominal clitic ṆA. Comparably to the situations with ENA and YAKAN, a special stipulation here restricts the values of τ and σ for which PF(⟨ṆA, τ⟩) is definable as PF(⟨ṇa, σ⟩). According to (27), PF(⟨ṆA, τ⟩) is undefinable as PF(⟨ṇa, σ⟩) unless (a) ⟨ṆA, τ⟩ is an instrumental content cell or (b) ⟨ṆA, τ⟩ is an accusative content cell having a masculine form cell ⟨ṇa, σ⟩ as its form correspondent.

(27) Defectiveness of ṆA in Prākrit

Where σ encompasses τ, PF(⟨ṆA, τ⟩) is definable as PF(⟨ṇa, σ⟩) only if
(a) τ encompasses {C:ins} or
(b) τ encompasses {C:acc} and σ encompasses {G:masc}.

Note that clause (b) of this stipulation defines ṆA's domain of defectiveness as excluding a certain sort of content cell having a certain sort of form correspondent. For this reason, the interaction between defectiveness and syncretism entailed by (27) is more complex than that entailed by (24) or (26): in particular, (27) defines a pattern of defectiveness that overrides the patterns of syncretism in (10a,b) (i.e. the patterns neuter nominative singular = neuter accusative singular and masculine nominative plural = masculine accusative plural) but is itself partially determined by the patterns of syncretism in (10c,d) (i.e. the patterns neuter nominative plural = neuter accusative plural and feminine nominative plural = feminine accusative plural).

Stipulation (27) defines the pattern of defectiveness represented in Tables 20 and 21, in which the labelled cells are those that (27a) and (27b) explicitly identify as non-defective. If σ encompasses τ and (27) identifies τ as non-defective, then σ is non-defective.

Table 20. Content paradigm of Prākrit ṆA

	Singular			Plural		
	m.	n.	f.	m.	n.	f.
Nom						
Acc	(b)	(b)	(b)	(b)		
Ins	(a)	(a)	(a)	(a)	(a)	(a)
Abl						
Dat						
Gen						
Loc						

Table 21. Form paradigm of Prākrit *ṇa*

	Singular			Plural		
	m.	n.	f.	m.	n.	f.
Nom					(b)	
Acc		(b)		(b)		
Ins						
Abl						
Dat						
Gen						
Loc						

5. Conclusions and Issues for Future Research

The early Indic evidence presented here demonstrates that defectiveness and syncretism may interact in more than one way. In particular, I have identified three canonical kinds of interaction: defectiveness may override syncretism, syncretism may override defectiveness, and syncretism may determine a domain of defectiveness. More complex kinds of interaction also exist.

I have proposed a theoretical explanation of these facts; crucial to this explanation is the assumption that the definition of a language's morphology makes reference to two distinct sorts of paradigm: (i) content paradigms, which express the range of syntactic uses to which lexemes may be put, and (ii) form paradigms, which express the range of inflectional realizations to which a root may give rise. I have argued that syncretism is a property of form paradigms, but that defectiveness is a property of both content paradigms and form paradigms. In particular, I assume that a lexeme's inflection exhibits syncretism if two of its content cells have the same form correspondent, and that a lexeme's inflection exhibits defectiveness if the realization of one of its content cells is not definable as the realization of a form cell. These assumptions predict a range of possible interactions between defectiveness and syncretism, including the three canonical interactions exemplified by early Indic.

The evidence examined here raises important questions for future research. First, are there limits on the sorts of interactions that may exist between defectiveness and syncretism? One would suppose that issues of learnability would impose such limits; nevertheless, it is not clear what sort of evidence could allow such limits to be characterized in absolute terms. Perhaps the most that could be established is simply that one sort of interaction is more complex than another, in the sense that it is more difficult to learn, and is therefore both less frequently observed across languages and less stable diachronically. As I have shown, the override of syncretism by defectiveness in the inflection of Vedic ENA erodes in post-Vedic Sanskrit, developing in the direction of an override of defectiveness by syncretism. If this same trajectory is observable elsewhere and the reverse trajectory is not, then the override of syncretism by defectiveness should be seen as a more complex, less stable relation than the override of defectiveness by syncretism.

A related issue concerns the role of word frequency in determining interactions between defectiveness and syncretism. In Vedic, the defectiveness of ENA's nominative cells overrides the five instances of nominative/accusative syncretism in (4). This state of affairs may have been tolerated because (i) the masculine accusative singular form *enam* is vastly more frequent in Vedic than all other accusative forms of ENA combined (Table 22), and (ii) a pronoun's masculine accusative singular form does not participate in nominative/accusative syncretism. Because the masculine accusative singular form acts as the paradigm's focal member, it is as though the paradigm's less frequent, less focal members in some sense share in its basic insusceptibility to nominative/accusative syncretism.

Table 22. Accusative instances of ENA in the *Ṛgveda*

			Instances	Percentage
Singular	Masc.	enam	76	77.6
	Neut.	enat	0	0.0
	Fem.	enām	3	3.1
Dual	Masc.	enau	0	0.0
	Neut.	ene	0	0.0
	Fem.	ene	2	2.0
Plural	Masc.	enān	8	8.2
	Neut.	enāni	0	0.0
	Fem.	enās	9	9.2

Clarification and resolution of these issues will depend on careful scrutiny of a wider sampling of interactions between defectiveness and syncretism in a range of languages. This research will provide further motivation for the already well-established theoretical program devoted to explicating the central role that paradigms play in the definition of a language's morphology (Stump 2001, 2006; Baerman, Brown, and Corbett 2005; Blevins 2006; Finkel and Stump 2007, 2009).

References

Baerman, Matthew, Dunstan Brown, and Greville G. Corbett. 2005. *The syntax-morphology interface: A study of syncretism.* Cambridge: Cambridge University Press.

Baerman, Matthew and Greville Corbett. 2006. Three types of defective paradigm. Paper presented at the LSA Annual Meeting, Albuquerque, NM, 5–8 January 2006.

Blevins, James. 2006. Word-based morphology. *Journal of Linguistics* 42. 531–73.

Burrow, T. 1965. *The Sanskrit language*, 2nd edition. London: Faber and Faber.

Corbett, Greville G. 2005. The canonical approach in typology. *Linguistic diversity and language theories*, ed. by Zygmunt Frajzyngier, Adam Hodges, and David S. Rood, 25–49. Amsterdam: Benjamins.

Dresden, Mark Jan. 1941. *Mānavagṛhyasūtra.* Groningen: J. B. Wolters' Uitgevers-Maatschappij.

Finkel, Raphael and Gregory Stump. 2007. Principal parts and morphological typology. *Morphology* 17. 39–75.

Finkel, Raphael and Gregory Stump. 2009. Principal parts and degrees of paradigmatic transparency. *Analogy in grammar: Form and acquisition*, ed. by James P. Blevins and Juliette Blevins, 13–53. Oxford: Oxford University Press.

Geiger, Wilhelm. 1994. *A Pāli grammar*, tr. by Batakrishna Ghosh, rev. and ed. by K. R. Norman. Oxford: Pali Text Society.

Johansson, K. F. 1907/08. Pali Miscellen. *Le Monde Oriental* 2.2. 85–108.

Juge, Matthew L. 1999. On the rise of suppletion in verbal paradigms. *Proceedings of the 25th Annual Meeting of the Berkeley Linguistics Society*, ed. by Steve S. Chang, Lily Liaw, and Josef Ruppenhofer, 183–94. Berkeley: Berkeley Linguistics Society.

Katre, Sumitra Mangesh. 1987. *Aṣṭādhyāyī of Pāṇini.* Austin: University of Texas Press.

Keith, Arthur Berriedale (ed., translator). 1909. *The Aitareya Āraṇyaka*, revised edition, 1995. Delhi: Eastern Book Linkers.

Keith, Arthur Berriedale (translator). 1920. *Rigveda brahmanas: The aitareya and Kauṣītaki Brāhmaṇas of the Rigveda translated from the original Sanskrit*, Harvard Oriental Series vol. 25. Cambridge, Mass.: Harvard University Press.

Macdonell, Arthur Anthony. 1910. *Vedic grammar.* Strasbourg: Trübner (2000 reprint, New Delhi: Munshiram Manoharlal).

Macdonell, Arthur Anthony. 1916. *A vedic grammar for students* [1977 reprint]. Delhi: Oxford University Press.

Pischel, Richard, ed. 1877–1880. *Hemacandra's Grammatik der Prākritsprachen*, 1969 reprint. Osnabrück: Biblio Verlag.

Pischel, Richard. 1981. *A grammar of the Prākrit languages*, 2nd rev. ed., tr. by Subhadra Jhā. Delhi: Motilal Banarsidass.

Sarma, E. R. Sreekrishna, ed. 1968–1976. *Kauṣītaki-Brāhmaṇa* (3 vols.). Wiesbaden: Franz Steiner Verlag.

Scheller, Meinrad. 1967. Das mittelindische Enklitikum se. *Zeitschrift für vergleichende Sprachforschung auf dem Gebiete der indogermanischen Sprachen* 81, 1–53. Göttingen: Vandenhoeck and Ruprecht.

Smith, Helmer. 1953. En marge du vocabulaire sanskrit des bouddhistes. *Orientalia Suecana* II, 2/4. 119–28.
Speijer, J. S. 1886. *Sanskrit syntax*. Leiden: E. J. Brill, 1980 reprint, Delhi: Motilal Banarsidass.
Stewart, Tom and Gregory Stump. 2007. Paradigm function morphology and the morphology/syntax interface. *The Oxford handbook of linguistic interfaces*, ed. by Gillian Ramchand and Charles Reiss, 383–421. Oxford: Oxford University Press.
Stump, Gregory T. 2001. *Inflectional morphology*. Cambridge University Press.
Stump, Gregory. 2002. Morphological and syntactic paradigms: Arguments for a theory of paradigm linkage. *Yearbook of Morphology 2001*, ed. by G. Booij and J. van Marle, 147–80. Dordrecht: Kluwer.
Stump, Gregory T. 2006. Heteroclisis and paradigm linkage. *Language* 82. 279–322.
Torp, Alf. 1881. *Die Flexion des Pali in ihrem Verhältniss zum Sanskrit*. Christiania: A. W. Brøgger.
Wackernagel, Jacob and Albert Debrunner. 1930. *Altindische Grammatik, III. Band: Nominalflexion, Zahlwort, Pronomen*. Göttingen: Vandenhoeck und Ruprecht.
Whitney, William Dwight. 1889. *Sanskrit grammar*, 2nd edition, Cambridge, MA: Harvard University Press.

Index of Authors

Abeillé, Anne, 153 n 4, 161 n 10
Ackema, Peter, 155
Ackerman, Farrell, 35
Adger, David, 155
Ahlborn, Gunnar, 165
Albizu, Pablo, 155, 175
Albright, Adam, 47, 48 n 12, 103, 105 n 4, 108, 116, 118, 119, 121, 152, 172
Anagnostopoulou, Elena, 155
Anderson, Stephen R., 6, 19–34
Andersson, Erik, 70
Araceli López, Serena, 121, n 23
Ariel, Mira, 162
Aronoff, Mark, 26, 35, 40, 103, 104
Arrivé, Michel, 38
Auger, Julie, 153 n 4, 158 n 6, 164, 170

Baayen, R. Harald, n 71, 125
Baerman, Matthew, 1–18, 29, 37, 126, 151 n 1, 169, 181
Bard, Ellen Gurman, 69
Battista, Marco, 39, 40
Bauer, Laurie, 71 n 4
Baxturina, R. V., 12
Bayer, Joself, 169
Béjar, Susana, 155
Benincà, Paola, 19, 24
Bermudez-Otero, Ricardo, 26
Bianchi, Valentina, 155
Bissel, Clifford, 160
Blanche-Benveniste, Claire, 154, 159, 160 n 9, 163, 170
Bogoras, Waldemar, 10
Bonami, Olivier. 35, 39, 40, 42, 43, 44 n 10, 47, 153, 158 n 6
Bonet, Eulàlia, 155, 157, 158, 159, 165, 168, 172, 175
Booij, Geert, 27
Boškovič, Željko, 155
Botelho de Amaral, Vasco, 117
Boyé, Gilles, 6, 16, 19, 35–52, 103, 153, 158 n 6, 174, 175, 181
Bresnan, Joan, 152, 175
Brooks, Patricia, 77
Brown, Dunstan, 4
Bürgi, Anne, 158 n 6, 165, 166 n 14
Butterworth, Brian, 125

Bybee Joan, 125, 148
Bye, Patrick, 27

Cabredo Hofherr, Patricia, 6, 16, 19, 35–52, 103, 174, 181
Cano González, Ana M., 117
Cardinaletti, Anna, 159 n 8
Carstairs, Andrew, 27
Carstairs-McCarthy, Andrew, 19
Corbett, Greville G., 1–18, 29, 126, 169, 181, 183 n 2
Corominas, Juan, 107 n 5, 119
Couquaux, Daniel, 155, 156, 160, 160 n 9, 163
Cunha, Celso, 117, 119

Daland, Robert, 49, 50, 106, 120 n 20
Debrunner, Albert, 189
De Calmès, Martine, 47
DeCurtins, Alexi, 30
De Figueiredo, Cândido, 117
de Kok, Ans, 153 n 4, 160 n 9, 161 n 10, 163, 167, 170, 170 n 17, 172, 173
Delfitto, Denis, 162
De Sá Nogueira, R., 111, 119
Di Sciullo, Anna-Maria, 169
Dobrovie-Sorin, Carmen, 174
Dressler, Wolfgang, 70

Elvira, Javier, 107 n 6
Embick, David, 151 n 1, 152
Endzelīns, Jānis, 53, 57
Espinosa, A., 117

Fellbaum, Christiane, 174
Fernàndez- Ordóñez, Inés, 174 n 19
Fodor, Janet Dean, 170
Ford, Michael, 125
Fraser, Norman, 4

Gak, Vladimir G., 53
Geniušienė, Emma, 55
Gilliéron, Jules, 15, 16

Giusti, Giuliana, 159
Godard, Danièle, 153 n 4
Gordon, Lynn, 6, 7
Green, Georgia M., 170
Grevisse, Maurice, 164
Grisch, Mena, 19, 24, 27
Grimshaw, Jane, 157, 159 n 8

Haiman, John, 20, 24
Halle, Morris, 116 n 16, 151 n 1
Hankamer, Jorge, 8
Hakulinen, Auli, 4
Harbour, Daniel, 155
Hare, Mary, 125
Hargus, Sharon, 9
Heath, Jeffrey, 9, 10
Heger, M. Klaus, 153
Heggie, Lorie, 167, 168, 172
Hellberg, Staffan, 70, 70 n 1
Herslund, Michael, 163, 166
Hetzron, Robert, 85 n 1
Hippisley, Andrew, 4
Holvoet, Axel, 54, 55
Hopper, Paul, 148

Inkelas, Sharon, 8
Inoue, Atsu, 170
Itô, Junko, 8
Iverson, Gregory, 85 n 1

Jacobson, Steven, 134,135
Johansson, K. F., 194
Jouitteau, Mélanie, 153
Juge, Matthew L., 191

Kager, René, 27
Kalnača, Andra, 11, 53–67
Kamprath, Christine, 26
Karlsson, Fred, 4
Katre, Sumitra Mangesh, 191
Kayne, Richard, 153 n 4, 155, 156, 159 n 7, 160, 160 n 9, 161, 161 n 10, 162 n 12, 166 n 14, 172, 174
Kim, John J., 125
Kiparsky, Paul, 4, 26
Kühner, Raphael, 15

Lambrecht, Knud, 153, 154 n 5, 171
Leclère, Christian, 153
Lepschy, Anna Laura, 162, 168 n 12
Lepschy, Giulio C.. 162, 168 n 12
Lieber, Rochelle, 71, n 4
Lokmane, Ilze, 11

Lindley Cintra, Luís, 117, 119
Littré, Émile, 164
Löwenadler, John, 4, 69–83
Lukács, Agnes, 6, 85–102
Lutta, C. Martin, 24

Macdonell, A. A., 185, 186, 187, 191
Machado, J. P., 107 n 5
Mackridge, Peter, 14
MacWhinney, Brian, 125, 159
Maiden, Martin, 6, 12, 19, 24, 39, 40, 48, 103–124
Manzini, Rita, 157, 158, 166 n 14
Marantz, Alec, 151 n 1, 152
Marslen-Wilson, William, 125
Mateo, Francis, 38
Matthews, P. H., 1, 2
McA'nulty, Judith, 167, 169
McCarthy, John J., 85 n 1, 152
McClelland, James, 125
Mendes de Almeida, Napoleão, 109 n 9, 117, 119
Mendikoetxea, Amaya, 174
Menn, Lise, 159
Mikheev, A., 47
Mīlenbachs, Kārlis, 53, 57
Miller, Philip, 151 n 1, 153, 153 n 4, 157, 158 n 6, 159, 160 n 9, 161 n 10, 163, 164
Mithun, Marianne, 3, 125–49
Monachesi, Paola, 163
Morin, Yves-Charles, 37, 38, 153 n 4, 158 n 6, 160 n 9, 161 n 10, 163, 166, 166 n 14, 168 n 15, 170, 171
Munro, Pamela, 6, 7

Neeleman, Ad, 155, 159
Neue, Friedrich, 2,
Nevins, Andrew, 157
Nicol, Fabrice, 160 n 9
Nītiņa, Daina, 57
Noyer, Rolf R., 169

O'Neill, Paul, 6, 12, 40, 48, 103–24
Ordóñez, Francisco, 167, 168, 172
Orgun, Cemil Orhan, 8, 85 n 1
Ormazabal, Javier, 155

Paegle, Dzintra, 57
Pascual, J., 107 n 5, 119
Paster, Mary, 27
Pérennou, Guy, 47
Perini, Mario A., 117, 119
Perlmutter, David, 155, 159
Pescarini, Diego, 157, 159 n 7

Pettersson, T., 70 n 1
Pierrehumbert, Janet B., 106
Piat, Louis, 166 n 14
Pinker, Steven, 125
Pirrelli, Vito, 39, 40
Pischel, Richard, 193, 194
Plag, Ingo, 71, 71 n 4
Plungian, Vladimir, 55
Pons, Rodríguez L., 121, n 23
Poser, William J., 175
Posner, Rebecca, 173
Postal, Paul M., 155, 156, 159 n 7, 160, 160 n 9, 161, 161 n 10 162 n 12, 173 n 18, 174
Prasada, Sandeep, 125
Prince, Alan, 85 n 1, 125
Pullum, Geoffrey K., 151 n 1

Raffelsiefen, Renate, 85 n 1
Rebrus, Péter, 6, 85–102
Rezac, Milan, 6, 151–80
Rice, Curtis, 85 n 1
Rivas, Alberto, 160 n 9, 173 n 18
Roetgiest, Eugeen, 160 n 9
Rohlfs, Gerhard, 165
Romero, Juan, 155
Rooryck, Johan, 154
Rouveret, Alain, 161, 162 n 12
Rowlett, Paul, 159, 171
Rubach, Jerzy, 27
Rumelhart, David E., 125

Sag, Ivan, 153, 160 n 9
Sastre, Antonio J. Rojo, 38
Savoia, Leonardo M., 157, 158, 166 n 14
Scheller, Meinrad, 194
Schreuder, Robert, 125
Seco, Manuel, 118
Signorell, Faust, 19, 27, 28
Simeon, Gion Pol, 19
Sims, Andrea, 14, 49, 50, 106, 120 n 20, 121
Siptár, Péter, 85 n 1, 88 n 9, 90 n 14

Smith, Helmer, 194
Smolensky, Paul, 85 n 1
Solà, Jaume, 173 n 18
Sonder, Ambros, 19, 27
Sportiche, Dominique, 159
Sprouse, Ronald. L., 85 n 1
Stemberger, Joseph Paul, 125
Stewart, Tom, 184, 195, 199
Stump, Gregory, 4, 35, 43, 181–210

Tasmowski, Liliane, 160 n 9, 161, 161 n 10, 162, 173 n 18
Teleman, Ulf, 70
Timberlake, Alan, 4
Tomasello, Michael, 77
Törkenczy, Miklós, 6, 85–102
Torp, Alf, 194
Trón, Viktor, 88 n 9
Trommer, Jochen, 151 n 1, 152
Tscharner, Gion, 31
Tschenkeli, Kita, 3
Tseng, Jesse, 151 n 1

Van de Koot, Hans, 159
Van der Veer, Bart, 27
Vázquez, Cuesta, Pilar, 109 n 9, 119
Veidemane, Ruta, 54
Vergnaud, Jean-Roger, 161, 162 n 12

Wackernagel, Jacob, 189
Wagener, Carl, 2
Walter, Mary Ann, 166
Whitney, William Dwight, 185, 186, 187, 192
Wierzbicka, Anna, 54
Wolf, Matthew, 85
Wuethrich-Grisch, Mena, 19

Zribi-Hertz, Anne, 174
Zwicky, Arnold, 151 n 1

Index of Languages

Bulgarian, 13

Catalan, 157, 158 n 6, 159, 168 n 15
   Barceloní, 157, 159, 165, 172
Central Alaskan Yup'ik, 126–36, 147–8
Chickasaw, 6, 7
Church Slavonic, 16, 17

Finnish, 5, 29
French, 12, 16, 35–51, 107, 151–75, 181, 186
   Old French, 169
Friulian, 19

Georgian, 3
German, 13, 169
Greek, 14, 50

Hungarian, 6, 85–101, 121

Indic, 182, 184
Italian, 27, 40, 107, 157, 159
   Castrovalvi, 157
   Conegliano, 159
Itel'men, 10, 11

Ladin, 19
Latin, 2, 11, 12, 15, 32, 104, 107, 108 n 7, 113,
Latvian, 11, 53–67

Macedonian, 13
Mohawk, 3, 126–48

Occitan, 165, 173, 174

Polish, 14
Portuguese, 12, 103–21
Prākrit, 184, 193–4, 206–7
Proto-Iroquoian, 145

Rumantsch
   Puter, 31–2
   Rumantsch Grischun, 32
   Surmiran, 19–32
   Sursilvan, 32
   Sutsilvan, 32
   Vallader, 31–2
Russian, 1, 12, 16, 49

Sanskrit, 184–208
   Classical, 184, 191–3, 205–6
   Post-Vedic, 184, 186, 188, 189–91, 208
   Vedic, 184–8, 194, 195–8, 203, 204, 205, 208
Spanish, 12, 35–51, 103–21, 157, 158, 159, 174
Swedish, 69–82

Tamashek, 9, 10, 169
Turkish, 8, 12

Valencian, 159

Witsuwet'en, 8

Yup'ik, 126–36, 147–8

Subject Index

acceptability test, 72–3, 91–101, 171
affix-based defectiveness, 6–7, 89–90, 91, 93, 100
allomorphy, lack of predicted, 109–10

Binding Theory, 154
borrowing, 12, 16, 107–9, 133, 135

case, 1, 2, 3, 14–15, 53–4, 57–9, 60, 61, 62, 63, 64, 127, 153–4, 157, 160–72, 184–94, 203–8
Case Filter, 154
clitics, 53, 151–80, 184–94
  clitic climbing, 160–1, 173 n 18
conjugation class, 12, 16, 21–3, 25, 29, 107, 112, 137
constraint-based analyses, 14, 19, 27–30, 70, 73–5, 80, 81, 82

default, 2, 35, 37, 39, 41–3, 45, 47, 50, 195, 197, 200
derivation, 4, 12, 134, 135
diachrony, 11–17, 30–2, 36, 40, 103, 107, 113, 143–7, 172, 189–91, 208
dualia tantum, 133, 136, 147

entrenchment, 77–8

frequency, 1, 70–2, 78, 78 n 11, 81, 81 n 15, 82, 94, 95, 96, 101, 106, 135, 148, 208

garden path, 154, 167–70
gender, 13–14, 47, 53–4, 57–9, 69–76, 78, 78 n 12, 79, 80, 81, 82, 136, 137, 144–7, 152, 172–3, 184–94

homophony avoidance , 10, 11, 10 5n 4

impersonal verbs, 3, 8, 37, 181
implicative relationship of stems, 41–3, 44, 45, 47
inferential-realizational morphology, 43–4, 182

kinship, 3, 139–47

Lexical Integrity Principle, 154
lexically specified (unmotivated) defectiveness, 2, 8–9, 11, 21, 87, 90

medio-passive, 173–4
Minimal Generalization Learner, 47, 49–50
mood, 20–1, 38–40, 47–8, 53, 56, 86, 87, 89, 104–5, 107–9, 112–13
morphology-free syntax, 2, 151–3, 157, 174–5
morphome, 25, 40, 104, 113, 116, 120

number, 1, 2, 8, 12–13, 14, 38, 48–9, 53–4, 57–9, 60, 129–36, 184–94
  see also dualia tantum, pluralia tantum

Obligatory Contour Principle, 157, 162, 166, 170
opaque cliticization, 156–60, 165

paradigm
  content paradigm, 4, 8–10, 195–207
  form paradigm, 4, 5–8, 9–10, 11, 195–207
  paradigm linkage, 199–203
Person Case Constraint, 154–64, 172, 174
person/number marking, 3, 7–10, 12, 20, 37–8, 38–9, 43, 44, 47–8, 56, 87, 89, 105, 107–8, 136–42
phonology, 8, 23–32, 70, 72–82, 87–90, 100–1, 104, 105, 113, 157
pluralia tantum, 2 n 2, 13 n 10, 133–4, 147

possession, 8, 126, 129–33, 137, 156
pragmatically motivated defectiveness, 3, 72
productivity, 4, 26, 69, 70, 71, 71 n 3, 73, 73 n 7, 74, 76, 79, 82
pronouns, 136–42, 151–80, 184–94, 203–8

Repeated Morph Constraint, 159

semantically motivated defectiveness, 2, 12, 14, 36–7, 72, 133–4, 186
singularia tantum, 2 n 2, 53 n 1
sonority, 94, 100–1
stem-based defectiveness, 5–6, 14, 15, 22–4, 26, 27, 29, 31–2, 35–51, 85, 86, 86 n 2, 87, 88, 90, 91, 93, 94, 95, 96, 97, 98, 99, 100, 101, 113–18
stress, 23–32, 48, 113, 117, 188

suppletion, 1, 11, 14, 23, 25, 28, 29, 35, 39, 40, 42, 43, 44, 50, 51, 73, 74, 104, 187, 191, 200
syncretism, 35, 58, 59, 61–3, 131, 152, 181–94, 196–7, 200–8
syntactically motivated defectiveness, 3, 154–6, 186

tense, 3, 10, 20–1, 38–40, 47–8, 53, 56, 105, 107–8, 112–13
Theta Criterion, 151, 154

vowel quality, 23–4, 30, 70, 77, 79, 106–8

word class, 13–14